Subjectivity

Subjectivity

Theories of the self from
Freud to Haraway

Nick Mansfield

NEW YORK UNIVERSITY PRESS
Washington Square, New York

For Bonny and I

First published in the USA in 2000 by
NEW YORK UNIVERSITY PRESS
Washington Square
New York, NY 10003

CIP data available from the Library of Congress

ISBN 0-8147-5650-6 (cloth)

ISBN 0-8147-5651-4 (pbk)

Set in 10.5/12 pt Bembo by DOCUPRO, Sydney
Cover design by Giulietta Pellascio, Designxbent

10 9

Foreword
Rachel Fensham

THEORIES OF SUBJECTIVITY have been crucial to the Cultural Studies project: from Raymond Williams' theorising of lived experience in 'structures of feeling' to the focus on identities by Stuart Hall and his 'minimal selves'; from feminist approaches such as Elspeth Probyn towards the 'sexed self' to the 'mimicry' of the colonial in Homi Bhabha's work.[1] And while Cultural Studies has produced its own theories of the subject, it has also been confronted by the 'death of the subject' (Foucault); the rejection of the 'subject of feminism' (Butler) or faced with the 'oriental other' (Said) who is never the subject of the West. Subjects have sought to enter culture through theory while others have exited. Indeed, it could be argued that Cultural Studies, even at its most political and deconstructive, is the intellectual field that has remained most concerned with theorising the subject. While contemporary discourses of medicine, media and the law have largely become postmodern, in the sense of strategic, global and effective, there is little left of the subject, or the question of the self, that is not also a disposable, reiteration of the same structures of power. Thus, the very idea of theorising the subject, of asking how the idea of a self has been thought and represented as this book does, can only

1   Raymond Williams *Politics and Letters* (Verso, London, 1979). Stuart Hall 'Minimal Selves' *The Real Me: Postmodernism and the Question of Identity* (ICA Documents, No. 6, Institute of Contemporary Arts, London, 1987). Elspeth Probyn *Sexing the Self: Gendered Positions in Cultural Studies* (Routledge, London and New York, 1993). Homi Bhabha *The Location of Culture* (Routledge, London and New York, 1994).

be productive where an idea of the cultural remains of value for mediating experience.

In this book, subjectivity is cultural theory in process. Whether the subject is political, or personal, our ideas and our experience of being a particular someone at a particular time and place in history have been shaped by theory. Adopting a genealogical approach, the book begins with a useful division of theories into those which foreground the subject as fixed, structures of meaning—the subject who knows and who speaks—including psychoanalysis, and to some extent, feminist arguments around sexual difference; and those which are anti-subjectivist, from Nietzsche to Foucault to Donna Haraway, where the subject is an effect of power, science or technologies. It also defers to Deleuze and Guattari whose theory radicalises the subject as a potential 'rhizomatics'. The chapters are divided between those which concentrate on a key thinker of the subject—Freud, Lacan, Foucault, Kristeva, Deleuze and Guattari—and those which concern complications of the subject within fields of social or identity formation—femininity, masculinity, radical sexuality, ethnicity, technology. Mansfield's special contribution to this topic is to demonstrate the ways in which the subject is implicated in and linked to other subjects, general truths and shared principles. He does not, fortunately, offer a theory of the subject. Rather, he suggests that modern and postmodern models have made the subject a central, if vulnerable, proposition without which Cultural Studies could not exist or proceed.

This book is addressed, however, not to the specialist but to the practitioner, student or teacher in the humanities and social sciences where a theory of the subject might come into play. It enables the question of who 'I' am to be brought into focus, and subjected to analysis, question and critique. And yet, it is an affirmative account that acknowledges that different theories will be useful for different subjects. Postmodernity notwithstanding, theories of the subject—linguistic, socio-political, philosophical, personal—are still necessary within culture, even if they are contested. This book offers a discussion of those theories we might encounter or need to address in relation to daily life, where that life involves reading, watching television, operating in many and varied relationships, working both globally and locally as well as feeling simultaneously constrained and liberated by the unsettling conditions of the contemporary.

Acknowledgments

THANKS TO THE staff and students of the Department of Critical and Cultural Studies at Macquarie University for their advice and enthusiasm, especially Elizabeth Stephens and Nikki Sullivan.

Contents

Introduction

This question of the subject and the living 'who' is at the heart of
the most pressing concerns of modern societies. (Derrida 1991, p.115)

What am I referring to when I say the word 'I'? This little word,
which is somehow the easiest to use in our daily lives, has become
the focus of the most intense—and at times the most obscure—
debate and analysis in *fin-de-siècle* cultural studies. Where does my
sense of self come from? Was it made for me, or did it arise
spontaneously? How is it conditioned by the media I consume, the
society I inhabit, the politics I suffer and the desires that inspire
me? When I use the word 'I', am I using it in the same way as
you, when you use it? Am I a different 'I' when I present myself
in different ways to my boss, my family, my friends, social security,
someone I'm in love with or a stranger in the street? Do I really
know myself? It is these difficult and open-ended questions that—in
different ways, and perhaps simply in different vocabularies—
occupy the theoretical reflection of intellectuals and the anxious
self-scrutiny of the citizens of the end of the twentieth century.

The 'I' is thus a meeting-point between the most formal and
highly abstract concepts and the most immediate and intense
emotions. This focus on the self as the centre both of lived
experience and of discernible meaning has become one of the—if
not *the*—defining issues of modern and postmodern cultures. As
many postmodern theorists have tried to point out, the contemporary era is an era in which we must consistently confess our
feelings: we answer magazine questionnaires about what we *want*,
surveys about which politicians we *like*, focus groups about how
we *react* to advertising campaigns; televised sport, war, accident and

crime are all designed to trigger emotion. The Olympic swimmer coming from the pool, the victim's relatives coming from court, the accident survivor pulled from the wreckage all must front the cameras and say how they *feel*. Our entertainment, our social values, even the work we do and the governments we elect are all to be understood in terms of satisfaction, pleasure, like and dislike, excitement and boredom, love and hate. A world where we once knew ourselves in terms of values and identities has given way to the uninterrupted intensities of elation and grief, triumph and trauma, loss and achievement; birth, death, survival, crime, consumption, career are all now pretexts for emotion. Even economics is driven by its painstaking graphs of consumer *sentiment*.

Things and events are now understood on the level of the pulsing, breathing, feeling individual self. Yet at the same time, this self is reported to feel less confident, more isolated, fragile and vulnerable than ever. Rather than being triumphant because of the huge emphasis it now enjoys, the self is at risk. Selfhood is now seen to be in a state of perpetual crisis in the modern West. Alienated intellectuals and suicidal youth; culture wars and volatile markets; endless addictions to food, work, alcohol and narcotics; sexual inadequacy and thrill killers—all feed into education and entertainment industries that keep the intensity of our selfhood perpetually on the boil, nagging and unsettling, but also inspiring and thrilling us with mystery, fear and pleasure. It is this ambivalence and ambiguity—the intensification of the self as the key site of human experience and its increasing sense of internal fragmentation and chaos—that the twentieth century's theorists of subjectivity have tried to deal with.

This book serves two purposes: to outline the various ways in which the issue of the self has been discussed; and to try to sketch some sort of account of how the self—more than family, locality, ethnicity and nationality—has become the key way in which we now understand our lives, in Western societies at least.

SUBJECT AND SELF

Before proceeding, it is worth dwelling on the word 'subject' and its meaning, since it is this term that is most often used in cultural theories about the self. Although the two are sometimes used interchangeably, the word 'self' does not capture the sense of social and cultural entanglement that is implicit in the word 'subject': the way our immediate daily life is always already caught up in complex political, social and philosophical—that is, shared—concerns. As Vincent Descombes has pointed out (1991, p.126–7), when philosopher René Descartes (1596–1650) wrote 'I think, therefore I am', the 'I' he described was not limited to René Descartes. Although it does not simply leave his own selfhood behind, this philosophical formulation claims to describe a faculty of reflection that links human interiority together everywhere.

'Subjectivity' refers, therefore, to an abstract or general principle that defies our separation into distinct selves and that encourages us to imagine that, or simply helps us to understand why, our interior lives inevitably seem to involve other people, either as objects of need, desire and interest or as necessary sharers of common experience. In this way, the subject is always linked to something outside of it—an idea or principle or the society of other subjects. It is this linkage that the word 'subject' insists upon. Etymologically, to be subject means to be 'placed (or even thrown) under'. One is always subject *to* or *of* something. The word subject, therefore, proposes that the self is not a separate and isolated entity, but one that operates at the intersection of general truths and shared principles. It is the nature of these truths and principles, whether they determine or are determined by us as individuals—in short, the range of their power—that has dominated theory and debate.

TYPES OF SUBJECT

It is probably impossible to produce an exhaustive list of the way the term subject defines our relationship to the world. For the purposes of summary, however, we could say it has four broad usages:

- Firstly, there is the *subject of grammar*, the initiating or driving principle of the sentence. We know and use the word 'I' first and foremost in this sense, as the origin of the actions, feelings and experiences that we collect together and report as our lives. As we shall see, this type of subjectivity is highly deceptive: it seems to bespeak the most simple and immediate sense of selfhood, but because we share the word with every other user of our language(s), it automatically entangles us in a huge and volatile, even infinite, trans-historical network of meaning-making.

- Secondly, there is the *politico-legal subject.* In various ways, the laws and constitutions that define the limits of our social interaction, and ostensibly embody our most respectable values, understand us as recipients of, and actors within, fixed codes and powers: we are subject of and to the monarch, the State and the law. In theory, in liberal democratic societies at least, this sort of subjectivity demands our honest citizenship and respects our individual rights. Because of this reciprocal obligation, we 'enter into' or at least 'agree to' what Jean-Jacques Rousseau (1712–78) first called a 'social contract' which asks certain responsibilities of us, and guarantees us certain freedoms in return.

- Thirdly, there is the *philosophical subject.* Here the 'I' is both an object of analysis and the ground of truth and knowledge. In a defining contribution to Western philosophy to which we will return in Chapter 1, Immanuel Kant (1724–1804) outlined the issues that defined the problem of the subject of philosophy: How can I know the world? How can I know how I should act in the world? And how can I judge the world? Here the subject is located at the centre of truth, morality and meaning.

- Fourthly, there is the *subject as human person.* No matter how exhaustive our analyses of our selfhood in terms of language, politics and philosophy, we remain an intense focus of rich and immediate experience that defies system, logic and order and that goes out into the world in a complex, inconsistent and highly charged way. Sometimes we seek to present this type of subjectivity as simple and unremarkable: we want to show ourselves as normal, ordinary, straightforward. At other times we long for charisma, risk and celebrity, to make an impression, to be remembered. Usually we live an open-ended yet known, measured yet adventurous journey into experience, one we see as generally consistent and purposeful. It is this unfinished yet consistent subjectivity that we generally understand as our selfhood, or personality.

To a linguist, political scientist, philosopher or therapist, the issues of subjectivity can be understood in terms of rigorously maintained disciplinary borders. What makes a sentence meaningful, a civic society stable, a philosophical thesis defensible or a personal problem solvable all contribute in different yet important ways to our lives as subjects. Yet the needs of each of these specialists often leads to hostility and scepticism towards the other equally useful approaches. This book, however, comes from the field of cultural studies. In the rich and unpredictable field of culture—where we make, perfect and communicate the meaning and meaninglessness that allow us to live—there can be no strict and simple demarcation between the subject of the spoken sentence, the citizen in court, the searcher after truth and the person walking in the street. Indeed, it is the way in which these different understandings of the subject interpenetrate and complicate one another that counts in the field of culture. In this way, our definition of the subject must remain speculative and incomplete.

In turn, this also explains many of the choices I have made about which theories and theorists to discuss in this book. On the whole, my discussion is dominated by those whose impact has been most keenly felt in the humanities, and in literary and cultural studies in particular. This leaves to one side many key figures in a more specific and more rigorous philosophical discussion, particularly in the tradition of phenomenology, which runs from Edmund Husserl, through Martin Heidegger, Maurice Merleau-Ponty and Emmanuel Levinas to Jacques Derrida. In Chapter 1, a brief discussion of Heidegger's highly influential contribution to theories of the subject will give some indication of the impact that phenomenology has had.

A GENEALOGY OF SUBJECTIVITY

The theorisation of subjectivity in the twentieth century has produced a range of different models and approaches. It is not even agreed with any certainty what the subject itself is. Different theories follow different paths to different ends. Yet a consistent set of disagreements always marks out an important zone of debate which can in turn clarify what has been important to us, and indeed the material of the oldest investigation in humanist and post-humanist culture: how is it that we live? This book attempts to map out the range and structure of the debate about subjectivity that has done so much to animate the contemporary humanities and the cultural politics it inspires. To use Michel Foucault's terminology, therefore, this project is *genealogical* rather than *metaphysical*.

A metaphysical investigation aims to determine by the systematic analysis and scrutiny of ideas what the truth of a certain argument may be. In this context, a metaphysician would analyse and critique theories of subjectivity in such a way that a preferred or ultimate theory could be derived. Psychoanalysts may say one thing and discourse theorists another, according to the metaphysician, but these various theories are just the stepping-stones to the inevitable final theory, shimmering tantalisingly on the horizon of our investigations: the goal that we will one day reach and discover. The genealogical approach, on the other hand, takes the theories themselves as the object of analysis. The question to be answered is not 'how do we get beyond these theories to the truth they aspire to but fail to reveal?' but 'what do the debates and theories themselves tell us about where we are placed in the history of culture and meaning-making?' The insight that the genealogist seeks is not the truth that will finally make further discussion redundant, but how the discussion itself—with its wild inconsistencies and its bitter antagonisms, in which the rivals, like enemy armies in some famous battles, never quite seem to catch sight of each other—defines the way we live and represent ourselves. In this sense, the purpose of this book is not to try to explain the subject itself, but to reach a better understanding of how the issue of subjectivity has become so important to us.

There are a number of reasons why I have adopted this approach. Firstly, I am not confident that the human subject is susceptible to final explanation. This is not to repeat the romantic idea that the human soul is so unique and mysterious that any rational or analytical process will never reveal its final determinants. Both sides of this particular debate—those who want to pin the subject down definitively, and those who resist them—rest on the same model of subjectivity: for those who believe that we will one day have an ultimate model of the self, subjectivity must be a consistent and quantifiable entity, a stable thing whose limits we can know and whose structure we can map. For those who believe the opposite, subjectivity is also a thing, but an ineffable one, producing intensities, emotions and values that are so beautiful or unique that they bear witness to an ultimate, irreplaceable and inexplicable individuality that is dazzling yet self-contained, like a precious jewel. Yet whether it is considered as scientific object or spiritual artefact, this model remains one of a unique and fixed subject: the only variation is whether it should be understood in rational-impersonal or spiritual-personal terms.

I do not believe that the subject is like this. Subjectivity is primarily an experience, and remains permanently open to inconsistency, contradiction and unself-consciousness. Our experience of ourselves remains forever prone to surprising disjunctions that only the fierce light of ideology or theoretical dogma convinces us can be homogenised into a single consistent thing. Perhaps each of the imperfect theories we will discuss in the course of this book accounts for, or at least provides a way of representing, some aspect or moment of our experience, giving us little flashes of insight or self-recognition that are sometimes pleasurable, sometimes reassuring but never the final resting-place for our reflection on ourselves. Indeed, even when we argue forcefully for a specific theorist or theory, we never go so far as to say that every aspect of our own subjectivity finds its value there. Many will know the famous anecdote about Freud's refusal to analyse his own cigar-smoking in terms of Oedipal and castration theory. 'Sometimes a cigar is just a cigar,' he is reported to have said. Even for the most ambitious and hubristic theorists, there is something about their own subjectivity that they refuse to pin down. In sum then, I would have to say that not only do I not believe that an ultimate theory of the subject is possible, I also do not want one. It is the discussion itself that is of interest. It is worth noting that a genealogical rather than a metaphysical approach to the subject flies in the face of one of the oldest duties of thought in the West, the Socratic/Platonic command, renewed in the Renaissance and the Enlightenment, to 'know oneself'. In postmodern theory, as we shall see, this very command has been seen as destructive. Much contemporary thought aims to protect us from anything as definitive as self-knowledge.

Of course, many theorists we will encounter in this book never aspire to or claim that they are developing complete models of the subject. There have been many global theories of the self, from Freud to Foucault, that have tried to explain either what the individual subject is and how it has come about (in the case of the former) or how we have been made to think of ourselves as individual subjects (in the case of the latter). This book covers these and other big-name theorists, whose ideas dominated discussions of subjectivity in the 1960s and 1970s. However, in the 1980s and 1990s, major theorists gave way to significant issues as the focus of debate. Instead of simply arguing through the work of Freud, Lacan, Foucault, Irigaray, Kristeva or Deleuze and Guattari, discussions started to focus on topics like gender, sexuality, ethnicity and technology. It is this shift from big names to big themes that explains the mix in this book of chapters addressed to thinkers and those addressed to topics. To pretend that discussion has always been derived from the work of major theorists or that it has always been simply teasing at key social/cultural issues would be to misrepresent the situation and pretend that there has been greater uniformity and consistency of discussion than has really been the case.

SUBJECTIVITY AND ANTI-SUBJECTIVITY

I have not, in this book, merely chosen to see this most crucial of discussions for modern culture as entropic and shapeless. Indeed, my argument is that the theories of the subject that have dominated debate in the field of literary/cultural theory and studies fall into two broad camps. Of course, the sort of schematic treatment that follows will not adequately show the internal inconsistencies and disagreement within each approach, but it will provide a shorthand overview of discussions that you may be able to use to map out the shape of what has been at issue.

I have linked these two approaches with the names Freud and Foucault for convenience more than anything else. The importance of Freud in the history of psychoanalysis cannot be doubted. Even allowing for all its tributary subgroups and schisms, psychoanalysis is a movement, with a generally consistent history and project. On the other side, Foucault's work is not the foundation of anything as consistent as a movement, does not really claim authority or allegiance, and operates more as a centre of influence—or, more accurately, as a point of transmission between earlier ideas like those of Nietzsche and later investigations.

What characterises these two broad approaches? Firstly, psychoanalysis generally understands the subject as a *thing*. This may sound obvious, but when we compare this approach to Foucault's, we will see how important this fundamental statement is. For Freud, we are not born with our subjectivity intact. Instead, it is instilled in us as a result of our encounter with the bodies—specifically the gender—of those in our immediate family environment, usually our parents. This encounter triggers a crisis that awakens our interior life, allowing us to feel we are separate from those around us, and gives rise to a complex, dynamic and sometimes obscure psychological structure—in short, the splitting of the subject into conscious and unconscious. Freud's ideas are dealt with in detail in Chapter 2.

Later psychoanalysts varied the Freudian model, sometimes quite radically, though the most influential either nominate Freud as their authority figure (for example, Jacques Lacan's call for a return to Freud: see Chapter 3) or else build their own arguments on a debunking of Freud (for example, Luce Irigaray in Chapter 5). Lacan translates Freud's model of subjectivity into the less realistic and more abstract domain of structuralist linguistics, though he does remain faithful to the model of a subject caused by the intersection between gender and power. Irigaray, on the other hand, draws attention to the crucial absences in the work of both of these psychoanalytic fathers, specifically their inability to provide a sensible model of the subjectivity of women. Julia Kristeva (see Chapter 6) splits the difference between the Lacanian and feminist approaches to psychoanalysis by using some Freudian ideas to develop a theory of a subjectivity that is more a process than a structure, though the coordinates on which it can be mapped remain parents (specifically mothers), bodies, gender and language.

Psychoanalysis cannot only be measured out through a sequence of major thinkers, however. The issues and terms that it has developed have also had a widespread influence on more general debates, not only about femininity but also about the politics of sexual 'orientation' (see Chapter 8), specifically in relation to Freud's term 'polymorphous perversity', in which perversion is seen as the obscure bedrock of everybody's sexual constitution. Freudian themes can also be traced through discourses on masculinity and its relation to cinema (Laura Mulvey's theory of the gender of the cinematic gaze) and, indirectly, through the anthropology of Claude Lévi-Strauss, Eve Kosofsky Sedgwick's work on 'homosociality' or the meaning of the relations between men, both of which are discussed in Chapter 7.

In sum, psychoanalysis is the key school of thought which attempts to explain the truth of the subject, how our interior life is structured, how it has been formed, and how it can explain both uniquely individual traits (for example, nervous habits and sexual tastes) and vastly public ones (for example, the politics of gender and culture). Its authority rests on the assumption, found nearly everywhere in Western thought in the modern era, that its object of analysis is quantifiable and knowable—in short, a real thing, with a fixed structure, operating in knowable and predictable patterns. Because of its commitment to this idea of stable and recognisable models, I understand psychoanalysis as the key *subjective* theory of the subject.

This near tautology begs the question: how can there possibly be an *anti-subjective* theory of the subject? Yet this is exactly what emerges in the work of Michel Foucault and others indebted to nineteenth-century German philosopher Friedrich Nietzsche (1844–1900). Nietzsche understood human life, and life in general, not in terms of the thinking and self-aware human person, lighting his or her way through the world by moral choices and discerning knowledges. Instead, we are each the embodiment of a quantum of force called 'will'. Those with little of this life-force—the herd of the weak—try to constrain those with more—the élite of the strong—by inventing all sorts of moral categories that assert doctrines of guilt and responsibility. In turn, the major vehicle of constraint is language, which petrifies the illusion that for every action there is a pre-existing subject responsible for it.

Foucault, although hardly partisan to Nietzsche's counter-democratic arrogance, has taken from him the idea that subjectivity is not a really existing thing, but has been invented by dominant systems of social organisation in order to control and manage us. We are educated and harassed till we believe that the proper organization of the world depends on the division of the human population into fixed categories—the sick separate from the well, the sane from the insane, the honest from the criminal—each exposed to different types of management, in the hands of doctors, social workers, police, teachers, courts and institutions (from schools to prisons, factories to hospitals, asylums to the military), all regulated according to rationalised principles of truth and knowledge. In this way, 'subjectivity' is not the free and sponta-neous expression of our interior truth. It is the way we are led to think about ourselves, so we will police and present ourselves in the correct way, as not insane, criminal, undisciplined, unkempt, perverse or unpredictable.

In sum, for Foucault the subject is the primary workroom of power, making us turn in on ourselves, trapping us in the illusion that we have a fixed and stable selfhood that science can know, institutions can organise and experts can correct. Nietzsche and Foucault's ideas are outlined in Chapter 4. These ideas have also been hugely influential, feeding into debates about gender (in the work of Judith Butler: see Chapter 5) and queer theory (see Chapter 8), and fuelling a fierce critique of psychoanalysis as the key example of subjective modelling (see Amina Mama and Hortense Spillers' work on psychology and ethnicity in Chapter 9, and Deleuze and Guattari's critique of psychoanalysis in Chapter 10).

These two approaches, the psychoanalytic/subjective and the Foucauldian/anti-subjective, will be the key landmarks of the discussion in this book. Like all work in the humanities, these models are offered up not because they are believed to be true, nor because they offer a complete account of all thinking on the subject. They are merely a useful schema that we can bear in our minds as we measure out the contributions of individual works to the debate about culture and subjectivity. I invite the reader to find the holes in this division. Psychoanalysis has to be seen as a school of thought with a wide variety of opinions and intense internal debate. Foucault's legacy could hardly be said to form anything as coherent as a school. But since we are dealing here not with a random and disconnected set of thinkers, but with a debate in which different points of view are aware of and contest one another, we must find some (albeit inadequate) way of mapping the patterns and consistencies we encounter. I hope and expect that better models than mine will emerge, but for the sake of intellectual work, which depends more than anything else on the tentative making of informed connections between things, I hope that it will be of some use to you.

THE SUBJECT IS A CONSTRUCT

What these two schools of thought do have in common is their separation from what we consider to be the commonsense model of the subject that we have inherited from the Enlightenment: the idea that we are possessed of a free and autonomous individuality that is unique to us, and that develops as part of our spontaneous encounter with the world. Martin Heidegger's contribution to the present-day crisis of subjectivity, as it has been called, was to propose that this model of the subject was a superficial illusion perpetrated on us by Descartes and the philosophers he influenced. It is with this issue that any treatment of modern and postmodern subjectivity must start, and it is to this we will turn in Chapter 1.

Yet before we do, something must be said about the consensus amongst theorists that the subject is *constructed*, made within the world, not born into it already formed. This is a difficult idea to accept at first, as it flies in the face of our assumption—probably derived from popular representations of the Nature described in Darwin and other Evolutionary theory—that the most intense of our feelings must be innate, natural or instinctive. This assumption is most often apparent in discussions of gender and sexuality: surely the aggression men feel or the statistical dominance of what has come to be known as 'heterosexuality' is evidence of the inclinations of Nature itself? Yet attempts to theorise subjectivity have almost always led to the opposite conclusion. In sexuality, for example, it is not Nature that is seen to appear at the core of our most deeply felt irresistible desires, but politics. Indeed, on reflection, perhaps it is the commonsense assumption of the power of Nature that seems most unconvincing. Surely we should not be surprised that it is the social and cultural pressures, inculcated by the uncodified but heavily reinforced rules of playground, street, family and mass media, by the intense pressure of social living for minutes, hours, days, weeks, months and years of our waking and even our sleeping lives, surely it is this ever-present, ever-reintroduced, ever-mysterious pressure, and the sanctions it can marshal—ostracism, mockery and violence—and not the absent imaginary impulses of a distant and hypothetical 'Nature' that would induce in us the most intense feelings of love and fear, of desire and danger? It is finally this belief that the problem of interior life is best understood in terms of culture and politics, rather than science and Nature, that provides this book with its material.

1 | The free and autonomous Individual

T HE THEORIES OF subjectivity that have dominated the last thirty years of literary and cultural studies all agree on one thing. They reject the idea of the subject as a completely self-contained being that develops in the world as an expression of its own unique essence. Uniformly, they identify this image of subjectivity with the Enlightenment.

THE ENLIGHTENMENT

The Enlightenment can be seen to span the period from Francis Bacon (1561–1626) to the French Revolution of 1789, covering developments as disparate as the origins of modern empirical science, the elaboration of universal ideals of political organisation (from totalitarianism to the liberal state) and the substitution of the cult of personal sensibility for collective religion. The Enlightenment is chosen as the target of contemporary critical thought because its ideals still underprop the institutions and processes that justify the way modern Western social and political systems operate. Yet, of course, the Enlightenment was not a single thing and is full of contradictions. Both the rationale for the modern liberal state and the ideology of its most vehement opponents can be traced to definitively Enlightenment thinkers.

The situation with subjectivity is similar: in the same way that key developments in Enlightenment thought, and early modern thought in general, first posed the question of the subject as a free, autonomous and rational being (what we call the individual), we can also find there the seeds of radical attacks on this model, which have aimed either to replace it with a different model, or to abandon the whole idea of subjectivity altogether. In other words, the very fact that it became necessary to define subjectivity at a certain moment in Western thought, that traditional practices and languages of selfhood were no longer to be taken for granted, opened up a field of contention, crisis and perpetual re-evaluation of the self. The self became an issue, a point of fundamental instability in the world. It was the Enlightenment that made the modern era the era of the subject.

DESCARTES AND THE *COGITO*

The work of René Descartes (1596–1650) represents major developments in the fields of mathematics (he invented the Cartesian diagram), scientific method and epistemology (the philosophy of knowledge). His most famous formula, *Cogito ergo sum* ('I think therefore I am'), stands at the head of the modern tradition in Western thought, that has seen the conscious processes of observation, analysis and logic as the key instruments in the search for objective truth. As we can see from the *Cogito*, as it is known, Descartes' philosophy considered knowledge in terms of the meaning of the word 'I'. Individuality, even the very existence of the individual, was not simply to be taken for granted as obvious, incontestable or even part of the revelation of Christian religion. Descartes' aim here was to throw everything into doubt, and only to accept that which could be verified from first principles.

That the key to knowledge was to be found in a formulation about the word 'I' shows the beginning of a new understanding of the human place in the world. Although the destination of Descartes' reflection was a restrengthening of his belief in God, its linchpin was a definition of the self. Such a definition had to come first. Knowledge of the world had to wait until selfhood was made philosophically secure. This emphasis on the self as the origin of all experience and knowledge seems glaringly obvious to us, but this merely indicates how much we still live in the wake of the mutation in Western thinking that Descartes' work represents. Yet, as we shall see when we look at other Enlightenment writings and in later chapters, this very assumption has been a fundamental bone of contention in recent debates.

The second key idea we can derive from the Cartesian *Cogito* is an emphasis on, or preference for, the conscious processes of thought over every other impulse or sensation. Descartes wrote: '"I am" precisely taken refers only to a conscious being; that is a mind, a soul (*animus*), an intellect, a reason—words whose meaning I did not previously know. I am a real being and really exist; but what sort of being? As I said, a conscious being.' (Descartes 1970, p.69). In context, when Descartes refers to consciousness, he seems to mean a general awareness of the world, rather than merely logical or rational thought. The Latin *Cogitare* (Descartes was writing in Latin), from which the term he uses is derived, includes the general idea of awareness, or 'experience' as it is sometimes translated. Yet in the above extract, a preference appears for certain 'higher', more active types of mental process. Conscious being may include, as it does in English usage, merely that of which one can be made aware. But increasingly from the Enlightenment on, and certainly since the Freudian naming of part of the mind as 'the unconscious', consciousness has been identified with the controllable, knowable, daylight functions that Descartes finds at the end of his list: intellect and reason. Certainly to later Enlightenment thinkers the operation of reason was the highest achievement of the human species, the final arbiter of every issue, even perhaps the very distinguishing feature that allowed us to know what was and what was not human.

In Descartes, therefore, we find together two principles that Enlightenment thought has both emphasised and adored: firstly, the image of the self as the ground of all knowledge and experience of the world (*before I am anything, I am I*) and secondly, the self as defined by the rational faculties it can use to order the world (*I make sense*). It is from these two principles that our summary of the Enlightenment will develop. Although, to our common sense, they seem to always everywhere go hand in hand, my aim is to show the potential contradiction between them—between the emphasis on selfhood, and the belief that it is most perfectly expressed by consciousness.

ROUSSEAU AND SENSIBILITY

First let us look at a later Enlightenment thinker, Jean-Jacques Rousseau (1712–78), whose work is the fruition of the new emphasis on the self as the ground of human existence in the world. Rousseau's work straddles the intense rationalism of Enlightenment thought, and the emphasis on feeling and sensibility that would arise in its wake in the Romanticism of the late eighteenth and early nineteenth centuries. His political thought, especially as expressed in *The Social Contract* (1762), argues for a rationalised, if not regimented, society under the authority of a despotic figure who embodies the popular will. As such, it has been often seen as a justification for modern totalitarianism.

On the other hand, his *Confessions* (1781) emphasises the uniqueness and autonomy, the absolute governing freedom, of individual experience. We can see this from its opening:

> I have resolved on an enterprise which has no precedent, and which, once complete, will have no imitator. My purpose is to display to my kind a portrait in every way true to nature, and the man I shall portray will be myself.
>
> Simply myself. I know my own heart and understand my fellow man. But I am made unlike any one I have ever met; I will even venture to say that I am like no one in the whole world. I may be no better, but at least I am different. Whether Nature did well or ill in breaking the mould in which she formed me, is a question that can only be resolved after the reading of my book. (Rousseau 1953, p.17)

People had written confessions and memoirs before. What was to be different about Rousseau's? How could he justify the claim that he was going to do something that had never been done before, and that would never be repeated?

Instead of emphasising a particular theme (the author's religious experiences or political career), Rousseau's aim is to give a complete, uninhibited and unapologetic representation of himself, not necessarily to make any point or even to justify himself (judgment, 'whether Nature did well or ill', will be up to others), but simply to present himself. To Rousseau, he as an individual is important and sufficient enough to justify hundreds of pages of painstaking exposition. It is not the significance of his life that makes it an adequate, even a necessary, object of description, but its uniqueness: 'I may be no better,' he writes, 'but at least I am different.' Any life is worthy of such treatment, because the individual at its centre will always tell a new and original story.

Furthermore, what binds together the disparate and disorganised places and events of this story will not be given by some theme, like a major historical event, or a particular experience (a victory in battle or a scientific discovery). The unity of the work is grounded in the feeling, living being at its centre. This sense of the *sufficiency* of individuality is the key to Rousseau's *Confessions*. The inclusion of any material—the author's exhibitionism and masturbation, his quasi-incestuous desires for the woman he called Mama, and the petty squabbles and rivalries of his later life—is justified by the simple fact that it all helps us get a complete picture of the 'I' who is writing about himself. Everything in the subject's life is of interest and value, because any omissions would result in distortion. The individual is a total and inclusive phenomenon, a sort of massive and dynamic unity.

The idea of the sufficiency of the individual is borne out in another way: Rousseau's trust in his own personal intuition as a way of judging the world. In a famous passage, he walks in the forest at Saint-Germain, contemplating the fallen nature of humankind. He writes:

> I dared to strip man's [sic] nature naked, to follow the progress of time, and trace the things which have distorted it; and by comparing man as he had made himself with man as he is by nature I showed him in his pretended perfection the true source of his misery. Exalted by these sublime meditations, my soul soared towards the Divinity; and from that height I looked down on my fellow men pursuing the blind path of their prejudices, of their errors, of their misfortunes and their crimes. (Rousseau 1953, p.362)

For Rousseau, humankind was born into the world in a state of more or less perfection that history and social life have debased, leaving us engulfed in prejudice, error and crime. Human beings have distorted and diminished their own natural potential by pursuing the unnatural demands of class, religion and ambition. If only they were able to liberate their true nature, they would free themselves of the suffering they now endure. Human beings should therefore recover the sanctity and promise of the individuality with which they were born.

This hymn to the natural human self is reinforced by what is perhaps the most significant feature of this passage: Rousseau's own dramatisation of the natural self, by withdrawing into nature and solitude in order to contemplate the truth of the human world. His insight is produced by his immersion in the very natural self he is praising. He does not derive his judgments from reading, nor from dialogue with other intellectuals, but by separating himself from the world and reawakening the individuality he sees as both humanity's birthright and its highest goal.

Here we can see clearly ideas about individuality that have become truisms in Western culture, and that are periodically rediscovered (as they were in the counter-cultural movements of the 1960s) with radical force: the idea that the individual is a naturally occurring unit, that it is preyed upon and entrapped by society, and that true freedom and fulfilment can only be gained by rejecting social pressures, and by giving individuality uninhibited expression. Not only is this the truth of the human species, but it raises the human to a transcendent status: Rousseau found his soul raised to the level of the Divine.

KANT AND THE UNITY OF REASON

The second attribute of individuality we derived from Descartes was the emphasis on the conscious as the defining faculty of the self. We now to turn to the late eighteenth century German philosopher Immanuel Kant (1724–1804) and his *Critique of Pure Reason* (1781) to see an important version of this idea.

This work attempts to describe what it is about human beings that allows them to know the world. For Kant, before we do anything, we must make at least some simple observation or impression of the world around us. We turn these observations into representations as they enter our minds and become things to think about. They circulate in our minds as images. Each and every representation a human being makes of the world, according to Kant, from the most simple sensory perception to the most complex formula, is understood to be grounded in the 'I' that perceives. Kant writes: 'it must be possible for the "I think" to accompany all my representations' (Kant 1929, p.152). Before we perceive anything, something must be there, in place, to do the perceiving. We do not open every observation or statement with the phrase 'I think', especially when we are merely communicating with ourselves. Yet, although it is unspoken, any dealing with the world is impossible without it being channelled through the 'I'. Furthermore, this 'I' at the heart of 'I think' is always 'in all consciousness one and the same' (1929, p.153). Since all our experiences are connected with this thinking self, they all appear to us to be happening to a single being. 'The thought that the representations given in intuition one and all belong to me, is therefore equivalent to the thought that I unite them in one self-consciousness . . . I call them one and all *my* representations, and so apprehend them as constituting *one* intuition' (1929, p.154). In sum, then, every relationship we have with the world, even the most primitive or abstract, must cross the threshold of the thinking 'I'. Before it does anything, however simple, the self thinks. What it thinks of at this primal stage is itself, which it conceives to be a unity. It is *self-conscious*, in the most intense meaning of the phrase. In order for us to be in any contact with the world, according to Kant, we must have an awareness of ourselves, and a sense of unity of self. This awareness is identified neither with a natural self-sufficiency (as in Rousseau), nor with a soul that has come into the world fully formed (as in religious discourse), but with thought. In fact, Kant would argue that before you can think the natural philosophy of a Rousseau, or the eternity of a religion, as with all ideas, impressions, impulses, representations and experiences, first you must think yourself. The self, then, is the feeling of connection or consistency between all your perceptions, the collection point of your thoughts.

If Rousseau fulfilled the first theme we discovered in Descartes (that the self is a sufficient starting-point for the analysis of the world), Kant fulfils the second: the equation between selfhood and consciousness. For Kant, subjectivity can only have content through awareness of the world. What circulates within our interior lives is a collection of mere representations. These representations meld with faculties that constitute us. Primary amongst these faculties, allowing us to have a relationship with the world, is a sense of 'I'. This I is much more fundamental than what we call a personality, or an identity. It operates before we discover all the things that make our I separate from everyone else's. This I is not really the fully formed individual. It is the bedrock on which that individuality is built, the sense that experience of the world is focused on a thing that is aware, that is processing the information it receives, that is turning mutations in the field of light into meaningful representations that can lead to judgment and action. Kant's understanding of that 'aware' entity is more intense than merely the word 'conscious' would allow. Kant's subject is not merely in the world, allowing its messages to cross back and forth across its senses. When it receives these messages, it is not merely passive. It grasps the outside world in a positive act of thought that not only connects it with things, but gives it a strong, unified and purposeful sense of selfhood.

THE LEGACY OF THE ENLIGHTENMENT

What is the relationship between the self-sufficient self of Rousseau and the conscious self of Kant? Do they fit together to complete a single workable model of the self that we have been able to build on, or is there some tension between them that may help to explain why the definition of the self has become the hidden but most persistent and compellingly urgent problem of the modern era and beyond? Rousseau's achievement was to imagine the individual in total terms, to conceive of subjectivity in all its manifestations as a whole—not always consistent, not always admirable, not always logical, but at all times worthy of study and description. The sheer scale and intensity of individual experience entitles it to be the basis, the starting-point and ground of all meaning. Kant, too, imagined a world that started with the individual's acts of perception, of the conscious subject as the origin of the human processes of meaning-making.

We don't have to take the comparison between Rousseau and Kant—or the comparison between the twin principles we derived from Descartes—very far before we see contradictions that have provided fertile material for subsequent thinkers. If Rousseau's model of the self is a total model, omitting nothing from its purview, then it already challenges Kant's emphasis on the conscious and intelligible as the privileged ground of the human relationship with the world. Already Rousseau must seek to include what Kant wanted to marginalise. In short, from the outset, *there is a contradiction between the attempt to grasp individual experience as a totality, and the belief that its essence and truth is to be found in conscious processes.*

The name now given to the whole irrational dimension of subjectivity works as a direct challenge to Kant and Descartes: the *unconscious*. If human beings seek to structure themselves on their awareness of the world around them, as empirical philosophers of knowledge seem to expect, they can only do this by attempting to suppress those parts of their subjectivity that are inconsistent, irrational, even obscure and unknown. Rousseau wanted to keep the door open to such emotions, and amongst those he most influenced were the English Romantic poets like Shelley and Keats who saw the truth as lying in their feelings and the highly aesthetic experiences they fostered, rather than in their rational faculties. This disjunction between the rational and irrational dimensions of subjectivity, between conscious and unconscious, represents the first profound challenge to the idea that the individual makes sense. With its emphasis on the unknowable dimension of our selves, it remains a challenge to us still. Its first major theorist was Sigmund Freud, the founder of psychoanalysis, and it is to his work that I will turn in Chapter 2.

Historically however, despite the contradictions between them, the two projects of Rousseau and Kant should be seen as coordinated. They are both part of the same shift of emphasis, not just towards the human (a human-centred model of the world had been dominant in Europe since the Renaissance) but to the individual self, to subjectivity. Rousseau's solitary walker, separated from his society and culture, assessing the world and its value, is an emblem of this emphasis on the individual as the fundamental material of the human world. We can see, when we look at this general level, that these two thinkers are part of the same broad discussion and redefinition.

Our philosophies of science, our theories of the organisation of society, our sense of morality, purpose and truth all partake of the same emphasis on the individual not only as a social quantity, but as the point where all meaning and value can be judged. This individuality is described as a freedom, and we still direct our most serious political ambitions towards perfecting that freedom. It also operates as a duty, however. Our personal desires must fuel the economy. Our individual ambition must make our nations rich and powerful. We are expected not only to mouth the right words at the death of heroes, princesses and children, or when our country loses a major sporting event, but to feel a sense of personal loss as well. Our shocked and dutiful sympathy for those killed by terrorists or in accidents and natural disasters hinges on the fact that they have families like ours, that feel like us.

Contemporary media honour individual response and intense personal emotion more than anything else, but only as they conform to clearly sanctioned patterns. A compulsory individuality is the measure of all things, from the lone researcher in the laboratory to the teenager answering the sex survey in a magazine, and it is an individuality that, in turn, must be repeatedly measured, assessed and normalised. Thus the question arises in our time whether this individuality is really built on the freedom and natural spontaneity that is supposed to be its origin. When we look at the Enlightenment dream of subjectivity through the lens of present experience, do we see the fruition of the dream that the individual would be able to shrug off the power of social institutions and inherited prejudices and superstitions? Whatever the fate of the high-minded sense of individuality that was the dream of eighteenth-century philosophers, we can see ourselves, in the absolute desperation with which we attempt to grasp, express and sell our subjectivity, very much in their wake, even if the type of freedom we enjoy sometimes looks like a parody of what they expected. The Enlightenment made the individual an issue, and although the philosophy and culture of the twentieth century has worked hard to complicate and interrogate its legacy, we can see in the thinkers of the eighteenth century the terms on which debates about subjectivity are still based.

HEIDEGGER ON THE ENLIGHTENMENT

It is worth mentioning the work of Martin Heidegger (1889–1976) because it is his understanding of the role of the Enlightenment—and the work of René Descartes in particular—that has defined the contemporary view of the history of modern thought about subjectivity. To Heidegger, philosophers from Descartes onwards had seen the human passage through the world as dependent on a fixable and self-aware entity called the subject that is the most fundamental form of experience—indeed, the very ground of the possibility of experience. They had not, however, looked beneath the structure of subjectivity to an even more basic and fundamental issue: we may be able to talk about how we experience and know the world, but what does it mean that we exist in the first place? What does the word 'is' really mean? What is the nature of our *being*? It is this most fundamental question that earlier philosophers had refused to grasp. In his major work, *Being and Time* (1926), Heidegger wrote:

> In the course of this history certain distinctive domains of Being
> have come into view and have served as the primary guides for
> subsequent problematics: the *ego cogito* [I think] of Descartes,
> the subject, the 'I', reason, spirit, person. But these all remain
> uninterrogated as to their Being and its structure, in accordance
> with the thoroughgoing way in which the question of Being has
> been neglected. (Heidegger 1962, p.44)

Philosophers had defined subjectivity in terms of reason, human spirit or the simple act of perception. These various subjectivities selected some arbitrary feature of human experience and chose it as the key or lodestone to all. This was highly artificial and selective to Heidegger. His project, therefore, was to define our place in the world not in terms of some artificial construct, but in terms of the most fundamental aspect of life: Being itself. There could be nothing more fundamental than the fact that we *are*. Any other determination of the basic structures of human life must come after that. Therefore, it is to Being that our attention should be addressed. Heidegger's term for the unique kind of human Being that could be theorised beneath the level of the artificial and selective subjectivities of earlier philosophers is the German word *Dasein*, commonly meaning 'existence', but literally *being-there* (Heidegger 1962, p.27 n.1), a term invariably left untranslated.

This introduces us to another point mentioned above: the assumption in inherited models of subjectivity that the human is defined by its separation from the world, that it has an interiority that is set off against the exteriority of the objective outside world. To Heidegger, there is no such simple separation from the world. *Dasein* is constituted by the fact that it is in the world and belongs to it. The world concerns us, and our relationship to it is one of care. We are not aliens enclosed within our fortress-selves, in a world that is absolutely foreign to us. Our experience conjoins us to the world.

As I have mentioned, this book is a study of the theories of the subject that have had a wide-ranging influence on theorists and critics who analyse culture, its complex conventions, politics and rituals, and the texts that inspire, challenge and entertain us. As such, our concerns will not be the same as the philosophers who seek to pursue the issue of selfhood towards absolute and abstract truth. Yet the debate about subjectivity and culture has been conditioned—indeed—is played out in the shadow of—the debates that Heidegger's work influenced. This is seen in three ways in particular: firstly, there is a widespread acceptance of Heidegger's argument that the subject is not a naturally occurring thing, but a philosophical category of thought that arose at a certain point in history, and that will be supplanted by more convincing models of what the human experience of the world is like. Secondly, Descartes is universally acknowledged as the pivotal philosopher of subjectivity. Almost all theory returns to him as the thinker to be debunked. And thirdly, the simple idea that we inhabit a world that is fundamentally separate from us (in some Christian rhetoric, that we are *in* the world, but not *of* it) is seen as an inadequate model of the complex and open-ended entanglements that condition our lives, and that provide the context in which we have always lived and must continue to live.

The Enlightenment model of the self has been complicated by more recent developments, especially the Freudian idea of the unconscious, but also by feminism and contemporary ethnic politics. Yet in our dealing with the social institutions of representative democracy (courts, parliaments and bureaucracies), our sense of selfhood is constantly falling back on Enlightenment motifs—for example, the tension between the strict sense of the demarcation of one individual from another, and a heightened awareness of the influence society has on us. Indeed, as we will discuss in Chapter 4, Enlightenment ideas are seen by Michel Foucault as trapping us in a selfhood that we convince ourselves is our most precious possession and freedom—our truth, in fact— but that actually functions to imprison us in a set of practices and routines that are determined for, rather than by, us. It is Heidegger who is now seen as the key figurehead of this new orthodoxy, according to which the writings of the Enlightenment define the inherited burden of both abstruse theory and daily life, as well as the attempts we make to shrug off this burden—both what it has meant in our culture to be a subject, and the various ways we imagine rethinking subjectivity.

FURTHER READING

Descartes, René, 1970, *Philosophical Writings* ed. and trans. Elizabeth Anscombe and Peter Thomas Geach, Thomas Nelson and Sons, Sunbury-on-Thames.

Heidegger, Martin, 1962, *Being and Time* trans. John Macquarrie and Edward Robinson, Basil Blackwell, Oxford.

Kant, Immanuel, 1929, *Critique of Pure Reason* trans. Norman Kemp Smith, Macmillan, Houndmills, Basingstoke.

Rousseau, Jean-Jacques, 1953, *The Confessions* trans. J.M. Cohen, Penguin Books, Harmondsworth.

2 | Freud and the split subject

No TWENTIETH-CENTURY discussion of what the subject is and where it comes from has been untouched by the theories and vocabulary of Freudian psychoanalysis. Similarly, the whole field of twentieth-century culture—from the shocking disconnections of surrealism to the DIY self-healing manifestoes of pop psychology—exhibits the fundamental insights of Sigmund Freud (1865–1939) and his followers.

It would be a mistake, however, to think that Freud burst on to the intellectual scene unanticipated. Nineteenth-century culture bears witness to a gradually intensifying anxiety about the structure of the self and the security of its lodgment in the world. Writers as diverse as Mary Shelley, Robert Louis Stevenson, Hoffmann and Dostoyevsky all in their own way produced images of an interior life that was potentially fractured, of a self prey to irrational impulses that threatened its usual role in the social order, and of a sexuality whose meaning was more psychological than procreative. In short, the nineteenth century, from its suicidal young poets to its booming brothels and wild hysterics, came increasingly to dramatise the self's radical distrust of itself, its fear of isolation, dark desire, hidden madness and easy breakdown—a version of subjectivity that has become ever more commonplace as the modern age has progressed.

Let us quickly review a couple of literary examples—firstly, Mary Shelley's *Frankenstein* (1818) and its much imitated story of artificial life born from a combination of artistic and scientific egotism and the flirtation with the occult. One way of interpreting the relationship between Doctor Victor Frankenstein and the monster he creates is as an analogy of the modern self. The scientist,

25

with his fierce vanity and his over-absorption in the quest for experimental power, is an almost pathological case of excessive involvement in the conscious mind's rational processes. The monster, with his primal innocence, vulnerability to corruption and intense, even malicious physical violence, embodies the dangerous and dark domain of the unconscious. Together, it is as if they form an image of a single mind, liberating its own unconscious energies only to find them uncontrollable and threatening. The only possible destiny for the relationship between scientist and monster—conscious and unconscious—is a shared annihilation. In Robert Louis Stevenson's *Doctor Jekyll and Mr Hyde*, a rational scientist experiments on himself until he is completely transformed into his own malicious and amoral double.

What we see in both these examples is not a conscious mind controlling its irrational impulses, but one that is fascinated and eventually consumed by them. In contrast to the eighteenth-century rationalists like Kant, who saw the conscious mind as the defining attribute of the human relationship with the world, nineteenth-century fiction often represents the rational as drawn towards the dark and uncertain impulses it was thought to rule. Now the rational and irrational have become inextricably bound up with one another, and the threat of the former being consumed by the latter is met with a mix of horror and longing. In sum, then, the appearance of Freud's writings at the very end of the nineteenth century and in the first few decades of the twentieth merely systematises a version of the self that had been accumulating for some time. The idea of the split subject was an idea whose time had come.

Freud's achievement was to intuit the understanding of self-hood that was coming to trouble his culture, and to give it a theoretical—even, as he claimed, a scientific—form. Freud stands, therefore, as a significant turning-point in an intellectual culture still committed to Descartes' identification of the self with the rational processes of the conscious mind. Jacques Lacan (see Chapter 3) has argued that the resistance, even mockery, still directed against Freud is not because of his infamous obsession with sex, but because his insistence on the inevitable force of the irrational in human life threatened the idea of a conscious mind always everywhere able to deal with itself. What, then, is Freud's view of the subject? Freud's work spans some thirty volumes and touches on an astonishingly wide range of topics, from the psychology of sex and gender to social anthropology, religion and aesthetics.

Similarly, in a long career, his ideas evolved and modified, producing a range of models and theories that are not easily assimilable with one another. For the purposes of this chapter, I will discuss two crucial versions of Freud's model of subjectivity, because they give the most important insight into its general meaning and because they have been the most centrally discussed in recent controversies in cultural theory. Firstly, what is the unconscious; and secondly, where does it come from?

THE UNCONSCIOUS

We are all familiar from our day-to-day experience with the way that ideas and images constantly pass in and out of our awareness. Usually, if we reflect on this, we assume that our preoccupation with the demands of the present means that our minds simply lack the capacity to be aware of the huge range of impulses, representations, emotions and inspirations that appear in it more or less constantly. On the other hand, we are equally familiar with the sudden irruption into our awareness of things far removed from what we were thinking about or busy with. At times, these flashes are pleasurable, at others menacing, but they are so much a part of our usual practice that, like our equally bizarre dreaming, we rarely bother with them, unless they become dominating, recurrent or uncontrollable.

The existence of ideas on the border of consciousness is hardly a radical idea. Freud, however, puzzled over the variety and the enigmatic nature of these experiences. Some seemed merely the recycling of conscious material from ordinary experience. You could not stop thinking about what you had said the previous day, how anxious you were at a meeting, how much you were looking forward to tonight's party and so on. But much of this material bore no apparent relation to real life. It was bizarre and unfamiliar, even threatening and confusing. The simple commonsense theory that there were ideas on the fringes of our minds that returned there, because of some ordinary, easy process of mental circulation, seemed inadequate to deal with the heart-stopping intervention into normal thought processes of what one could not—perhaps even did not want to—understand. Another mental domain must exist, with its own unfamiliar logic, that was releasing messages, or at least images, into the conscious mind.

These insights of Freud's found their most complete expression in his reflections on the nature of dreams. In fact, Freud's most important early work, and still one of his most read and readable, is *The Interpretation of Dreams* (1904). Freud saw in dreams the existence not only of a part of the mind in the shadow of conscious awareness, but one that was radically different, even opposed to consciousness. So unfamiliar was this domain that it could not enter into consciousness on its own terms, but chose as its costume images and symbols which, on first acquaintance, seemed merely insane, but from which analysis could disentangle some personal significance, if it knew enough about the individual. It was the exotic and chaotic nature of dream material that had allowed it to be traditionally interpreted as either prophecy, fantasy or the more or less accidental and trivial reprocessing of mental material. The first two of these explanations seemed too unscientific to Freud, and the last provided no explanation for the intensity—even terror—dreams could provoke. In short, there were not only vague and leftover thoughts on the periphery of the human mind, there were also strong—even menacing—thoughts that consciousness did not merely ignore, but that it struggled with, tried to push away and suppress.

Dreams, however, were not the only place that such unconscious investments reappeared. Slips of the tongue—still referred to in common speech as Freudian slips, especially when they have some sexual ambiguity—and jokes are common daily occasions when surprising or incongruous material surfaces unexpectedly and without easy explanation in the conscious mind. Most urgently, unconscious material reappears in the symptoms of neurosis, a term with a harder clinical meaning in Freud's time. Neurotic symptoms can be as simple as a peculiar nervous way of scratching your nose, or pushing back your hair. They can be as terrifying as a panic attack, obsessive tidying and washing—even to the point of personal injury—or the appearance of the symptoms of all sorts of diseases and conditions. Such behaviour, if a manifestation of the unconscious, is beyond the control of the individual, who does not fake symptoms, but experiences them as intensely as any other sufferer, only without the same pathology.

All of these events were evidence of an unremitting tension in normal life that was most manifest in the behaviour of clinical patients who presented themselves for therapy. But these experiences and behaviours were not restricted to those whose lives they had made nearly impossible. Dreams are experienced by the least-troubled individuals on an almost daily basis, showing Freud that the complex structures that neurotic symptoms revealed in an extreme form were merely the universal qualities of human mental life. Neurotic patients were not marginal or idiosyncratic; they were the key to the truth of human subjectivity. Their symptoms were the action of the unconscious in a louder, clearer language, but not one at all foreign to the vagaries of the less urgent experience of those who did not turn up asking for help.

OVERDETERMINATION

One of the most common objections to Freud's work on the unconscious is that it takes the accidental and trivial and turns it into the significant, dramatic, even tragic. This objection brings us to one of the most important ideas in Freudian psychoanalysis, and especially in its use as a theoretical model for the analysis of culture. Analysis of a television program or an ad seems to many people to be an incredible act of forced reading, and must always involve the importing into a small container of a lot of material that is not really there. University seminars are often interrupted by a half-complaining, half-pleading cry: 'But aren't we reading too much into it?' Freudian theory meets this objection head on, by arguing that all psychological (and, by corollary, cultural) material is *over-determined*. This means that even the most trivial behaviours—biting your nails, disgust at the skin on the surface of warm milk, anger and impatience in traffic—are the focus and expression of the most plural and deep psychological complexity. Indeed, so rich is our unconscious life, and so closely do we live with it—so ordinary is it, in fact—that even allowing for its highly charged, even mur-derous, material, it rarely produces crises. Its only presence in the conscious mind—and its impulse is always to push into the con-scious mind—can be in the trivial impulses and surprising disjunctions that we live with every day. It is no surprise, therefore, that the unconscious we do not want to be aware of should appear in trivial things, though the truth may well be the inverse. Perhaps our need to trivialise the obscure material at the root of our minds makes us want to see the surfacing of the unconscious in everyday life as accidental and unimportant, rather than the product of our deepest experiences and investments.

It is clear that we have come a long way from the simple forgetfulness of day-to-day life. When we talk about over-determination, we are seeing the most intense psychological energies invested in the smallest behavioural space. What Freud presents, therefore, is a subjectivity not of simple presences and absences, but of potentially violent energies and conflicts, where negative feelings do not merely lapse from the conscious mind, but where they are kept in place by a force against which they constantly struggle. In their endeavour to enter the conscious mind and gain expression and fulfilment, unconscious ideas meet the barrier of *repression*. A huge amount of psychological energy is expended on keeping unconscious investments in their place. In fact, so important is this energy in maintaining a semblance of subjective stability that it signals to the therapist the location of the most unstable unconscious material. Resistance, whether it is to an experience in day-to-day life or to a suggestion of the analyst, is a sign of the proximity of something the subject is unable to face.

In sum, if you look at the Freudian version of the subject topographically, we have an interior life split between the socially and culturally integrated processes of the conscious mind, and the threatening or unconfessable impulses of the unconscious, which the conscious hopes to keep in its place by a quantum of mental force called repression. The nature of repressed material is to defy repression and to seek to express itself, either in dreams or in neurotic symptoms, slips of the tongue and so on. Usually, the mind is able to accommodate this. Dreams, in fact, usually function as what Freud called 'wish-fulfilment', allowing repressed material an adequate enough expression so that it need not interrupt the subject's daily practices. In nightmares, the repressed material has proven too strong for the subject. Wish-fulfilment breaks down, and you wake, unable to face the proximity of unconscious material to the conscious life you are struggling to protect. Neurotic symptoms function in the same way—although they are a near-inevitable part of subjective experience, at times the machinery of repression is not strong enough, and clinical help is required. Yet, in the same way that dreams are so similar to nightmares, neurotic patients are never far away from the 'normal'. Indeed, only the success or not of repression and the ease of management of unruly unconscious material in day-to-day life distinguishes psychological illness from health.

THE OEDIPUS COMPLEX

Although much Freudian theorising is dedicated to evolving models of the topography of the subject, an equal amount of work goes into explaining how the subject ends up with this particular configuration of identities and energies. The explanation for the derivation of subjectivity—what is generally known as the Oedipus complex—is not only one of the most famous aspects of Freudian theory; it is significant for two other main reasons. Firstly, it argues that the subject is *produced* in conjunction with the specific set of familial and social relations dominant in culture. This idea that subjectivity is neither innate nor inevitable challenges the model of personal or spiritual life as a privileged essence, subsisting well in advance of the historical conditions in which it appears.

Secondly, the Oedipus model understands that the key contributing factors to the production of subjectivity are the gender relations and sexual identifications of the child's environment. Subjects are not born into an undefined world that they then order according to their own priorities. The world we enter is already structured according to cultural traditions and a civil politics laden with significances and imperatives with which we must deal. For example, although the child only has its gender stabilised after the Oedipus complex, it arrives in a world where certain biological attributes are read as naturally and necessarily connected with the particular set of behaviours, feelings and appearances we call gender. Although his theories have been used to argue for the relativity of gender, Freud himself remained loyal to the gender politics of his own society. Thus his theory of subjectivity is firstly a theory of masculinity and a treatment of the development of the boy child. For that reason, my discussion of the Oedipus complex uses the masculine pronoun.

The basic form of the Oedipal drama is well known. Freud's usage is derived from Sophocles' tragedy *Oedipus Rex*, in which a young man, despite attempts to resist the incontrovertible prophecy that has foretold what he will do, unwittingly murders his father and marries his mother. Oedipal theory emphasises the uninterrupted immediacy with which the boy experiences his mother in the earliest stages of his development. In fact, it is as if the separation from the mother's body in birth does not take on a psychological meaning until much later. The boy feels an almost idyllic unity with the mother's body and reality. This idyll cannot last, however, and is interrupted by the recognition of the masculine principle in the boy's awakened interest in his own genitals. He connects ownership of the penis with the presence of his father, both as an increasingly important influence on his own identity, and also as a complicating factor in his relationship with his mother. The lasting significance of the Oedipal relationship emerges, therefore, as the intimacy with the mother begins to break down.

According to Freud, the boy becomes interested in his penis, and starts to see it as a significant force in his emotional life. Why this happens is not clear. Freud chooses merely to rely on what he reports to be empirical observation. Nevertheless, the penis becomes a preoccupation. Yet this interest attracts negative attention, usually from women, who are the most common carers of young children. The boy is threatened with a range of punishments for his interest in his penis, sometimes with the invocation of the father as the ultimate sanction. These threats are always interpreted by the boy as the danger of castration. His fear that his penis may be taken from him is reinforced by the fact that, 'sooner or later' (Freud 1977, p.318), he sees the genitals of a girl or woman. According to Freud, his response is to see the girl as already castrated. The female body is a site of lack, therefore—a lack that the boy interprets as an ever-present danger for himself. The castration he has been threatened with has, it seems, already been carried out on others.

In sum, then, the boy recognises that there is a difference between genders, and the mark of that difference is the presence or absence of the penis. Ownership of the penis is not permanent. The boy, therefore, is faced with two alternatives: he can either identify with the father who owns the penis and seems to be the policeman of the very principle of penis ownership, and imagine having sex with the mother, as the father does; or he can identify with the mother who has lost the penis, and imagine being the object of the father's sexuality. Freud calls these alternatives the active-masculine and passive-feminine. The problem is that, although one seems to lead to the heterosexual normality Freud was so desperate to promote, both these options remain under the persistent threat of castration. If he chooses the active path, he will be punished for excessive interest in the penis. Similarly, he can only choose the passive path if he has lost the penis already. Neither alternative offers an escape from castration. The boy is presented with a no-win situation. Instead of confronting this dilemma, a whole new zone of the mind is created in which the problem can be installed. The Oedipal material is repressed into the unconscious.

Thus what is considered heterosexual normality is not a fixed and predictable path dictated by nature. It is the result of a complex series of developments within the subject himself, which remain problematic and unresolved. Even the most apparently stable and normal male subject has only a fragile hold on masculine identity. The threat of castration is ever-present, and must be dealt with again and again in adult life. In other words, the Oedipal drama, the resulting fragility of gender roles and anxiety about castration have not been resolved for the male subject, but merely hidden away in a domain that may allow them to be temporarily controlled, but is not strong enough to resist their constant drive towards re-enactment. The man repeatedly projects aspects or fractions of this drama on to his adult world, by seeking parent substitutes or conquering the threat of castration over and over again in the triumphs and competitions that are seen as the most essentially masculine behaviour. Sometimes these identifications and projections are played out within the individual subject himself. For example, when Freud later complicated his model of the subject by splitting the conscious into ego (the part of the subject that organises the self in its day-to-day, hopefully stable relationships in the world) and superego (the higher faculty of moral reflection and judgment), he saw in the latter the danger of the subject internalising the strictest forms of parental authority, and inhibiting the ego by excessive self-critique, guilt and inhibition.

FREUD AND FEMININE SUBJECTIVITY

As I have mentioned several times, the model of subjective development outlined above is specifically for boys. What about feminine subjectivity? Here we encounter one of the most notorious aspects of Freudian theory, and the one at the heart of postmodern revisions of psychoanalysis (see Chapters 5, 7 and 8). According to Freud, the girl also experiences a version of the Oedipal complex. However, her comparison of her own genitals with those of boys makes her feel as if she is already castrated. The fear of future castration does not operate for her, but she does seek a substitute for the lost penis. She progresses 'along the line of a symbolic equation, one might say' (Freud 1977, p.321), replacing the missing penis with a baby, that she imagines she receives from the father. It is this process of substitution that is repressed in the feminine unconscious.

Freud was the first to admit that feminine subjectivity was a mystery to him, though it does seem to have been impossible for him to think of it other than as a variant of the model he had already established for the masculine. This emphasis on the masculine as the standard produces some quite bizarre results. For example, in his 1919 paper on masochism, 'A Child is Being Beaten' (1979), Freud considered himself limited in having a preponderance of female case studies from which to theorise. His impulse was to develop a theory of the male masochist from this material, and then develop his model of female masochism from the male. The idea of developing a female model first does not seem to have been possible for him. In general, the emphasis on the genitals means that, despite the fact that subjectivity is seen as constructed and not innate, the biological differences between the male and female bodies are paramount. In practice, this difference comes down to the ownership or not of the penis. As Freud says, misquoting Napoleon, for psychoanalysis, 'Anatomy is Destiny' (Freud 1977, p.320). Freud recognised that the subject was constructed according to family relations, yet—perhaps because of his ambition to create what could pass for general scientific truth—he universalised the specific social practices not only of his own time, but also of his own city and class, until they stood in his mind as a model of the practices of human families at all times and everywhere. Recognising that gender and sexual identities had been and would be vastly different from those that he knew would have called for a more pluralistic understanding of how subjects develop—a breadth Freud, striving for a universal and transhistorical theory, was reluctant to consider. Ironically, however, as we shall see in later chapters, the very historically specific nature of the parameters Freud chose have allowed more recent feminist theorists, such as Luce Irigaray, Elizabeth Grosz and others, to identify his model not with a universally valid truth, but with the structure of the gender values and politics of the West in its modern history. This has opened up a whole tradition of productive debunking that has found means both for critically analysing the politics of our subjectivity, and for defining the huge varieties of possible subjectivities lived in its gaps and shadows.

Given the nature of the material that has been buried in the unconscious, it is no surprise that the pressure exerted on the conscious mind by repressed material carries with it an element of danger, ambiguity and obscurity. The very issues that define and anchor subjectivity in Freudian terms—gender, sexuality, the body, family relationships—have all proven to be ambiguous, unstable and threatening. At the heart of the boy's subjectivity is the feeling that the masculinity he has inherited from his father, and whose emblem is the male genitals, can easily be taken away from him. He feels as good as castrated, and is locked in a life of desperate compensation and reassurance, seeking everywhere the certainty and stability of gender on which he can ground some sense of capable selfhood. We will see in later chapters how other theorists have seen this anxiety about the fragile presence and easy absence of the phallic defining principle of masculinity as the key to understanding such diverse things as human language (in Lacan, in Chapter 3), or cinema (see the discussion of Laura Mulvey in Chapter 7). Freud's own work saw the Oedipal drama not only as the key to the neurotic symptoms of individual patients, but as explanations for religion, art and the structure of societies from the tribal to the industrial.

FREUD, ART AND TEXTUALITY

What is the implication of Freudian theory for the study of texts? One of the most straightforward adaptations of Freudian theory in aesthetics sees the artwork as analogous to the dream. In the same way as the dream attempts to placate unconscious material by giving it some temporary outlet, and conjuring for it some image of its possible satisfaction, the artwork reprocesses in a disguised form the most troubling Oedipal obsessions of the artist, and indeed of readers, viewers and audiences. This version of psychoanalytic aesthetics is the most simple and primitive. Since Lacan identified the Oedipal drama with the acquisition of language, psychoanalytic textual analysis has become infinitely more supple.

In the high modernist period between the First and Second World Wars, however, there was no shortage of artists interested in using art as a way of exploring their own unconscious. In this way, the idea of the repression of unconscious material took on a significant historical, even political, meaning. In surrealism, the evocation of nightmare as a kind of hidden truth was intended as a direct challenge to the daylight knowledges on which an overly rational and technocratic, decadent and doomed modern world was seen to depend. In a very different way, but to a similar end, a novelist like D.H. Lawrence (1885–1930) read the unconscious as a kind of primeval and authentic animality that needed to be liberated in all its sexual glory and charisma. Other artists experimented with automatic writing—the rapid spontaneous production of whatever words occurred to the writer. This was understood as providing direct expression of unconscious material. In films like *Un chien andalou* (1928), Luis Buñuel (1900–83) attempted to enact the sort of identifications and transitions that the unconscious used in producing dream material. All these experiments are approximations of Freudian theory, inspired more by its endless metaphoric potential than by its precise doctrines. In a sense, artworks—if they did what dreams did, as Freud himself believed—did not need to be aware of Freudian theory in order to illustrate psychoanalytic truths. But it is important for us to see the widening ripples of Freudian influence if we want to understand twentieth-century culture, even if some of the practices involved are only vaguely connected to the Freudian project, or the finer points of its theory.

There is much we have not said about the work that Freud himself has done. His work on the stages of sexual development (oral, anal and genital) in *Three Essays on the Theory of Sexuality*, the death drive in 'Beyond the Pleasure Principle', and the rich range of subjective feelings that are conventionally divided up into religion, art and culture in works as diverse as 'The Uncanny', *Moses and Monotheism, Totem and Taboo* and *Civilization and Its Discontents*, are all of significant interest, and are often used as touchstones in analyses of culture and art. All that has been possible above is to sketch out the most general of Freud's theories about the structure of the subject and where it comes from. For the purposes of this book, however, it should be clear that Freud is the most important and influential exponent of what I have called 'subjective' theory. To Freud, the subject has a knowable content, and an analysable structure. In other words, the subject is full to the brim of identifications, emotions and values, separating it from the subjects around it, even though the processes from which this subjectivity is derived are seen to be as good as universal experiences. In Chapter 4, we will begin to look at quite a different understanding of subjectivity in the work of Nietzsche and Foucault, whose theories of the self I have labelled 'anti-subjective'. Here, subjectivity is not fixed and individual, but is a ruse of power. According to these theories, the whole idea of a fixed and knowable, autonomous subjectivity is an hallucination contrived by power in order to isolate and control us in the cage of individuality. In this contrast between a model of subjectivity of which the self-sustaining individual is the goal, and one that views it as the ultimate prison we can see the outline of the struggle over selfhood that is the hidden yet desperate tension that defines modern and postmodern experience. Firstly, however, I want to turn to Jacques Lacan, whose work is the bridge between Freudian and postmodern psychoanalysis.

FURTHER READING

Freud, Sigmund, 1976, *The Interpretation of Dreams* trans. James Strachey, Pelican Books, Harmondsworth.
——1977, 'The Dissolution of the Oedipus Complex' *On Sexuality* trans. James Strachey, Penguin Books, Harmondsworth, pp.315–322.
——1984, 'A Note on the Unconscious in Psychoanalysis' *On Metapsychology* trans. James Strachey, Penguin Books, Harmondsworth, pp.50–57.

3 | Lacan: The subject is language

FREUD ARGUED THAT subjects could only deal effectively with unconscious material when they could talk about it with their analysts—by bringing it into language, in other words. It took the work of Jacques Lacan (1901–81) to draw out fully the significance of language for psychoanalysis. In doing this, Lacan was in tune with other major developments in twentieth-century thought. Indeed, it is hard to overstate the importance to the modern era of the idea that language defines human life. Ludwig Wittgenstein's (1889–1951) idea of the 'language game', and Martin Heidegger's identification of language with the limits of (human) Being both in very different ways and in very separate traditions propose language as the centrepiece of the interactions of consciousness with both the world and others.

In the 1950s and 1960s, structuralism and semiotics encouraged the use of the linguistic theories of Swiss linguist Ferdinand de Saussure (1857–1913) as a general model of all human culture. The human being was to be seen as the *signifying animal,* and all human rituals and behaviours could ultimately be *read.* The anthropological work of Claude Lévi-Strauss (b. 1908) and the cultural analysis of Roland Barthes (1915–80) were pivotal in the application of structuralist models of the sign to human behaviour in general.

Lacan's ultimate and most influential conclusion is that *the unconscious is structured like a language.* The aim of this chapter is to give an outline of Lacanian thought in relation to its forebears: Saussurian linguistics and Freudian psychoanalysis. It must be said that Lacan's writing is notorious for its ambiguity and its intentional obscurity. Given that Lacan's aim was to challenge the common-sense idea that language exists in order to communicate, and is instead the very material of subjectivity, it seems logical that he chose to use language himself in the most intense and self-conscious way. He was merely drawing attention to language's material density, rejecting the platitude that language is at its best when it is used most clearly and transparently. His writing, then, illustrates the understanding of language that has become common amongst philosophers and cultural theorists. It is not that subjects exist in the world and then use language as their tool. This may seem at first glance a logical explanation for how language came into being in the first place, but it does not represent the relationship we have with language as individual subjects. The sequence is, in fact, reversed. Language existed before any of us was born, and we must locate ourselves in the field of language in order to take up a place in the human world. As the post-structuralist philosopher Jacques Derrida (b. 1930) has pointed out in his influential *Of Grammatology* (1967), it is impossible to isolate a moment that could be called the origin of language. Yet we still continue to think of it as a tool under our control, as if we give rise to it ourselves for our own purposes. Lacan's work reverses this unthinking assumption, reminding us that our subjectivity has had to emerge in a world in which language is always already established.

SAUSSURE AND STRUCTURALISM

Behind Lacan's ideas about language lies, as I have said, the linguistics of Ferdinand de Saussure, as found in an edited version of his lecture notes, *The Course in General Linguistics* (1916). To Saussure, language is a system of signs, each of which connects a material form, the *signifier* (written marks on a page or spoken sounds in the mouth) with an abstract concept, its *signified*. This last is not a material thing in the world as much as the idea of the thing as it forms in the mind of the language user. Signs are not directly anchored in reality, therefore, but in the conceptualisation of reality in the human mind. The relationship of each signifier is thus not with the object in the outside world with which it is supposed to connect, but with other signifiers, as they form a systematic world-view.

Language is not a medium, then, but a *system*. This system is not determined by what happens outside of it, in some pre-linguistic space. It is built around an internal arrangement of *differences*. In a famous analogy, language is compared to pieces in a game of chess. You can use anything as chess-pieces (medieval figurines, dolls based on your favourite sit-com, buttons found in the street), as long as it is clear to the players what defines the system of differences between the various pieces that allows them to move in specific ways (small identical pieces are pawns, larger individual ones are knights, bishops, the king, etc.). It is not important what you use as king, queen, rook and pawn, as long as everyone knows which is which. In the case of signifiers, it does not matter which particular marks or sounds are used to denote a certain object. What makes language work is the difference between one signifier and all others. Language efficiency depends not on the perfect way the marks 'cat' define a certain quadruped, but on the complex web of differences which allows us to recognise the minute but crucial distinction between 'cat', 'bat' and so on. Indeed, although this distinction is minute, we are so sensitised to language as a system of differences that we consider those who cannot recognise the distinction to be either non-users of our language or suffering from a learning disorder.

This leads to another important point. The relationship between signifier and signified is not inevitable, but is governed by convention; it is *arbitrary*. There is nothing in the pre-linguistic nature of a set of railway carriages that forces us to use the signifier 'train' to denote it. Onomatopoeia may give us the illusion that signs imitate things, but they too prove to be merely conventional on closer inspection (guns go 'bang!' in English and 'pan!' in French, for example). In sum, to Saussure, language is not a set of tools haphazardly connected, but a concrete system of conventions built around two relationships: the difference between one signifier and another and the arbitrary relationship between signifier and signified. Language is thus a complex cultural order.

Lacan aimed to use these ideas about the sign as a way of recovering what he saw as Freud's essential insight: the relationship between the subject and signification. Lacan always presented his project as a 'return to Freud', saying that he was merely drawing out ideas already present in the earlier theorist's own writings. Many of the famous seminars which Lacan conducted in the 1950s and 1960s were based around the close reading of Freudian texts. Indeed, Lacan's work can be seen as a direct adaptation of key Freudian models and motifs into mid-twentieth-century controversies about language and its importance.

THE MIRROR-STAGE

What is Lacan's understanding of the nature of subjectivity? The most famous and accessible idea in the writing of this most infamous and inaccessible theorist is the 'mirror-stage'. We remember that, for Freud, the boy-child's subjectivity is the result of a charged engagement with the figures around him, especially his physical relationship with the bodies of his parents. Before the Oedipus complex entered its final crucial phase, the boy felt himself in direct unmediated relationship with his mother. His separation from his mother's body is not yet complete. Something intrudes from 'the outside' to disrupt this secure relationship: the penis—firstly, the boy's own, as the focus of his own illicit preoccupation; secondly, his father's, as the sign of the distinction between masculine and feminine, and of the gender hierarchy that will bring the boy's sense of self into crisis, and lead it into the highly fraught field of subjectivity.

The boy's subjectivity, then, is constructed as the end of a complex and scary game, where the physical body's vulnerability intersects with the phantom body of the ideal gender types. The residue of volatility, frustrated dream, and lost security haunt human subjectivity everywhere and forever. Even as an adult, you endlessly recycle the imagery of this drama. A chaotic set of signs, linked to the Oedipus complex and reproducing the phantom parent-figures and their meaning, governs the subject's interior life.

Lacan also describes the development of subjectivity as the result of the intrusion of something external into the ideal space of the pre-Oedipal subject. In his work, the Freudian intuition that subjectivity is ruled by signs and images—the father-*figure*, the phallic *symbol*—becomes a complete theory of signification. In Lacanian theory, the critical stage for the development of subjectivity is called the 'mirror-stage' and it occurs usually between the ages of six and eighteen months. Prior to the mirror-stage, the child has no sense of itself as a separate entity. There is no understanding of the limits of the individual body, nor that there is necessarily anything external to it. The many surfaces that the child touches—the mother's skin, clothing, carpet—are all felt to be part of a continuous, uninterrupted, limitless being, so amorphous and open-ended that it cannot be compared to anything as located, specific and defined as selfhood. At this *pre-Oedipal* stage there is no subjectivity, therefore. An aspect of this undefined state is that the child has no sense of the coordination of its limbs. In the same way that no surface with which the child comes into contact is felt to be necessarily alien to it, outside of the 'self', the child does not experience its body as its own, with a fixed perimeter and working as a unified system.

All this begins to change in the mirror-stage. Now, for some reason, the child starts to see an image of itself from outside of itself, perhaps in a mirror, perhaps reflected in an adult's eyeball, perhaps by suddenly recognising some similarity with a playmate. In Lacan's words, 'the *mirror stage* . . . manufactures for the subject, caught up in the lure of spatial identification, the succession of fantasies that extends from a fragmented body-image to a form of its totality' (Lacan 1977, p.4). The visual field plays a crucial role in the development of subjectivity, offering the subject an image of wholeness, unity and totality to replace the fragmentation and dissociation that has dominated so far.

IMAGINARY AND SYMBOLIC

The sense of unified selfhood is one of the most crucial defining moments in the development of subjectivity, according to Lacan. For the first time, the child understands itself as separate from the world around it, that there are objects in the world with which it may come into contact and that there are other people with whom one is involved, but who are physically distinct. Linked to this sense of the separation of what is outside (or 'otherness', as it is commonly referred to) is the climactic intuition of the wholeness and completeness of the self.

Because of their location, human eyes are unable to provide the consciousness that inhabits the human body with an immediate awareness of that body's shape. The eye merely returns disconnected flashes of the line of the arm, the shape of the shoulder, the distance of the feet. To the eye, the body is a collection of disproportionate moving objects, shifting in and out of perspective in apparently random ways. The mirror-stage compensates for, and overturns, this lack of perspective, this sense of disproportion and randomness. The mirror image supplies the self with an image of its own coordination, of system and unity. The limbs are no longer part of the outside world. That world is separate, and the limbs now seem part of a simple unified whole that is set off against that world. This complex experience, where the subject feels its unity and separation in response to what it has seen of itself in the mirror, becomes—because it is governed by the image—the *imaginary*.

This wonderful sense of unity and oneness is not as simple as it may seem, however. The image of the self as separate has not been something that the subject has developed for itself, from within, as a result of its own creativity, or as an expression of its own interior, naturally occurring truth. The self's new understanding of itself has come to it from the outside, in an image it has seen in the external world. This image may provide it with a sense of its own unity, but the image has an external source: it comes from, and remains part of, otherness itself. The complication here is of huge significance in Lacanian theory. The subject, at its very birth, only gets a sense of its own definition from the outside, specifically from an image of itself returned to it from the world. The subject does not define itself. Instead, it is defined by something other than itself. Put in Lacanian terms, *the subject is the discourse of the other*.

The subject, then, is in a state of contradiction. It sees itself as unified and whole, as autonomous and complete, but this very imaginary identity subverts that wholeness. Your selfhood—your subjective centre of gravity—is grounded outside of you, in the very field of images from which you first gained a sense of separation. In short, your selfhood makes you alien to yourself. You are radically *decentred*. In Lacan's words, the mirror-stage ends in 'the assumption of the armour of an alienating identity, which will mark with its rigid structure the subject's entire mental development' (Lacan 1977, p.4). Almost as soon as it has happened, the subject is tipped out of the heroic sense of unity and completeness provided for it by the imaginary. It realises that the image in which the imaginary was grounded instantly throws into doubt the security it seemed to provide. Your sense of self is outside of you, projected at you from a world over which you have minimal control. The system of meanings and identities from which your selfhood derives is not your own. This system is what Lacan calls the *symbolic order*.

This over-arching order is structured as a field of signification, defined in terms of the difference of each of its elements from the others. It is the field that Saussure had defined as language, a system of circulating signifiers. The self's mirror-image of itself that it had discovered in the imaginary finds its archetype in the signifier. The word 'I', for example, provides an image of the self, but only when that selfhood concedes its meaning and definition to the system of signification, of which the signifier 'I' is a part. The imaginary unity it seems to provide is sucked away by its alien nature, the fact that it is part of a system that pre-exists the subject, that other subjects also use, and over which no individual subject has control. The subject's sense of itself is lost in the very field of signs that seemed to provide it in the first place. It is this paradox that governs human subjectivity.

THE REAL

As well as the imaginary and the symbolic, there is a third order in the Lacanian system: the *real*. The real is not reality as we conventionally describe it. Our notion of reality is really a shared cultural construct, a consensus about the material world and how it is to be measured, as an agreed limit to the point-of-view of the individual. Lacan's real is something else, and has to be understood in relation to the imaginary and the symbolic: it is simply that which lies outside of these two domains, and is unapproachable by them.

Subjects only exist in the tension and interplay between imaginary and symbolic. In this way, for Lacan as for Freud, subjectivity is not automatic or spontaneous. It is not simply as if there is always a subject where there is the biological entity we call the human being. Subjectivity is attained only at the end of a process which has many complex and dangerous passages. Subjectivity is always, therefore, problematic. We have become used to simply identifying the separate body with the individual subject as if the two always everywhere went together as the result of their spontaneous self-generation. But according to Lacan, the subject arises in the exchange between two orders whose material and impetus are from the shared, autonomous field of language. Language, if you like, inhabits the body as the subject. There is no simple individual, operating its body like the ghost in the machine, to use a famous metaphor. The subject is merely a fragment of a dynamic field of endless incompletions and disjunctions. The individual body is the hardness which makes this subjectivity appear in its illusory separation. The body is therefore the limit of the interplay of the imaginary and the symbolic, the sort of inert outside that language cannot reach. This is what Lacan calls the real, the irreducibly separate and unsignifiable asymptote of subjectivity.

To recap, then, the subject's mature life is dominated by the demands of the symbolic order. In the symbolic, things appear to make sense, hierarchies of meaning are established, and society functions in a tense but efficient manner. All the identities, systems and priorities we associate with the rational and liberal functioning of a stable social order require the subject to agree to the logic of the symbolic. The essence of the symbolic is the promise that language makes sense—in Saussure's terms, that for every signifier there is a signified. Social processes and institutions, whether they are as amorphous as the gender hierarchy of masculine over feminine, or as specific as the courts of law, rely on and claim to reproduce the same logic. At the heart of every process, it is assumed, is an agreed and rational meaning.

Yet our involvement in the symbolic order is the result of an imaginary identification. The subject enters the symbolic thinking that what it will gain is the intense self-identity it thought it found in the mirror-image. This image seemed to offer the sense of unity, totality and completion that the uncoordinated, fragmented pre-Oedipal child discovers as the first token of its identity. It is only when it finds that this image is not its own—that it is the play of light on a mirror, the gaze of a completely separate subject or a word in the mouth like 'I' that may seem to represent the self, but is equally the property of others—that it senses its identity is being sucked away from it into a public, shared world of orders and hierarchies.

DESIRE AND DEMAND

The subject seems to agree to inhabit the symbolic order, but maintains, at an unconscious level, its pursuit of the intense satisfaction, the sense of completion and self-identity, that it felt it had momentarily in the imaginary, but that it has lost. Indeed, the success of the symbolic is explained by the fact that it seems to hold out for the subject the intense identifications that will return to it the sense of completeness it now lacks. Here we encounter the crucial Lacanian distinction between *desire* and *demand*.

The subject's entry into the symbolic order is at the expense of the magical feeling of oneness it had in the imaginary. At the heart of its very being is a sense of *lack*. It endlessly seeks to compensate for this lack, to fill the hole at its core. This longing for self-completion is Lacan's definition of *desire*. The subject is propelled into and through the world, into its emotional and sexual relationships, its fraught group identities with nation, race and political party, its careerism and material acquisitiveness, all as a result of this insatiable need to fill up the lack at the centre of its being. Each separate thing we pursue is called a *demand*. None of them will satisfy desire, which is by definition insatiable. Each demand offers momentarily the possibility that it will satisfy desire. We go shopping for clothes, electric with the sense of the new self our purchases will offer us. When we get home, we lay our new things on the bed, exultant in the new horizons of selfhood, the sense of identity and completion they seem to offer. But, after we have worn them once or twice, we put them away and the excitement soon passes. This is the drama of demand and desire. We are endlessly drawn towards the selfhood each new success, sexual relationship or night of intoxication may offer. But they are all illusions. There is no new self, except as the endlessly receding horizon of desire.

The tension between the endless desire that is the source of human motivations, and the hopeless demands that fail to appease it, is the very heart of the human tragedy, according to Lacan. We feel desire only because the imaginary has escaped us, because we are lost in the symbolic. In other words, the very fact that we feel desire means that we are part of the order in which desire cannot be satisfied. All the demands we pursue arise only in the symbolic. They are doomed to inevitable frustration, because we cannot fulfil what desire really seeks from us: to return from the symbolic to the imaginary we have always already lost.

THE OTHER AND THE *OBJET PETIT A*

Lacanian jargon is also worth noting here. What we seek is the image of completion that was coming to us from the world outside, specifically from other subjects—what, in general terms, the Other (French *l'Autre*) seemed to offer us. Each small transitory object that we mistake for the Other is called an *objet petit a* (literally, 'object little a [from autre]') by Lacan. This refers to another sort of other, an other so inconsequential it is not to be written with a capital letter. The motivations that fuel and guide our daily lives are each and every one the pursuit of one *objet petit a* after another. These objects in turn are mere substitutes for the huge and miraculous Other hovering on the horizon of human possibility, always beckoning us as the ultimate object of desire, the lure of a complete satisfaction that would also be the stabilisation of a complete and meaningful selfhood. It is this dream of a great and glorious Other that would restore the subject's miraculous unity that explains the religious belief in a patriarchal God, and its rhetoric of purity, completion and totality.

THE NAME-OF-THE-FATHER

Here, we are very distant from the commonsense understanding of language as a human tool. We are used to thinking of words as subordinate to the essential ideas and meanings that we generate through our immediate and intense relationship with the world. We tend also to think of our relationships with others as a complex but rewarding adventure that we, as separate and autonomous individuals, undertake after we have attained our sense of self and personal identity. For Lacanian psychoanalysis, these ideas are reversed. It is impossible to gain any sense of selfhood outside of relationship with the Other. Selfhood, in fact, can only come to us in relationship. The ground on which this relationship develops is language. Language is not a transparent system of meanings and messages. In fact, this image of language as a system of communication is one of the ruses of the symbolic order, its perpetual offering of a stable meaning that perpetually eludes us. Language is an unstable and obscure system, offering us identities and simultaneously drawing them away from us. It seems to offer us imaginary individual completion, while entangling us in a shared symbolic order.

In Freud, the penis operates as the marker of sexual difference. Men aspire to ownership and control of the penis, which they identify not only as the site of pleasure, but also the symbol of masculine power. They are aware that their possession of the penis is not certain. They have been threatened with castration, and they believe that the female body is already castrated. They interpret this to mean that women cannot gain access to power, because they lack its symbol and instrument. Only ownership of the penis guarantees the certainty of power and stable identity and order. Masculine subjectivity is governed by the pursuit of this certainty, by the unconfessed anxiety about the ownership of the penis and a need for continual confirmation of masculinity itself and all its prerogatives. Control of the penis seems always available to the man, but is never completely stable and certain.

Lacan's view of subjectivity repeats the Freudian schema, but with one major variation: the drama of gender and power is displaced from anatomy to language. Subjectivity still has the same dramatic gender inequity. It still operates with the same threat of loss and incompletion. It is still a pursuit of stable identities and structures. Yet all this takes place in language and not in mere biology. For Freud, the penis operates as the essence of the system of gender order. Subjectivity and all its material—gender, sexuality, pleasure, desire, power—perpetually return to the penis as the logic of identity and order, particularly the defining identity of masculine and feminine and their inextricable relationship with power. To Lacan, language defines gender, keeping identity, order, meaning, reason and truth firmly on the side of the masculine as they were in Freud. Yet it is not the literal penis that is the essence, symbol and guarantee of this process.

Where the masculine subject had pursued control over the penis in Freud, as the imaginary image of his totality and authority, of his *meaning*, in Lacan he is pursuing that ideal moment of language use that draws him ever on into the field of language, with the ever-postponed but ever-renewed hope of a complete and efficient image of himself appearing to stabilise his subjectivity. For Freud, it was the father's penis that functioned as the basis of the social law. For Lacan, it is the signifier of the father that seems to hold all charisma and power. In other words, what takes the place of the penis for Lacan is the Name-of-the-Father—in French, *le nom-de-père*—or the *transcendental signifier*. In the same way that the social order for Freud was governed by the masculine principle—and masculinity was in turn defined by ownership of the penis—for Lacan, the symbolic order is a masculine domain, governed not by the penis, but by the symbol of the penis, the phallus. The symbolic order is thus commonly described as a *phallocentric* order.

LANGUAGE AND SUBJECTIVITY

Freud provided a model of the construction of subjectivity that emphasised the place of gender in influencing family relations and defining social place. Although he came to the conclusion that 'anatomy is destiny', he did end by separating the formation of gender—and indeed of selfhood—from the inevitability and spontaneity of Nature. Instead, obscure and fragile social processes were involved—ones that often went wrong, leading to neurosis, maladjustment and mental illness. Lacan both generalised and intensified this model. Although the family supplies some of the imagery for the development of the subject (the archetypal Other remains the mother, the law is the Name-of-the-Father), it is the amorphous and ubiquitous field of language that determines the development of the self. The gender politics of subjectivity are played out in every aspect of human culture and society, because always and everywhere human interaction must rely on shared symbolic processes of exchange and mediation.

Lacan shared with semiotics the conviction that every social process was a symbolic process. Even your relationship with yourself involves the dramatisation of images and identities projected into your interior life by the great field of otherness that is co-extensive with language. In other words, selfhood is never spontaneous and always derivative. Only in our fantasies of a return to the imaginary do we encounter an image of the subject as self-generating and complete. In the symbolic order in which we must live, we are separated from that imaginary completion; even though our desire drives us forever on to try and recover it, it will always elude us, forging the contradiction with which we all must live.

It is no wonder, given the intense pathos of the human condition as Lacan has defined it, that his work is often criticised for its conservatism and pessimism. In later chapters we will meet other adaptations of Lacanian theory that use its terms and schemas to propose ways of subverting the phallocentrism of the symbolic order (see the discussion of Luce Irigaray in Chapter 5, Julia Kristeva in Chapter 6, and the work of Gilles Deleuze and Felix Guattari in Chapter 10). We will also see how Lacanian theory, and the reaction to it, together provide insights into the gender politics of cultural practices like literature and film. What is important to recognise in Lacan is a major step forward in finding a theoretical framework in which to talk about something as notoriously hard to pin down as subjectivity: for this theorist, the key is in reversing commonsense logic and seeing the self as a by-product of the language it thinks it uses for its own ends.

FURTHER READING

Lacan, Jacques, 1977, 'The Mirror Stage as Formative of the Function of the I as Revealed in Psychoanalytic Experience' *Ecrits: A Selection* trans. Alan Sheridan, Tavistock, London, pp.1–7.
——1979, *The Four Fundamental Concepts of Psychoanalysis* trans. Alan Sheridan, Penguin, Harmondsworth.

4 | Foucault: The subject and power

THE THEORIES OF subjectivity that have dominated the second half of the twentieth century fall broadly into two categories: those that attempt to define the nature or structure of the subject (its 'truth'), and those that see any definition of subjectivity as the product of culture and power. The former is associated with Freud and psychoanalysis, and the work of Jacques Lacan; the latter with the work of Friedrich Nietzsche (1844–1900) and Michel Foucault (1926–84). Both these models may seem surprising to those coming from outside of the discussion. Where is the image of the subject as autonomous and free, as authentic and naturally occurring—the subject of Rousseau and of Romantic poetry; the thinking, feeling, agent making its way through the world, giving expression to its emotions and fulfilment to its talents and energies? In short, despite the fierce antagonism between the different theories in the debate around subjectivity, they agree in seeing this older form of the subject—the 'individual'—as a mirage or even a ruse, either of language's symbolic order or of power.

Chapter 3 introduced Lacan's theories of the subject and its relation to language. This chapter outlines what Nietzsche, and especially Foucault, had to say about power, showing how their view diverges from that of Rousseau.

THE SUBJECT AS A CONSTRUCT

As I have mentioned, both the Lacanian and Foucauldian points of view dispute the model of the subject as a free and autonomous individual. They also see the subject as a *construct*. For both, the subject does not come into the world with all its nature and scope encapsulated within itself in embryonic form. Subjectivity is made by the relationships that form the human context. To psychoanalysis, dominant amongst these are family relationships defined in terms of gender and sexuality. For Foucault, they are the broad relationships of power and subordination that are present everywhere in all societies.

Both approaches also pinpoint the key mechanism by which this context forms the individual: language. Their understandings diverge in terms of what it is about language that most systematically affects the subject. As we saw in the last chapter, for Lacan it is what Swiss linguist Ferdinand de Saussure called the 'signifier', the very functioning material of language. For Foucault, it is the discourses of truth and knowledge from which are derived our models of normal and abnormal behaviour.

Yet this is as far as the similarity between the two groups goes. To psychoanalysis, the Foucauldian tradition omits a fully fledged definition of the nature of the subject. To Foucault, it is this very need to derive a final and complete understanding of the nature of the subject that makes psychoanalysis what he calls a 'totalitarian' theory, collaborating with power rather than revealing some way of frustrating it—his understanding of the ultimate purpose of theoretical work.

ALTHUSSER AND THE INTERPELLATED SUBJECT

It is important to recall that Foucault's theory of the relationship between the subject and power was not the first political theory of subjectivity to be influential. Marxist philosopher Louis Althusser (1918–90) was developing a definition of the subject's place under capitalism in the late 1960s, at about the same time as the post-structuralist theorists who would soon attract far more attention. His most important treatment of the issue comes in the long essay, 'Ideology and Ideological State Apparatuses' (Althusser 1971, pp.121–73), written in 1969. The purpose of this essay is to investigate how the structure of capitalist society reproduces itself. How do successive generations become the docile workers and consumers the capitalist system needs? This cannot simply be explained by the repressive forces that the capitalist state has at its disposal—what Althusser calls the Repressive State Apparatuses, like the army, police and prison system.

The answer is to be found in the institutions that reproduce the values, meanings and logic of the capitalist system—what are called Ideological State Apparatuses, like the church, family and especially the school (more recent commentators would, of course, add the mass media). These institutions endlessly reinforce capitalist values—or, at least, the right degree of docility and fatalism in us, making us useful to the dominant order. Thus, capitalism does not simply operate on the level of industries, classes and structures. It succeeds by creating subjects who become its instruments and bearers. Ideology *needs* subjectivity. It constitutes us as subjects by 'interpellating' us, according to Althusser—calling out to us in the way a policeman calls out to someone in the street, to use his most famous example. He writes: 'the hailed individual will turn round. By this mere one-hundred-and-eighty-degree physical conversion, he becomes a *subject*.' (Althusser 1971, p.163) By calling out to him, the policeman creates from the solitary walker in the street a certain type of subject—one answerable to the law and to the state and system behind it. This subject does not develop according to its own wants, talents and desires, but exists for the system that needs it. Its only public reality is determined for it by the social apparatus that calls it into a certain kind of being. Subjectivity, therefore, is the type of being we become as we fit into the needs of the larger political imperatives of the capitalist state. It requires us not only to behave in certain ways, but to *be* certain types of people.

Althusser's influence has steadily declined since the late 1970s, reflecting the decline of Marxism's academic prestige and the rise of other types of politics, specifically those of gender, sexuality and ethnicity. It is important to note some crucial distinctions between his ideas and Foucault's, however. Althusser's theory contrasts ideology (the false consciousness capitalism instils in us so that we cooperate with it) and science (the insights into the true nature of the social order that Marxism can produce). The latter is a model of a truth that can contribute to the correct revolutionary species of power—a new social order, in fact. To Foucault, there can be no such impersonal 'scientific' truth. Ever mutating and ever dangerous, power and the so-called truth it uses to justify and extend itself are always in all of their forms to be met with scepticism and resistance.

FOUCAULT ON THE FREE AND AUTONOMOUS SUBJECT

Let us turn to a summary of Foucault's work, by way of quick
reference to Rousseau. As we saw in Chapter 1, Rousseau saw
the individual as self-sufficient. Walking in the woods of Saint-
Germain, he contemplated the true nature of the human self,
descended from its original form to a state of prejudice and
confusion by the working of human culture and society. Not only
was this natural self the subject of Rousseau's contemplation, but
he was also giving it dramatic form. His solitary walking was itself
a reanimation, a rediscovery, of the same individual self-sufficiency.

This image of the self as compromised by the world, yet
recoverable beneath the detritus and inauthenticity of day-to-day
life, still has a powerful attraction. From the counter-cultural call
to act purely according to spontaneous desire, to the pop psychological truism that you should 'be yourself', the modern era has
been saturated by the dream that social life is a place of compromise
and debasement, but that—somewhere—your true self remains
hidden, free and available, if only you can find the right social
group, language or personal style. According to this model, the
individual is self-contained and complete, and society presses in on
it from the outside, frustrating its dreams and restricting its ability
to express itself.

This is the very model of individuality that Foucault disputes.
He writes in a very clear statement of his position:

> The individual is not to be conceived as a sort of elementary
> nucleus, a primitive atom, a multiple and inert material on which
> power comes to fasten or against which it happens to strike, and
> in so doing subdues or crushes individuals. In fact, it is already
> one of the prime effects of power that certain bodies, certain
> gestures, certain discourses, certain desires, come to be identified and
> constituted as individuals. The individual, that is, is not the *vis-à-vis*
> of power; it is, I believe, one of its prime effects. The individual is
> an effect of power, and at the same time, or precisely to the extent
> to which it is that effect, it is the element of its articulation. The
> individual which power has constituted is at the same time its
> vehicle. (Foucault 1980b, p.98)

This extract stands at loggerheads with Rousseau's model of the
self, which it clearly identifies in its first sentence: the individuality
we dream of, that primitive, elementary and self-contained form
that society and politics stand outside of and oppress. According

to Rousseau's model, this oppression arises after the subject has been made complete by Nature. The individual comes first, almost producing itself. Power comes after, confusing and limiting the individual. It is this intervention by power that we so often dream of resisting: from within the limitations imposed on us by power, we seek—like Rousseau—to recover the true self that predates it.

Foucault sees this narrative the other way round. Power comes first, he argues, and the 'individual'—and all the things we identify as making up our individuality (our separate body, its idiosyncratic gestures, its specific way of using language, its secret desires)—are really effects of power, designed for us rather than by us. As a result, we are not the antagonists of power, standing opposite (or '*vis-à-vis*' it). We are the very *material* of power, the thing through which it finds its expression. What makes us such an effective 'vehicle' for power is the very fact that we seek to see ourselves as free of it and naturally occurring. For Foucault, Rousseau's free and autonomous individual is not merely an alternative, outmoded theory of subjectivity, a quaint forerunner to contemporary discussions. This very model is the one that allows power to conceal itself, and to operate so effectively.

The dream of individuality denies power, and encourages the individual to become preoccupied with itself—in short, to monitor its own behaviour. Kant saw 'self-consciousness' as the basis of all human experience of the world. Slightly later, G.W.F. Hegel (1770–1831), the highly influential German philosopher who had such an impact on nineteenth-century thought, including the work of Karl Marx, described in his mammoth work *The Phenomenology of Spirit* (1807) how self-consciousness was the destiny of human history, its highest form and purpose. To Foucault, all these images of human self-consciousness ended up as the modern individual endlessly turned in on itself, supposedly discovering its unique truth, but really making itself prey to a power that asks it to be forever aware of and assessing its desires and inclinations. The aim of this chapter is to fully explain what Foucault means here, and to illustrate the most significant ways in which this power operates us.

NIETZSCHE ON SUBJECTIVITY

Before we go into Foucault's work in detail, however, it is worth briefly investigating the ideas of Friedrich Nietzsche, one of the key forerunners of Foucault's work. Nietzsche remains a controversial figure in Western popular history at least, because he was claimed as an influence by the Nazis. How accurately they represented his work is still a subject of debate. In terms of the history of ideas, however, Nietzsche's work stands as a stark rejection of the Enlightenment's faith in reason and universal principles of human value and rights.

In contrast to a society built on impartial and equal commitment to freedom and justice, Nietzsche lauded force, and its essence, will. The human species was divided into those who mindlessly aped convention, and those who, because of some lionine interior power, reached towards a superhuman capacity that was the harbinger of a coming stage of development where the human species as we know it will be surpassed by a higher form. This image of herd behaviour being superseded by a history-smashing élite seems obnoxious to the democratic rhetoric around which we build our judgments in public life. Yet it has had a huge impact on twentieth-century culture. The cultural and social avant garde (from Dadaism at the time of the First World War, through various counter-cultures to the present) have long abominated bourgeois conformity as a life of mindless and mean vindictiveness. Still, in contemporary advertising and pop psychology, the imperative to transcend all opposition by believing in yourself and relying on personal willpower tries to catch the echo of the élitism Nietzsche hoped would usher in a new era. Certainly, it is no more respectful of egalitarianism.

Foucault's work does not share Nietzsche's disdain for the majority of people, but it does present a portrait of a heroic self-creating force, challenging the restrictions of conventional life. In Nietzsche, also, we find the origins of Foucault's understanding of subjectivity and its relationship to language. Let us look at Nietzsche's opinions here, and show how they relate to the crucial Foucauldian notion of power/knowledge. In *On the Genealogy of Morals* (1887), Nietzsche writes:

> A quantum of force is equivalent to a quantum of drive, will, effect—more, it is nothing other than precisely this very driving, willing, effecting, and only owing to the seduction of language (and of the fundamental errors of reason petrified in it) which conceives and misconceives all effects as conditioned by something that causes effects, by a 'subject', can it appear otherwise. For just as the popular mind separates the lightning from its flash and takes the latter for an *action*, for the operation of a subject called lightning, so popular

> morality also separates strength from expressions of strength, as if
> there were a neutral substratum behind the strong man, which was
> *free* to express strength or not to do so. But there is no such
> substratum; there is no 'being' behind doing, effecting, becoming;
> 'the doer' is merely a fiction added to the deed—the deed is
> everything. (1989, p.45)

Here, Nietzsche challenges the commonsense notion of cause and
effect as it appears in 'popular' judgments of human behaviour.
Traditionally, we see an event as an expression of the inner reality
of the thing that causes that event. Things exist in the world; they
have an essential nature. When they act on the world, the effects
that they give rise to are a result of that inner nature. In moral
terms, a criminal deed is performed by someone who has a criminal
nature, whether it has been born in them or is the result of their
experiences. This makes them answerable for the disastrous consequences of their action.

This morality had been given extra force by the Enlightenment's focus on the individual. But this logic is an illusion,
according to Nietzsche. It is quite wrong to assume that behind
every effect there is a human 'subject' intending it, and therefore
answerable. Lightning, in his analogy, is not something that exists
permanently, occasionally flashing in the sky to signal its presence.
Lightning is only this flashing, and it is a mistake to separate the
two. The phrase, 'lightning flashes' is a tautology. Lightning can
do nothing other than flash, and exists only in its flashing. It is
language that gives the illusion that something called lightning exists
separate from the fact of its flash. Grammar gives the impression
that lightning is a thing, and flashing merely something that it may
or may not sometimes do.

Similarly, it is 'a seduction of language' to think that subjects
exist who can choose or not choose to act in certain ways. Force,
will, energy and power circulate in—indeed define—the universe,
unable not to produce dramatic and violent conflicts and impacts.
Grammar, with its imaginary subjects, is an attempt to constrain
those powerful figures who are in tune with this will, and give it
its fullest expression—who are indeed, for Nietzsche, the hope of
a higher life. The 'weak', unable to partake of this higher will,
have invented morality, and embedded it in the categories of
language to give the impression that the powerful could choose
not to be strong. But this is quite false. Strength can only be
strength, and the morality that tries to constrain it is an obstacle

to the ascent of the élite, out of the morass of history that is the legacy of the pettiness and vindictiveness of the meek. In short, morality, and its instrument language, are not universal systems of absolute truths and values, but weapons in a power game where one group in the human world tries to constrain another.

THE SUBJECT AND DISCIPLINARY POWER

The primary idea that Foucault has derived from Nietzsche's argument is that 'subjects' only come into existence through the complex interplay between power and language. According to Foucault, pre-modern modes of power, which relied on a religious obedience and vicious force, by the late eighteenth century could no longer cope with the mobile and fractured nature of the human population. A new type of power arose, one invested in systems of social administration rather than lodged in individuals and titles—in other words, a power built around institutions (prisons, workhouses, schools, factories, hospitals, barracks) rather than around kings and aristocrats. In order that human populations could be better organised, new mechanisms of power needed to be developed.

We remember how, in Nietzsche's argument, morality contrived the category of the subject, and lodged it in language to foster the assumption that individuals existed who were responsible for their actions. The new impersonal power growing with the modern age did something similar, according to Foucault. It developed new truths about human beings which distinguished normal from abnormal behaviour. New academic disciplines appeared, like psychology, sociology and criminology. These disciplines started to produce new arguments and counter-arguments that supposedly provided a scientific insight into the truth of human behaviour. The range of discussions, studies, surveys, theories and reports (collectively called 'discourses') produced by these disciplines were not always consistent. They were often the site of bitter dispute. But they were able to coordinate with the institutions that were springing up at the same time to justify various types of therapy, from re-education to isolation and drugs. These discourses are large and amorphous fields of writing, claiming to deliver the 'truth' about individuals: what makes us sane or insane, criminal or law-abiding, sick or well.

The linchpin of these new knowledges is, as in Nietzsche, the 'subject'. Where the prejudice that every action was the effect of its cause, the subject, was petrified in the grammatical subject of the sentence, modern discourses invented the subject as the imagined origin of all behaviour and thus the ultimate object of analysis. The justification for this was the much-lauded 'self-consciousness' that had been one of the dreams of the Enlightenment: theories of what made the individual what it is would provide an insight into the truth of human nature. But in the same way that, for Nietzsche, morality was a counter-strike against the strong, for Foucault, discourses of knowledge are merely instruments in power's dream of totally organising human populations.

POWER/KNOWLEDGE

The subject does not exist as a naturally occurring thing, but is contrived by the double work of power and knowledge to maximise the operation of both. Indeed, so coordinated are power and knowledge that Foucault collapsed them into a single term: power/knowledge. It is impossible, according to this argument, for one to exist without the other: systems of power require some truth to be derived to justify what they seek to do. Disciplines of knowledge always divide the human population into distinct categories that are one of the prime instruments of power.

One of Foucault's clearest examples of how power/knowledge operates is in the development of the prison. Prisons do not function here as an institution on the margins of social life, but as one that is absolutely central to the day-to-day management of our subjectivity. This is because of the impact the existence of prisons has on us as individuals, but also because the development of the prison is typical of the changes that have been taking place in the politics of the subject since the Enlightenment. In the early modern era, according to Foucault, crime was controlled by spectacular and public displays of absolute power, performed importantly on the transgressor's body—the public dismemberment, torture and execution of the transgressor brought the normally invisible power of the sovereign into the marketplace for all to see. This power was dramatic and stunning, but more or less absent from the routines of the ordinary day. The gradual development of the prison and the systematisation of court proceedings rationalised crime and punishment, making it an inextricable part of the public logic of society.

The physical presence of the prison, and similar institutions (the asylum, the workhouse, even the school and factory), did transform the urban landscape. Yet this was not the mechanism that allowed the meaning of the prison to become such an important factor in modern life. The prison operates, according to Foucault, on the level of the subject. This happens in two ways: firstly, by way of the forms of truth that develop around the reality of crime and the criminal; and secondly, by way of the methodology used within the modern prison. Let us study these one at a time.

Firstly, the prison does not simply incarcerate people arbitrarily. It depends on a system of proper proceedings that in turn must be justified by codes of law or legal precedent. According to the Enlightenment model of subjectivity, the 'individual' is the focus of proceedings, prone before the weight of the institutions of law, but also—in theory, at least—protected by rights. At a deeper level, however, this isolation allows the individual to become an object of study and analysis. What was once a person becomes a phenomenon. The person who has committed a crime becomes something else altogether: the criminal. As a type, the individual becomes subject to analysis, according to ostensibly scientific models. What personality traits make you a criminal? What social conditions lead to crime? What cultural factors (age, class, gender, even ethnicity) predispose individuals to antisocial behaviour?

Here, the 'individual' is not free and autonomous, but the focal point of larger forces, analysed by systems of knowledge in what they claim is an impartial quest for truth. Your interior life is not your own property, with its own logic and inner truth, that you bring into society as a free agent. It is a permanently open display case of psychological and sociological truths, to which you always remain subordinate. Whether we commit crime or not, we are never out of reach of the psychological and sociological theories that circulate about crime. The criminal is a type of person, a mode of subjectivity, and we seek evidence of it within ourselves. We feel that we may always be under the scrutiny of others—of strangers, of hidden surveillance or of tabloid TV cameras. This results in us exaggerating to this hypothetical audience the legality and normality of our behaviour.

PANOPTICISM

This sort of casual yet compulsory paranoia attunes normal day-to-day life to the routine of the prison, our second point. Here, Foucault has famously chosen the liberal economist and social reformer Jeremy Bentham's (1748–1832) design of a model prison—the panopticon—as a summary and image of how the putatively criminal subject is managed. In Bentham's prison design, tiers of cells open on to a central courtyard, in the middle of which is a guard tower. With the cells open at the front, a single guard placed in the tower is able to look into dozens of cells more or less simultaneously. Prisoners will never know if they are being observed or not. Furthermore, if some sort of opaque window-covering is fitted to the tower, it may never need to be occupied at all. Since they may be under observation all the time or never, the prisoner becomes responsible for *appearing* to behave acceptably. Behaviour, according to the logic of the new sciences of psychology, has only one meaning: it is a sign of the nature of the subject within. The prisoner behaves correctly if they have been reformed, or are penitent. The new names for prisons in the nineteenth century (reformatories and penitentiaries) clearly exhibit this new focus not on punishing the body as spectacular early modern punishments had done, but on correcting the soul. These institutions are not interested in merely making sure 'criminals' will not repeat certain acts, but in curing them, changing the nature of their subjectivity. The isolation and monitoring of the body, placing it in a context of maximum visibility, serves merely to allow the subject to be analysed, according to the reigning knowledge about what is and is not illegal or antisocial behaviour. In an important formulation, Foucault reverses the Christian platitude to say 'the soul is the prison of the body' (Foucault 1979, p.30).

Thus the subjectivity of both the citizen in the street and the prisoner are constantly being analysed and measured. The functions of this analysis are threefold: *to individualise, normalise and hierarchise*. Firstly, the subject is to be seen and to feel separate from others. Our primary reality ceases to be derived from a locality, religion, or even an ethnicity. In the modern era, subjects are isolated before the psychological truth they exhibit. Secondly, this allows us all to be measured according to standards of behaviour. There is a healthy, a legal, an acceptable form of behaviour, and the behaviour of individual subjects can be plotted against it. This takes place not just at the level of crime, but in the most trivial behaviour: running in a crowded street, laughing too loud, shouting in public are all seen as potentially dangerous, and are notionally connected with violence and crime, especially in social groups that are already considered suspect, like teenagers. Thus, with the application of norms, certain behaviours—and thus certain subjects—can be compared with one another. Hierarchies of the more or less criminal, the more or less acceptable can be designed.

According to Foucault, the panopticon is typical of the processes of subjectification that govern modern life. Power organises the population into individual units that are then subject to monitoring in a system of maximum visibility. This works most effectively in institutions. Hospitals, schools and universities, banks, departments of social security and tax all keep files on us. We simply forget about these files, or accept them as a necessary and inevitable part of the operation of these institutions. Yet they are our effective social reality, and contain 'truths' about us that can be manipulated outside of our control. Like the files themselves, the truth they contain about us is not our property.

Each of these institutions operates according to its own theories and knowledges: the remedial reader, the uncooperative adolescent, the hysterical patient, the credit risk—these are all types of subjectivity that we may or may not occupy, sometimes even without knowing it. You can see here the coincidence of power and knowledge, as Foucault has theorised it. Each of these institutions has classes of persons into which everyone who deals with them is distributed. The apparently simple and necessary logic of this categorisation—it is not a conspiracy to oppress us, our common sense says, how could these institutions operate otherwise?—already separates us from one another, isolating us, opening up and closing off opportunities, destining us for certain rewards and punishments. The system of truth on which each institution depends is always already a power at work on us.

This is what our individuality has become. We can see here the logic of the quote from Foucault with which we began: individuality is not something free and naturally occuring, as Rousseau had imagined it, that is then affected by society. Social institutions need to define us as individuals, separate from one another, all in our own individual files, all in fear of the tax audit we must face alone, or glancing nervously at the security camera that may or may not be filming us at the ATM. Individuality, therefore, is not the highest possibility of human life, if only we could attune society to allow it expression. Instead, the individual is the thing social institutions need us to feel we are, so that we remain vulnerable to the truths they have contrived for their own efficiency. The power at work here is not the power of the absolute monarch, who appears dramatically in the marketplace to display his might. Instead, it is an anonymous and impersonal power that saturates the pettiest and quietest moments of our personal lives, pressing us with what we should be—at the height of its operation, even becoming us.

THE AESTHETICS OF EXISTENCE

What can we do about it, then? The answer to this question leads us to one of the most important themes of Foucault's later work, the 'aesthetics of existence'. If power/knowledge works at the level of the subject, then it is at the level of the subject that it will most effectively be resisted. Since there is no authentic or natural self that we can simply recover or struggle to liberate, subjects should be geared towards a dynamic self-creation, an experimental expansion of the possibilities of subjectivity in open defiance of the modes of being that are being laid down for us constantly in every moment of our day-to-day lives.

Interestingly, Foucault rediscovered some sympathy for the Enlightenment project of critical self-consciousness, particularly as he found it in Kant. His famous essay, 'What is Enlightenment?', (1984) suggests that if subjects are really to deal with their situation in the modern world, they need to make themselves aware of the sorts of selfhood that are being constructed for them, all with the aim of contriving some alternative, albeit fanciful or ephemeral. His own work, with its analysis of the subjectivities demanded of us by institutions and, towards the end of his life, of the abstract concept sexuality (see Chapter 8), aimed to trace the haphazard historical development (or 'genealogy') of these subjectivities. Armed with this self-awareness, we can construct a fictional or hypothetical selfhood outside of, or in pure hostility to, the conventions modern life seeks to normalise.

In this way, Foucault found in his project of an experimental selfhood the way of forging a connection between aesthetics, ethics and politics. His study of the sexuality of Ancient Greece and Rome revealed a subjectivity that was managed according to an 'ethics of pleasure' (Foucault 1990, p.239). The self constantly problematised its place in the world and its relationship to others and to inherited codes of behaviour. As a result, the subject would not simply rely on some unknowable notion of a pure natural selfhood, but would produce itself endlessly as a response to its cultural and historical context. This ethical preoccupation with the responsible management of the self touches on politics on the one hand (with its attempt to frustrate power/knowledge), and aesthetics on the other, with its willingness to embrace the fictional and fantastic. In the classical context, this self-management sounds dour, but Foucault's idea of self-creation has inspired performance artists, radical fashion designers and major cultural festivals like the Sydney Gay and Lesbian Mardi Gras, with its charged engagement with the imagery of popular culture and its dramatic revealing of the hidden breadths of Western sexual practice. Foucault himself experimented with sado-masochism as a way of imagining new forms of selfhood that transgressed the rules of what modern discourse and its ironic police force, tabloid news culture, has laid down as acceptable sexual practice.

It would be a mistake to describe the influence these ideas have had on recent theories of the subject as forming a school or movement. Foucault's work is, however, a key reference point for those who want to engage with the way subjectivity has become a mode of social organisation and administration. In this way, it is a great resource for those who reject both the Enlightenment model of the free and autonomous individual, combatting a society that seeks to oppress it, and that it in turn seeks to attune to its own freedom and self-expression, and the psychoanalytic model of a subject formed around desire and lack by a family politics of gender and language. To those who work with Foucault's ideas, subjectivity is always everywhere a fiction, and has no intrinsic reality or structure, neither one given to us at our birth or as a result of the relationships and experiences of our early lives. This fiction may be exploded, or remodelled as a subversion of the demands power places on us.

Yet, however we choose to respond, Foucault's ideas encourage a rigorously sceptical attitude towards subjectivity, one that I have called in the introduction 'anti-subjective' because it will always see any statement that claims to speak the truth about our subjectivity as an imposition, a technique of power and social administration. In sum, the intensity of this scepticism is designed to match what is seen as the almost immeasurable cynicism of a power that controls us most effectively by making us believe in a uniquely contemporary and absolutely desperate way in our own freedom.

FURTHER READING

Foucault, Michel, 1979, *Discipline and Punish: The Birth of the Prison* trans. Alan Sheridan, Penguin Books, Harmondsworth.

———1980, *Power/Knowledge* ed. Colin Gordon, Pantheon Books, New York.

———1984, *The Foucault Reader* ed. Paul Rabinow, Penguin Books, Harmondsworth.

5 | Femininity: From female imaginary to performativity

So FAR I have outlined two broad approaches to theorising the subject. The first approach—identified with psychoanalysis and the work of Freud and Lacan—attempts to present a model of the nature of the individual subject, and how it is formed. For these theorists, the subject has a knowable content, and is measurable against a normative path of development. This development is influenced by a variety of factors: for Freud, gender identity and family politics define the immediate hothouse context that brings the nascent self to an early crisis, from which the normal masculine subject emerges, laden with complex and ambiguous identifications but motivated by a clear sense of its needs and purposes. Lacan's approach is far more mythical, in the sense that for him subjectivity is a product of the self's appeasement of huge incontrovertible and superhuman forces, that underpin gender and family positioning as they do for Freud, but whose domain is language, the systems of symbolisation and mediation which structure human culture. Language defines the subject from the outside, instilling in it a sense of lack, which it perpetually tries to satisfy through an endless and constant desire.

The second approach to the subject, which I have identified with the work of Foucault, believes neither that the subject has a fixed or knowable content, nor in fact that subjectivity exists outside of the demands power places on individual bodies to perform in certain ways. Power, in its drive to administer human populations, contrives the subject as an ideal mode of being to which we must conform. We define ourselves according to authoritative notions of what it is to be well and not sick, sane and not mad, honest and not criminal, normal and not perverted. These ideas circulate in the pettiest forms of social exchange, from the discipline of the playground to the hysterical categories of tabloid journalism. Their end result is the feeling of separation and vulnerability that has become the modern experience of individualism.

Indeed, in contrast to the Enlightenment thinkers who first systematically proposed the problem of subjectivity, Foucault sees the 'individual' not as a naturally occurring entity that needs to be protected—even 'liberated'—but as power's prime instrument in manipulating us to behave in certain ways. As long as we believe that the issues of social behaviour (mental illness, sexuality, crime) are played out in our behaviour as individuals, then we will perpetually judge each other—and indeed ourselves—in terms of publicly sanctioned codes of being, whose map is the discourse of 'truth' developed by the human sciences and whose prime aim is the pacification of populations.

Neither of these approaches deals adequately with the issue of gender. Psychoanalysis identifies gender relations as absolutely fundamental to the construction of the subject, yet either chooses to present gender as determined by biology ('Anatomy is destiny', Freud said), or sees the feminine as a by-product of the necessarily dominant masculine. Foucault, on the other hand, is almost completely silent about the issue of gender, even though he does list changes in 'relations between the sexes' as an example of the sort of political transformations he prefers (Foucault 1984, pp.46–7). The aim of this chapter is to see how these problems and omissions in the approach to gender have been dealt with by feminist thinkers, specifically Luce Irigaray's response to Lacan and Judith Butler's use of some Foucauldian themes for her reconsideration of gender identity. I recognise that this broad-brush approach is not a complete treatment of the variety of feminist discussions of subjectivity, yet it will elucidate both the problems and limitations of some of the key positions in the postmodern discourse of the subject, as well as signalling some of the important trends in the relationship between gender politics and cultural theory.

THE SEX/GENDER DISTINCTION

Before we discuss each of these thinkers, it is worth reminding ourselves of one of the most important ideas that has governed all recent theorisation of gender: what is referred to as the sex/ gender distinction. Since the major theoretical breakthroughs of nineteenth-century science, the concept of Nature has occupied a unique position in Western culture. Whether the buzzword has been race, hormones or genes, we have usually looked to Nature as the explanation for what we believe to be fundamental in our behaviour: to late nineteenth-century psychology, racial inheritance explained individual dispositions; to more recent thinkers, measuring hormone imbalances or seeking the gay gene, there is an absolute belief that our social behaviours are not social in their origin but are inborn, and thus inevitable and incontrovertible. The idea of gender 'roles', whether the issue is childcare, the violence of male sport or the suitability of women to fight in the front line, has been particularly prone to this idea of a natural determinism.

Feminist thought has consistently challenged this idea that our gendered behaviour is dictated to us by Nature, however, by separating biological reality from cultural identity. According to this argument, the gender identity and behaviour you manifest are products of a socially and culturally sanctioned system and hierarchy, and not the inevitable result of naturally occurring differences between men and women. In one of the most influential formulations of this argument, Simone de Beauvoir writes: 'One is not born, but becomes a woman. No biological, psychological, or economic fate determines the figure that the human female presents in society: it is civilization as a whole that produces this creature, intermediate between male and eunuch, which is described as feminine' (de Beauvoir 1952, p.249). Here, the social behaviours and identities that we define as feminine are seen as the product of purely cultural and historical forces, rather than any natural propensity or essence. Gender behaviour is the result of purely human factors, and is not pre-programmed in us by our chromosomes, our genes or our genitals. We may be born with certain body types, but these do not define the modes of appearance, patterns of behaviour, distribution of social and economic power and opportunity that together form the gender structure of a given society. Such a structure is the product of a specific political history and specific institutions.

This distinction between biological sex and cultural gender rejects theories—even feminist ones—that fall back on the biological difference between the male and female bodies as an explanation for the different behaviours of men and women. The latter are to be seen as artificial and thus changeable. Monique Wittig has put it like this:

By admitting that there is a 'natural' distinction between women and men, we naturalize history, we assume that 'men' and 'women' have always existed and will always exist. Not only do we naturalise history, but also consequently we naturalise the social phenomena which express our oppression, making change impossible. (Wittig 1992, pp.10–11).

The arguments that gender is an inevitable outgrowth of biology (whether they argues that men are naturally dominant because they hunt, or that women are naturally more caring because they give birth) disguise politically and culturally determined differences as something inevitable and immutable.

IRIGARAY AND PSYCHOANALYSIS

I want to turn now to some arguments about femininity that confront and challenge the psychoanalytic tradition, specifically in the work of French psychoanalyst and philosopher Luce Irigaray. Irigaray was trained and worked as a Lacanian analyst until irreconcilable differences over the issue of feminine identity and sexuality made a continued alliance with the Lacanian movement impossible. My aim here is to introduce the reader to Irigaray's disagreement with the dominant psychoanalytic project by a close reading of the early article 'This Sex Which is Not One' (see Irigaray 1985). Although this article does not provide a complete overview of Irigaray's work, its clear argument and direct address to problems in earlier psychoanalytic theorising recommend it as a starting point.

Some of the key points of the argument here are captured in the carefully chosen title. The French title 'Ce sexe qui n'en est pas un' is intentionally ambiguous. In French, every noun and pronoun is gendered. The word 'sexe (sex)' is gendered masculine. By way of this pattern of grammatical gendering, the feminine will always be a subset of a masculine category. Irigaray's title denotes the feminine as the sex which cannot be assimilated or subordinated to the masculine. It is not 'un' (masculine for 'a') sex. In fact, it is this very automatic and unthinking inclusion of the feminine as a secondary part of a system defined first and foremost in masculine terms that her article sets out to contest. The second meaning of the word 'un' is the one the English translation is able to capture: 'one'. As we shall see, Irigaray's argument revolves around the distinction between the masculine idealisation of the singular and unified, in contrast to the feminine immersion in plurality and difference. The feminine gender is thus separate from the totalising logic of oneness that so mesmerises masculine culture.

Irigaray argues that feminine sexuality has never been theorised on its own terms. For Freud, as we saw in Chapter 2, an understanding of feminine sexuality must always wait until a complete model of masculine sexuality has been produced. Freud followed this pattern even when the evidence before him involved female patients. He first translated their experience on to a masculine template. This dominance of masculine models and paradigms results in either a forced reading of female sexuality as if it is a mere echo of masculine sexuality (the clitoris is a penis substitute); or the representation of female sexuality as implicitly inadequate (female genitals are defined as lacking by comparison to the penis). Irigaray writes: 'Woman and her pleasure are not mentioned in this conception of the sexual relationship. Her fate is one of "lack", "atrophy" (of her genitals), and "penis envy", since the penis is the only recognized sex organ of any worth' (Irigaray 1980, p.99).

The significance of this subordination of female sexuality in Western sexual culture goes well beyond sexual relations and practices. As in the psychoanalytic tradition in general, sexuality, its imagery and the relationships that form around it are influences on, and emblems of, a wide variety of cultural and social practices. This emerges in the reading Irigaray provides of masculinity, specifically its obsession with the phallomorphic (the shape and symbolism of the penis).

Phallomorphism saturates the dominant masculine culture of the West. The penis is seen as the sexual organ *par excellence*. The symbolism it drives emphasises erection, unity, strength and, above all, visibility. To this phallic culture, female genitals are invisible. They represent, as Irigaray puts it, 'the horror of having nothing to see' (Irigaray 1980, p.101). As a consequence, the masculine is an 'economy', in Irigaray's terms, that emphasises the visual. This emphasis on the visual produces an aesthetic orthodoxy that idealises formal structural qualities above all others. This formalism in turn seeks unity, stability, consistency and completion everywhere as its highest values. The incongruous, jarring, asymmetrical, arbitrary and unfinished become terms of criticism, not praise. In the abstract, this emphasis on unity and stability of form sees the production of fixed and final meaning as the highest and most necessary goal of either philosophical reflection or scientific investigation. The idea that anything may have a dynamically changing or inconsistent identity, or have contradiction as its very essence or animating principle, is defined as monstrous and abominable to a phallomorphic culture that can tolerate only the homogeneous, the defined, knowable and consistent.

Irigaray's attack on the stability of identity in masculine culture also represents an assault on language as Lacan has defined it. To Lacan, the engine of language is the transcendental signifier, the ideal of the symbolic order, the possibility of stable and complete symbolic meaning, embodied in the Name-of-the-Father. To Irigaray, this obsession with 'the proper name, [and] the literal meaning' (Irigaray 1980, p.101) as the essence of language represents not so much an insight into the necessary reality of language itself, but more a peculiarly masculine anxiety about the phallus and its privileges, an anxiety from which the feminine always stands apart.

The logic of Irigaray's argument, therefore, leads inevitably to the definition of a 'female imaginary' (Irigaray 1980, p.102). The female imaginary, like the masculine, replicates the meaning of the genitals. However, unlike the male genitals, which are understood obsessively as a symbol of unity, totality and purpose, the female are to be read as plural and dynamic. Irigaray writes: 'A woman "touches herself" constantly without anyone being able to forbid her to do so, for her sex is composed of two lips which embrace continually. Thus, within herself she is already two—but not divisible into ones—who stimulate each other' (Irigaray 1980, p.100). Because the female genitals are a variety of surfaces forever in contact with one another, they cannot be reduced or compared to the simple, single logic of the masculine. The consequence of this plurality is a culture not of the visible and the preference for unity of form, but of the tangible, of continuous touching. The contiguity here is forever open, in terms both of time (women cannot not touch themselves) and space (there is no perimeter to the possibilities of connection that touching opens up). 'Woman has sex organs just about everywhere,' Irigaray writes (Irigaray 1980, p.103).

We noted that, in masculinity, the emphasis on phallomorphic form and visibility in general was merely part of a culture that included certain priorities in language, truth, meaning and identity. The ramifications are equally widespread for the feminine. Because it always involves plurality, feminine culture is built around an implicit difference from itself. This subverts the traditional emphasis on unity and consistency of meaning and identity in Western culture. Feminine culture seeks no such simplicity, according to Irigaray. She writes of the typically feminine, '"She" is indefinitely other in herself' (Irigaray 1980, p.103). The feminine does not insist on a strict dividing line between the self, and what is outside of it (the other). This sort of fortress-like exclusion is identified with the tension, paranoia and self-obsession of masculine culture. Similarly, this inclusion of the other within the subject is a challenge to identity itself, a process which is here represented as indefinite and open to an endlessly renewable difference. In linguistic terms, feminine language also represents a threat to the idealised stabilities of the symbolic order. Irigaray writes of feminine language: '"she" goes off in all directions . . . in which "he" is unable to discern the coherence of any meaning. Contradictory words seem a little crazy to the logic of reason, and inaudible for him who listens with ready-made grids, a code prepared in advance' (Irigaray 1980, p.103). Language, as Lacan has defined it, dreams of the possibility of meaning as a way of stabilising the fleeting identities that seem available in the imaginary. This understanding of language is represented by Irigaray as completely masculine. Feminine language stands against this, exulting in an internal difference and ambiguity, which is a reflection of the difference implicit to feminine being.

Irigaray is at pains to point out, however, that what we are dealing with here is not some naturally occurring essence of the female. Indeed, since the feminine stands against identity and definition, it is important not to allow her insights to petrify into fixed and predictive categories, insisting on what women are and should be everywhere. In short, the feminine and its fluidity and open-endedness form a position in the dynamic field of gender identity and meaning as it has been structured in a specific historical context, a context that includes a type of masculinity, the cultural values of that masculinity, and the theories that set the two against one another. It would defy the fundamentals of the argument to insist that there can be no other types of masculinity and femininity. This would deny the open-endedness and ambiguity that at least the feminine allows to operate in Western culture.

DECONSTRUCTING THE SEX/GENDER DISTINCTION

It is important to remember that Irigaray is writing in and against a tradition that sees the purpose of theorising as providing the subject with some sort of content, however provisional or culturally contingent that content might be. In the work of Judith Butler, we see a suspicion—reminiscent of Foucault's—towards even this carefully modulated understanding of the content of the subject.

Let us begin with Butler's response to the sex/gender distinction, as outlined by de Beauvoir. We recall that the purpose of this distinction was to sever the automatic relationship between the nature of the biological body with which you are born and the social and cultural identities you attain as masculine and feminine. The conservative commonsense idea that your gender is immediately and automatically determined by the sort of genitals, hormones or genes you have implies that the social distinctions and inequalities between men and women are inevitable, and merely a fulfilment of Nature's own logic. Feminism consistently draws attention to the way gender definitions change radically from culture to culture and era to era. We may be born with male or female bodies, the argument goes, but the way these are interpreted, and the roles and meanings ascribed to them, are purely a function of the politics and superstitions of each era. Biology appears here as the fixed and immutable separation of the human species—and indeed of all species—into two rigid categories, a separation that culture then claims to be interpreting when it assigns various roles to men and women. Feminism argues simply that culture's gender roles are imposed on Nature, not derived from it. Biology ('sex') comes first, and then culture ('gender').

Butler argues, however, that the situation may indeed be the other way round (Butler 1990, pp.8–9). We can only theorise about biology and nature from the side of the great nature/culture divide on which we live: the side of culture. By the time we start to speculate about nature and biology, we are completely saturated by the values, structures and priorities of the gender system within which we live. It is from within this system that we look back to find the biological 'truth' we imagine to exist before culture started to make its arbitrary rules. It is no surprise, therefore, that if we begin our theorising from within a cultural system that divides gender into two strict categories, the most significant markers we find in biology are the ones that divide all living things into the same twin categories. In other words, we can only view the world through the prism that has already refracted everything we see into two separate frequencies. When we see nature always and everywhere producing the same two categories, it is a reflection of the gender logic in which we are so deeply immersed, not a revelation of the basic structure of nature. Butler writes:

> Always already a cultural sign, the body sets limits to the imaginary meanings it occasions, but is never free of an imaginary construction. The fantasized body can never be understood in relation to the body as real; it can only be understood in relation to another culturally instituted fantasy, one which claims the place of the 'literal' and the 'real'. The limits of the 'real' are produced within the naturalized heterosexualization of bodies in which physical facts serve as causes and desires reflect the inexorable effects of that physicality. (Butler 1990, p.71)

Here, Butler argues that the very identification of a nature and a reality that pre-exist culture is itself a model produced within culture, another 'culturally instituted fantasy'. The belief that there are categories that exist independent of and prior to the systems that theorise them is an act of faith, produced within a specific culture at a specific time in its history.

The idea of a 'real' biological body, which depends on culture's guesswork about what exists outside of culture, must equally be seen as an object of belief, rather than an immutable fact. Gender, therefore, is neither a result of nature's own categories, nor an interpretation appended to them. Distinctions attributed to nature are only produced from within culture—in other words, within gender. Gender comes first, operating an all-pervasive system of binary oppositions that constructs nature in its own image, as well as colonising every aspect of social life. Indeed, the tyranny of gender over social behaviour can hardly be overstated. Everything from the way you dress, eat, laugh, talk and touch others to the videos you like, the ambitions you have, the desires you feel, even the shape of the body you diet and exercise to produce, are all governed by gender. At almost every level of culture, from commercial TV to parliamentary power-play, gender is thoroughly visible, and enters consciously into our response to almost every social situation. There is a horror at the use of the word 'it' as a general term for human beings, rather than the more conventional 'he' or 'she': it seems that the failure to ascribe gender in the usual way is interpreted as a denial of your very humanity.

GENDER AND PERFORMATIVITY

What is the logic of this massive system that governs our subjectivity, our bodies and even the definition of nature itself? Butler's
answer is to argue that gender is performative. We will see how
she draws on some motifs in Foucault's work to develop this
argument, but first we should mention an influence on the idea of
gender as performance or masquerade, from the Freudian tradition:
the psychoanalyst Joan Rivière, in her paper 'Womanliness as a
Masquerade' (1929).

Rivière analyses the case of a highly successful woman profes-
sional who, after delivering a presentation to a public forum, would
seek out older men and act in a highly flirtatious manner towards
them. Rivière argued that the purpose of this behaviour was to
disavow ownership of the phallus to the man seen as most identified
with masculine authority. The woman's success in her profession
represented momentary accession to the power of the phallus,
which must be compensated for by extra-feminine (in Freudian
terms, castrated) behaviour towards a substitute father-figure.
Rivière's generalisation, on the basis of this case, is very striking.
She writes:

> Womanliness, therefore, could be assumed and worn as a mask,
> both to hide the possession of masculinity and to avert the reprisals
> expected if she was found to possess it—much as a thief will turn
> out his pockets and ask to be searched to prove that he has not the
> stolen goods. The reader may now ask how I define womanliness
> or where I draw the line between genuine womanliness and the
> 'masquerade'. My suggestion is not, however, that there is any such
> difference; whether radical or superficial, they are the same thing.
> (Rivière 1986, p.38)

In contrast to the Freudian argument that the Oedipal drama
distributed subjects into the stable categories of masculine and
feminine, Rivière proposes that, for women at least, gender is a
costume worn as part of the sequence of micro-dramas that
constitute daily life. Rivière does not dispute the phallocentric logic
of Freud's definition of gender, but it no longer seems to occupy
the structured being of the subject. It is a disguise, yet one worn
over an apparent void. We do not meet here a man pretending to
be a woman, or even a woman pretending to be a woman, but a
womanliness that is nothing but pretence.

Butler further develops this argument by linking it with the

Foucauldian idea that subjectivity lacks any interior structure, and is always everywhere a position in a field of possible behaviours constituted by power/knowledge. We recall Foucault's statement that 'the soul is the prison of the body' (Foucault 1979, p.30) from Chapter 3. The conventional Christian imagery Foucault is parodying here proposes the reverse: the body entraps the eternal soul in its transmigration through and beyond the world. To Foucault, however, modern systems of truth and institutional operation expect the body to operate as a clear sign of the internal state of the subject. A disciplined and hygienic body is the sign of a correct subjectivity. As a consequence, the body's movements, routines and presentation are all subordinate to the subject's need to represent itself as proper.

To Butler, gender works in exactly the same way. Gender is a correctly coordinated set of acts and gestures that link the subject to clearly defined parameters of healthy and normal identification. To be masculine or feminine does not involve giving expression to a naturally developing interior truth. It means performing and representing yourself in sanctioned and expected ways to give the impression that your interior life is organised around the acceptable poles of gendered being. Yet what counts is the correct performance alone. The inner essence does not exist except as the fantasy of a gender system that needs to present its policed and disciplined behaviours as natural. Butler writes:

> Such acts, gestures, enactments generally construed, are *performative* in the sense that the essence or identity that they otherwise purport to express are *fabrications* manufactured and sustained through corporeal signs and other discursive means. That the gendered body is performative suggests that it has no ontological status apart from the various acts which constitute its reality. This also suggests that if that reality is fabricated as an interior essence, that very interiority is an effect and function of a decidedly public and social discourse, the public regulation of fantasy through the surface politics of the body, the gender border control that differentiates inner from outer, and so institutes the 'integrity' of the subject. (Butler 1990, p.136)

Cultures whose distribution of labour, power and meanings are built around the normalisation of a compulsory heterosexuality require that all gendered behaviour be judged according to its connection with two broad but clearly defined categories: the masculine and the feminine. As in all the categories we have met through the work of Foucault (madness, crime, sexuality and so on), the distinctions this sort of distribution depends on must disguise the fact that it is primarily the expression of the political structures of a certain culture at a certain phase in its history. It must represent these definitions as natural and inevitable—in short, as *true*. Each of us as subjects needs to repeat this logic by pretending that our gendered behaviour and self-presentation are spontaneous and authentic. We think we walk, talk, dress and mock in the way we do because we are naturally that way, regardless of any social needs and pressures.

It is this sense of the spontaneity of gendered behaviour that Butler most rigorously rejects. Giving the impression we have the correctly gendered interiority is another of the acts which we perform in the service of the gendered system. Yet this is not mere laziness or conformism on our part. As Butler reminds us (1990, p.140), failing to perform gender in the right way can meet with social isolation and mockery, violence, rape and even death. Gender performance is not just a question of dressing or behaving in a way acceptable to a peer group. Nor is it a simple matter of not standing out in the crowd. We are imprisoned within endlessly repeated and endlessly reinforced messages from the media, schools, families, doctors and friends about the correct way to represent our gender. The collective energy put into this regulation is probably unmatched by any other social or cultural practice. The seriousness with which it is taken surfaces in the trivial mockery of those who are seen to wilfully defy commonsense gender self-presentation, but also in the most ruthless and impersonal violence to which we all know somewhere in the back of our minds that we are vulnerable.

To Butler, then, gender is a regulated system of performances. In short, it is built on the correct repetition of behaviours. Yet each of us, in some small or trivial way, sometimes fails to repeat perfectly. This failure to repeat is not only more evidence of the artificiality of the gender system, but it also shows that there is inevitably—even accidentally—a continuous, even unplanned resistance to the norms of gender. We may all be subject to these norms, but we cannot stop ourselves violating them as well. We are soldiers of gender, but we are also subversive of it as well. It is in drag that this failure to repeat reaches its most clear and significant expression. Butler acknowledges that drag has traditionally been seen by feminists as the celebration of the most misogynistic stereotypes of a misogynistic culture. Yet she argues that it sends a double signal: the feminine appearance never completely disguises—in fact, invariably signals as part of its routine—the fact of an anatomically male body beneath. Drag thus demonstrates the artificial and performative nature of gender, distilled into a set of speech patterns, bodily movements and styles of dress separable from any natural determinant, and perfectly performable by those who, according to the logic of compulsory heterosexuality, are least qualified to do it.

In the contrast between Irigaray and Butler, we see another version of the contrast between subjective and anti-subjective theories. To Irigaray, the feminine must reveal its distinctive identity and its separation from purely masculine determinants and descriptions, which make it subordinate to masculine identity. To Butler, anything as abstract as a female imaginary contributes to the belief that the controlled and monitored gender behaviours of a culture are grounded in something outside of its particular historical context and its disciplinary systems. The tension here is again between, on the one hand, the construction of a theoretical model (in this case, of gender)—not because it is absolutely true, but because it provides some leverage for a suppressed identity in the corrupt and cornered marketplace of identities—and, on the other hand, the argument that any and all identities inevitably stabilise and restrict, discipline and control a being-in-the-world whose only hope can be in the perpetual subverting of all identities. In short, it is a struggle over whether any identity—or any model of subjectivity, for that matter—can ever make you free.

FURTHER READING

Butler, Judith, 1990, *Gender Trouble: Feminism and the Subversion of Identity* Routledge, New York.

Irigaray, Luce, 1980, 'This Sex Which Is Not One' in Marks, Elaine and Isabelle de Courtivron eds *New French Feminisms: An Anthology* University of Massachussets Press, Amherst.

6 | Kristeva and abjection: Subjectivity as a process

JULIA KRISTEVA (b. 1941) was one of the most influential theorists of the 1980s and 1990s, linking post-Lacanian psychoanalysis with topics as diverse as semiotics, love, melancholy and migration. She has written on writers as dissimilar as Marcel Proust, Louis-Ferdinand Céline and Phillippe Sollers, and also published her own fiction. It is her work on abjection and horror, specifically in *Powers of Horror* (1980), that has been the most influential, however, with its rich theorising of the interconnection between subjectivity, the body, textuality and the law.

Debates in psychoanalytic feminism in the 1980s were dominated by the contrast between Kristeva's work and Irigaray's (see Chapter 5). Lacan had taken an emphatic line on the centrality of the masculine in the construction of subjectivity and, in turn, on masculine dominance over the symbolic. It quickly became clear in an era of feminist politics that this was a wholly inadequate account of the feminine, and thus of gender altogether. Yet Lacanianism was an opportunity for feminist theorising as well. It made clear that gender inequities in a society could be viewed not only as a matter of restrictive social roles and limited opportunities; nor was it simply exclusive economic and educational institutions that produced masculine dominated gender power structures. This politics could be detected at the very heart of human interaction, and the machinery that Lacan saw as its basis: language itself.

Yet if the symbolic order was inalienably masculine, what possible change could be promised to those entrapped by an atrophied patriarchy? As we have seen, Irigaray answered this question by proposing a 'female imaginary', matching the Lacanian transcendental signifier with something of equal applicability and dexterity. In some ways, although it was rigidly circumspect, this was a utopian move, projecting feminist psychoanalysis into a wholly new domain of possibility, giving a theoretical frame to the feminist drive for change and reinvention.

Kristeva chose a much more ambiguous—even dangerous—approach, seeing in the more dark and unresolved mechanisms of the subject an opportunity for subversion of, and freedom from, the masculine dominance Lacan had celebrated. This chapter provides an outline of Kristeva's argument about the subject of the *abject*, because of its highly original contribution to debates about gender in human culture and because of its impressive ability to theorise subjectivity as incomplete and discontinuous, as a *process* rather than a fixed structure. Kristeva's modelling does not diverge from Freud and Lacan as much as you might expect. Yet she supplies a series of emphases that these two lack, especially in terms of a willingness to embrace the ambivalent, unresolved and dangerous. The fathers of psychoanalysis are committed to stability, order and a fixed and constant identity. The daughter, on the other hand, is able to develop a detailed model that reveals, beneath the father's ordered world, a host of uncertainties and unresolved images and emotions. Implicit in this contrast is a whole cultural politics: the contest between a traditional power hoping to be able to control and manage a stable and knowable world, and a subversive force seeking to set the future of the world in motion again, into a hopeful and productive uncertainty.

REPRESSION IS NEVER COMPLETE

Let us start with the unconscious, with which we are familiar from the discussion of Freud in Chapter 2. Kristeva repeats much of what Freud says of the unconscious, retracing his argument about the repression of material that resurfaces in dreams, slips of the tongue and neurotic symptoms. Yet, she argues, there is a zone in which the repression of unconscious material is incomplete, where the dividing line between what the conscious mind does and does not admit is weak or blurred. It is in this incomplete repression that we find the beginning of the process of abjection:

> The 'unconscious' contents remain here *excluded* but in strange fashion: not radically enough to allow for a secure differentiation between subject and object, and yet clearly enough for a defensive

position to be established . . . As if the fundamental opposition were between I and Other or, in more archaic fashion, between Inside and Outside. As if such an opposition subsumed the one between Conscious and Unconscious. (Kristeva 1982, p.7)

For Freud, the formation of the subject reaches a stable state when a meaningful and predictable dividing line forms between the individual's very proper rational and social concerns, and the private and obscure remnants of the cruel but inevitable Oedipal drama. For Lacan, the subject establishes itself by entering into the symbolic order, which condemns it to a life of loss and a specific type of insatiable nostalgia called desire. Lacan's was a grim, even pessimistic, view of a limited and always already defeated subject, yet it did promise a resolved and stable model.

For Kristeva, subjectivity never necessarily stabilises. The attempt to repress may lead to the exclusion of unconscious material, but this is not inevitably propelled into a closed box whose lid is more or less secure, as Freud imagined it. Unconscious material is not stored away, but hovers on the very fringes of the subject's self-definition. This definition in turn is not complete. A defensive position is taken up, but not one that produces a subjectivity rigorously and completely separated from the world around it. As Kristeva says, no absolute distinction between subject and object results. The subject is merely the hypothetical inside of an imagined container whose walls are permeable. The subject tries to stabilise itself as this inside, yet supposedly unconscious materials are forever pressing in on it, threatening the consciousness that earlier psychoanalysis had hoped to promote as stable and meaningful.

The subject is thus not a fixed system, prone to the occasional outburst of incomprehensible and irrational displacement, the odd outlaw thought or image crossing the boundary fence from the unconscious to the conscious. Its incomplete and unresolved nature permanently accompanies it. In fact, subjectivity never quite forms. The boundary fence is never finished. Yet it is important to emphasise that the dramatic nature of this subjectivity is experienced as an intense ambivalence. The subject never feels itself to be ordered and knowable. It is always under threat, in an unresolved state that is exciting as well as dangerous, 'as tempting as it is condemned' (Kristeva 1982, p.1).

THE CLEAN AND PROPER BODY

In our fantasy of an autonomous selfhood, we normally imagine our subjectivity to be identified with the uniqueness and separateness of our individual bodies. We draw an imaginary line around the perimeters of our bodies and define our subjectivity as the unique density of matter contained within that line. When we operate in society as voters, taxpayers, welfare recipients and consumers, our identity seems to be married to this autonomy: we front up for interviews, check-ups and interrogations as the content of our bodies. The physical presence they provide us with is taken everywhere to be the absolute and final validation of who we are. In court, at the doctor's, in line at the social security office, we cease being a name on a piece of paper and, presenting our bodies, appear as ourselves. As we have seen with Foucault (in Chapter 4), when institutions seek to know and control the subject, they manipulate the body, fixing it strictly in place, watching and measuring it.

Kristeva claims an even richer, more exact, politics of the body. She seeks to see in the very processes of the physical body itself the whole drama of subjectivity and its meaning. The imagined line around the perimeter of the body is not just the demarcation of some social unit, easy to fit into the routines of public administration. Our very sense of selfhood at its simplest and most primitive level is connected with the separation and integrity of the body. This separation is flawed and questionable, not because there are larger group identifications that subvert its autonomy, but because the unity of the body is never more than fragile and provisional.

Kristeva calls the unique and separate body 'le corps propre'. In French, the adjective 'propre' has two meanings, depending on where it is positioned: firstly, it is translated as the English word 'clean' and, secondly, it denotes ownership (linked to the English word property). The phrase 'le corps propre', then, defines the body as something that the subject owns and maintains in hygienic order. This 'clean and proper' self-controlled body is the one we imagine we are referring to when we use the word 'I'. It is the one social institutions demand of us when they check on our cleanliness, our truthfulness, our hard work and honest citizenship.

Yet this selfhood to which we cling is unstable. It never forms outside of our idealism and ideology. As mentioned above, we forever try to shore up a defensive position, strictly mapping a fixed line between inside and outside, but the correct perimeters of our clean and proper bodies are forever broken, punctuated by the physical flows that cross them: flows of urine, tears, shit, vomit, blood (especially menstrual blood), sweat and semen. These flows challenge the clean and proper body, undermining both its hygiene and the security of its ownership. They threaten to contaminate our sense of individual identity and security, by making the dividing line questionable. Does my vomit belong to me? Is it part of my body? I expel it in a climax of humiliation and insecurity. Why is my response to a regular, necessary, universal human activity, a response of fear and loathing? Of shame and infantilisation? I work hard to alienate those parts of myself that disgust me. To Kristeva, this desperate pushing away of what the body produces, the gag reflex with which we turn on our own bodily refuse, is evidence of our violent attempts to strengthen the subjectivity— or, more accurately, the 'defensive position', which is all we have of subjectivity.

ABJECTION

This defensiveness is the most literal, physical form of the drama of abjection. We thrust away the evidence of those flows which puncture our skin and make us—despite ourselves—doubt the integrity and autonomy of the selfhood which we identify with the wholeness and closure we look to our bodies to define. The self, for Kristeva, seeks to establish itself by this process of alienation. She writes: 'I give birth to myself amid the violence of sobs, of vomit' (Kristeva 1982, p.3). But neither the establishment nor the alienation is ever complete. The subject remains in process, forever trying to establish itself, forever pushing away at those things that relentlessly challenge its limits: 'unflaggingly, like an inescapable boomerang, a vortex of summons and repulsion places the one haunted by it literally beside himself' (Kristeva 1982, p.1).

The anxiety grounded in the permeable dividing line between the inside and the outside of the body is replicated endlessly in unease over frontiers and separation in general. We are unsettled by things that cross lines, especially those that seem to belong to both sides, that blur and question the whole process of demarcation. Some of these lines are physical; some are abstract or metaphorical. Some reach us at the level of our very bodies; some challenge our sense of meaning and truth, though it is almost always impossible to separate these two dimensions of abjection.

Two examples Kristeva offers of the former, more physical, processes of abjection are the skin on the surface of hot milk, and the corpse. It is a common enough phobia to gag at the skin on the surface of hot milk. Kristeva seems to experience it herself. This thin layer of fat is the objective correlative of the dividing-line between physical states: it is the separation of liquid and air made palpable. Yet it is also an analogy of the barrier between self and other, between the child and the parents with whom we associate the sometimes pressured offering of milk. The gagging is a re-dramatisation of these separations and the intense questions they awaken, about the self and its involvement with others, and about the interpenetration of separate states in general.

The corpse is perhaps the strongest manifestation of the problem of abjection, the 'utmost of abjection', as Kristeva calls it (1982, p.4). The corpse is something that was living but now is dead. It is the very presentation of death, but what it presents is in fact something that we are familiar with as living. Our dead relative appears in the corpse, both as the living person we remember and can still identify with, and the death we cannot adequately signify. The physical reality of the corpse brings together life and death, presence and absence, love and repulsion, happiness and dismay in an endless, chaotic alternation and confusion. The dividing line between our own life and its extinction is reasserted amidst our comfortable and conventional daily preoccupations. The fear of the dissolution of our subjectivity, its very ambiguity, can only be withstood by a religious rhetoric of transsubstantiation that offers to preserve us forever, or by a science that smothers our loss in an impersonal logic that subordinates us to a higher evolutionary destiny. The corpse defies both these systems. It is the uncertainty of the life/death dividing line, literally in our faces.

ABJECTION AND AMBIGUITY

Yet all these physical experiences are powerful sources of horror and phobia, not because of the intense bodily reactions they provoke, but because they are a subset of the abstract process of ambiguity, uncertainty and inter-pollution that is the core meaning of abjection. Abjection is not just about the bodily feeling of uncleanliness, or even unstable subjectivity-in-process. It is the destabilisation of all systems of order, meaning, truth and law that is at stake. It is not the subject's relation with the body that counts. The ownership of the clean and proper body is merely the most intense and emotional example of the orders of law and laws that produce a controlled and manageable subject. Kristeva writes: 'It is thus not lack of cleanliness or health that causes abjection but what disturbs identity, system, order. What does not respect borders, positions, rules. The in-between, the ambiguous, the composite. The traitor, the liar, the criminal with a good conscience, the shameless rapist, the killer who claims he is a saviour' (Kristeva 1982, p.4).

We saw in Lacan that physical experiences like the reflection of a mirror-image in the eyeball of the other had consequences that linked the establishment of an insecure personal identity with shared structures of symbolic order and patriarchal law. To a post-Lacanian thinker like Kristeva, therefore, shifts in the quality of selfhood are like tugging on the weave of a complex fabric. Inevitably, abstract systems of order, meaning, truth, authority and power will be affected too. Thus the meaning of the abjection of the individual subject and its clean and proper body is entangled in the abstract and general sphere of truth and power. Put simply, the stability of both the dominant symbolic and the political order relies on individual subjects' commitment to the desperate self-discipline of the clean and proper body.

What abjection unleashes, then, is the internal ambiguity and uncertainty that logical systems try to deny or disguise. In fact, the first and fundamental purpose of systems of order is to repress ambiguity and contradiction, to assert the singularity of truth, the certainty of law, the inevitability of order against the abominations of contradiction, mixture, incompletion and difference in general. Behind the solipsistic drama of our individual shame and disgust at the flows that accompany bodily life are the desperate politics that demand one law, one God, one answer and one nation.

Kristeva traces this struggle between law and abjection through a variety of domains, from Old Testament prohibitions to modernist fiction. *Powers of Horror* shows how the concept of abjection can be used to detect the intricate entanglement of a subjectivity-in-process and a fragile socio-symbolic order, not only in the way the body is represented but in religious systems, and even in the unusual punctuation of an avant garde writer. She analyses Biblical prohibitions on food preparation to show that they are governed by an anxiety about the crossing of boundaries. Animals are classified according to what is imagined to be their proper domain: sea, air or pasture. The pure are those which keep within their ostensibly pre-set domain. Those that cross between domains and do not conform to the rules of a governing taxonomy are impure, and lead only to mixture, disorder and confusion (Kristeva 1982, p.98). Animals which transgress boundaries are therefore not to be eaten. Here, dietary regulation projects anxieties about abjection onto the natural world. Food in fact brings together the order of the material world with the regulation of the individual body and subject. It is a sensitive point of application of law, allowing truth (systems of classification of animals), religion (the order created by God), the patriarchal symbolic order (regulations as written by traditional authority) and the body (what nourishes it and the subject identified with it) all to be coordinated in a single mutually supporting system.

ABJECTION IN TEXTS

One of Kristeva's most famous case studies analyses the work of the French modernist author Louis-Ferdinand Céline (1894–1961). Kristeva detects in Céline's unusual style, with its self-interruption and gaps in logic and order, the proximity of the coordinated breakdown of bodily stability and symbolic order that is abjection in its acute form. Here is an example of Céline's prose, from his novel *Rigadoon*, a narrative of the violence and death of the Second World War:

> let them rot, stink, ooze, end up in the sewer . . . they keep wondering what they can do in Gennevilliers . . . easy! fertilize the fields . . . the true sense of History . . . and what we've come to! jumping this way! . . . whoops! and that way! . . . the death dance! impalements! purges! vivisections! . . . twice tanned hides, smoking . . . spoiled, skulking voyeurs, let it start all over again! guts ripped out by hand! let's hear the cries, the death rattles . . . a national orgasm! (Céline 1974, p.179, ellipses in original)

Here, there is a promiscuous crossing between sex and death, violence and meaning, horror and thrill. The vicious dismemberment of dead bodies combines with a libidinous excitement that shocks and threatens conventional sensibility. Céline's writing surfs what Kristeva describes as 'the fascinating crest of decomposition–composition, suffering–music and abomination–ecstasy' (Kristeva

1982, p.153). This breakdown of order allows the abject to surface in all its criminality and force. Yet the abject is not only to be found in the meaning of Céline's words, but also in the way they are deployed: the repeated exclamation marks and ellipsis points. Both of these usages bring the prose to its limits, either in terms of intensity, which is kept at fever pitch, or breakdown, where gaps constantly surface in the representation and in the logical unfolding of meaning. It is emotion in its most unrationalised and under-represented form that surges through these gaps, and that Céline's style is able to evoke.

This wrecking of the neat order of patriarchal logic always attracts us at some level. Kristeva points out from the very beginning of *Powers of Horror* that abjection both threatens and thrills us, dramatising the insecurity of our subjectivity and the possibility of its loss, but also offering us a freedom outside of the repression and logic that dominate our daily practices of keeping ourselves in order, within the lines, heads down. This ordered subjectivity is a comfort, but it is also a burden, and we flirt endlessly with what may be outside its limits. Here we can begin to trace why our entertainment—for which we sacrifice huge amounts of money and time—is not dominated by stories and games built around simplicity and unambiguous pleasure. Instead we are fascinated by horror, violence, death and danger, by the movie screen we watch between our parted fingers, lost in the suspense that threatens our control over our bodies. In the horror and violence of novels, movies and video games, we can see the commodification and commercialisation of abjection, whether in the form of Freddie Krugers who emerge from our nightmares, natural born killers, or the 'rogue cops and shakedown artists . . . [the] wiretappers and soldiers of fortune and faggot lounge entertainers . . . [the] bad men'—in short, the killers and sadists to whom James Ellroy dedicates his political crime novel *American Tabloid* (Ellroy 1995, p.5).

Before the attraction of abjection carries us away, it is worth noting, as Kristeva does in her discussion of Céline, that what we are touching on here is the emotional raw material that allowed itself to be manipulated by Fascism and Nazism (Kristeva 1982, pp.155–6). In fact, she presents Céline as a writer capable of doing justice—in a way that realist or conventional writers could not—to the immensity of the horror and energy of the Second World War, because he captures both the mayhem of the period and the political seductions that gave rise to it.

ABJECTION AND GENDER

The more specific political connection for abjection is with the gender politics of the symbolic order. Lacanian psychoanalysis defined the subject in the symbolic order as a kind of fortress-self (Lacan 1977, p.5). According to Kristeva, the most complete stage that the subject reaches in the endless instability and near break-down that abjection makes of it is a defensive position. In sum, the self that is committed to the symbolic order, and on which the latter depends, is fragile and vulnerable. It contains within it a plurality and uncertainty that is always threatening to tear it apart.

If the symbolic order that represents the conservative pole of this process is connected with the masculine—even patriarchal—principle, can a similar political value be connected with the other pole of the struggle, the pre-Oedipal indefiniteness that is preserved in the forces and flows that defy the clear perimeter of the clean and proper body? It can: the abject impulse is inalienably connected with the feminine, specifically the maternal. As it forms out of the undefined morass of relations, surfaces and currents that existed before the Oedipal or mirror-stage coordinated them, the subject seems built around a primal sense of loss. The developing sense of the limits of the body is focused on those holes in its surface through which the outside becomes inside and vice versa: the mouth, anus, genitals, even the invisibly porous surface of the skin. It was the mother's body that was most connected with these crossing-points, as it fed and cleaned the undefined infant body. The sense that boundaries and limits are forming around this permeable flesh is interpreted then as the withdrawal, or even loss, of intimacy with the body of the mother, firstly in the increasing distance of the practical hygiene operations it performs, and secondly, more remotely, beyond that in its archaic ur-form as the body through which the child entered into the world. The abject subject is emerging 'out of the daze that has petrified him before the untouch-able, impossible, absent body of the mother, a daze that has cut off his impulses from their objects' (Kristeva 1982, p.6).

As we have seen, the stronger the sense of demarcation from the world, the stronger is the young subject's location in the symbolic order, and the stronger its commitment to a paranoid masculine dominance. Yet the subject will never be completely at one with the symbolic. To Lacan, desire always sought some return to the imaginary. To Kristeva, this longing to break down neat limits and ordered processes is a functionally indistinguishable part of their very operation. There is no selfhood without a simultaneous abjection. In gender terms, there is no commitment to masculine subjectivity without a simultaneous subversion of that subjectivity's wholeness and completion by an impulse to fragmentation, ambiguity and ambivalence that is connected with the maternal (Kristeva 1982, p.6). The maternal comes to represent freedom from a burdening meaningfulness, logicality and purpose that entrap not only maturing subjects, but the soul of whole cultures. At the heart of this freedom, however, must also lie a horror and foreboding that is strong enough to resist the carping seductions of practicality, effective communication and common sense.

Yet we make a mistake if we follow the conventions of post-Enlightenment liberal politics and think that this sort of alternative is a choice we can make. We do not decide whether to commit ourselves to the symbolic or the abject. They never separate into discrete options, nor do they ever depend on us, as individuals, making some sort of willing and conscious commitment to them. The impulse of the subject is always to accept the terms of the symbolic order. That is indeed what subjectivity is to post-Lacanian psychoanalysis: the creature and servant of a vast impersonal even inhuman machine called language. Yet this acceptance is always fringed around, harassed, sometimes even overwhelmed by the abjection which permanently accompanies it. The politics of abjection, and consequently one of the core versions of gender politics, can be located in this continual struggle between the subject and the abject.

This is not to say that Kristeva's thinking here fits neatly into discussions of gender and contrasts with the positions adopted by Irigaray and Butler. As we have seen, to Irigaray an understanding of the feminine as merely the subversive undershadow of the symbolic order frustrates any attempt to delineate a completely or even functionally autonomous female imaginary. And to a thinker like Judith Butler, any attempt to provide a transhistorical definition of the feminine (or masculine) is merely to deny the varied versions of gender discipline whose only constituting factor is the culture and politics of specific phases of the history of power. Criticisms have been made of Kristeva's apparent reduction of the feminine to the maternal, which is seen to be little different from the patriarchal understandings of the female 'role' that feminist and gender politics have sought from the very outset to struggle against (see Oliver 1993, pp.48ff.). Similarly, it seems wildly general to claim that the theory of abjection is applicable to all cultures and eras.

Yet despite these clear limitations, like most psychoanalytic work, Kristeva's provides an insightful reading of themes in its own culture. The linking of the experience of horror to the corpse and to the maternal arises again and again in Western representation. The *Alien* series of films, for example, link danger with a maternal force that can penetrate the individual (clean and proper) body and pulp it from within, whose most dangerous function is its uncontrolled procreation and whose most memorable physical feature is its gaping, drooling mouth. Similarly, in Jonathan Demme's *The Silence of the Lambs* (1991), the career of a young female FBI agent has to be painstakingly negotiated between two abject serial killers—one, obsessed with the limits of the human body, is making a costume of human skin for himself; the other combines the abjection of the corpse with the abjection of food by cannibalising his victims. Clarice Starling's membership of a meaningful social order must be achieved by the elimination of one of these principles of abjection (she kills Buffalo Bill), and the neutralisation of the other (her relationship with Hannibal 'the cannibal' Lecter becomes almost fond). Interestingly, this struggle is supervised by her superior, who maintains a rational if somewhat colourless connection with the logical and responsible world of her dead police officer father. Her mother is completely absent from the text, allowing for the effeminate and sexually 'ambiguous' serial killers to drive the notionally feminine motivation whose source is the abject.

These readings, and the legion of others performed on literary and popular culture using the theory of abjection, remind us that the ground of Kristevan theory is textuality. This is not surprising considering that post-Lacanian psychoanalysis views the subject as a part of language. Yet Kristeva's work has provided much more productive tools for the analysis of texts than, say, Lacan's, even allowing for the influence Lacan had on early film theory, such as that of Christian Metz. Kristeva argues that if abjection is a signified, then its signifier is literature (Kristeva 1982, p.5). This is one of the key moments in the dominance of post-structuralism over literary studies, which reached its high point in the 1980s. Indeed, one could even say that Kristeva's achievement here is to renew the claim of literature to a central place in human self-analysis, over and above the effete humanistic claims about literature as the repository of moral values that have dominated English studies from the period of Leavisism and New Criticism on. Whether Kristeva's work maintains this centrality in the broader domain of cultural studies remains to be seen.

FURTHER READING

Kristeva, Julia, 1982, *Powers of Horror: An Essay on Abjection* trans. Leon S. Roudiez, Columbia University Press, New York.

7 | Masculinity: Saving the post-Oedipal world

MASCULINITY WAS NOT considered much worth studying by cultural studies academics before the explosion of men's movement literature at the end of the 1980s and into the 1990s. After all, since masculine values were the dominant ones in the society, it was considered that all traditional study had been unselfconsciously the study of masculinity anyway. The rapid progress of feminist thinking, however, soon made this tenet too general. The feminine as an object of analysis had produced complex insights into gender politics, and made masculinity appear as a set of historically and culturally specific formations. In turn, the traditional dominance of the masculine made these insights a defining clue to the meaning and structure of culture in its entirety. Masculinity, therefore, started to appear in its specificity. Since this was happening at the same time as the men's movement was seeking to retrieve some semblance of a new positivity for men from a severely compromised history, the 1990s has seen an upsurge in theorising of the masculine.

This chapter firstly surveys the representation of the masculine in psychoanalysis, especially since Lacan, because it has been in feminist psychoanalysis that some of the most important insights into phallocratic culture have emerged. This is followed by a discussion of some other theories of the masculine in the work of Eve Kosofsky Sedgwick and Fred Pfeil, to enable some evaluation of the men's movement and its significance. Though this second group is not strictly speaking Foucauldian, it does take as one of its assumptions the inextricably political entanglements of subjectivity. In this way, it represents a progression beyond the 1970s model of masculine domination that conceived of it as a single and uniform patriarchy. The challenge of theorising the masculine beyond the 1990s is to define how masculine power operates in not so much a post-feminist, but a post-Oedipal culture.

At the same time, the thin disavowals of many contemporary apologists for masculinity, who want to see it now as victimised or suppressed, have to be seen as an attempt to reinvent a masculine power that no longer carries the baggage of its traditional form. There is no denying that being a man in our time is not easy, but it is one of the longest unbroken traditions of masculine culture to blame masculine suffering on women. This takes the form of blaming feminism for all deleterious social change. The greater suffering and struggle of men is more the result of the intensification in the late twentieth century of the culture of dominance and subordination, winners and losers, competition and humiliation which has been masculinity's modern form. That feminists are blamed for this seems to me part of masculinity's self-reinvention. Unlike the patriarchy that is being replaced, contemporary masculinity wants to exercise its power, but it no longer wants to admit to being powerful.

MASCULINITY IN PSYCHOANALYSIS

We have noted already that, for Freud, the major determinant of subjectivity was the gender formation dominant in the middle-class family. This formation was distributed around the corners of the Oedipal triangle. What distinguished each position in the triangle was its relationship to the dominant sign of sexual difference: the paternal penis. In the way the Oedipal drama unfolded within each (boy) subject, the father was seen to be defined by his ownership of the penis, the mother by her lack of the penis, and the son by his need to choose between the relationship to the penis that each of these positions seemed to offer. In this theory, the masculine is the defining norm of subjectivity, distributing positions around its fixity. These other positions lack a way of defining themselves. They can only be known in terms of something that they are not, or do not have.

The feminine, therefore, is defined by what is absent from it, and the success of all subjective formations is assessed in terms of what exact relationship each has to the marker of the masculine. This is perhaps one of the clearest examples of what is called the self/other or same/different dialectic, where a fixed or normal position is identified as the standard, self or same, and the other or the different is measured against it. This automatically subordinates the other to the self, making it appear to have either too much or too little of something, and therefore to be inadequate or imperfect. Whatever gets chosen somewhat arbitrarily as the norm immediately arrogates to itself the prestige of being natural and right. In the case of Freud, even women's desire was to be defined in terms of the want of a penis, even though it was not part of the female body—hence the doctrine of 'penis envy'.

Irigaray is one of the most eloquent critics of Freud here. In an interview published as 'The Power of Discourse and the Subordination of the Feminine', she states:

> female sexuality . . . is never defined with respect to any sex but
> the masculine. Freud does not see *two sexes* whose differences are
> articulated in the act of intercourse, and, more generally speaking, in
> the imaginary and symbolic processes that regulate the workings of a
> society and a culture. The 'feminine' is always described in terms of
> deficiency or atrophy, as the other side of the sex that alone holds a
> monopoly on value: the male sex. Hence the all too well-known
> 'penis envy'. How can we accept the idea that woman's entire sexual
> development is governed by her lack of, and thus by her longing for,
> jealousy of, and demand for, the male organ? Does this mean that
> woman's sexual evolution can never be characterised with reference
> to the female sex itself? All Freud's statements describing feminine
> sexuality overlook the fact that the female sex might possibly have its
> own 'specificity'. (Irigaray 1985, p.69)

Lacan's work has made clear that this male-centred way of thinking in psychoanalysis was more than a mere oversight. The reinterpretation of the significance of the penis in the form of the phallus and the transcendental signifier (as we have seen in Chapter 3) made the feminine appear as a mere adjunct to a dominant masculinity. In the same way as the Freudian family defined itself by reference to the penis of the father, the Lacanian symbolic order is always and everywhere governed by the hypothesis of an absolute signification, linked to a paternal principle or Law—the Name-of-the-Father. The defining ideals for Lacan, therefore, resonate with the glamorous transcendental signifier, and its commitment to unity of form, the final revelation of truth and a meaningful principle of order.

In the wake of Lacanian psychoanalysis, these have been seen to define the cultural logic of masculinity. The Freudian male subject hoped to believe in his ownership of the penis as a way of stabilising his subjectivity. Analogously, the Lacanian male subject, lost in the symbolic, believes in the fixed principles of phallic order that are offered him as the guarantors and meaning of the whole phallocratic system. He believes that the world can be known, represented and, as a result, controlled by a strict system of signing. This system holds out a dream of truth, of logic and order as final achievable results, even if they always remain the mirages of desire. The masculine, therefore, believes in finality, purpose, truth, stability, principle and communication: all the buried dreams and assumptions of the symbolic order. This masculinity in turn abominates the feminine as provisional, irresolute, irrational, ephemeral and deceptive. Again, behind psychoanalysis's modelling, we can see at least the lineaments of a diagnosis of a whole modern history of Western cultural practice, and its misogynistic clichés: in masculine culture, a male heroism shoots for the glorious final moment when its enemies are killed, its motives known and justified, and the world finally reordered—a resolution all women admire as they get out of the way, recover their true place and keep their opinions to themselves.

Psychoanalytic feminism sees in this phallic principle of order and truth the carnage of human history. Commitment to stable order built around inflexible traditional principles results inevitably in the frustration and suppression of the uncertain, the ambiguous and the different. The ideal of an impersonal and absolute truth abominates anything incomplete, double or provisional. Any open-ended reflection is interrupted endlessly by the masculinist insistence: *'But what is your point?'* Hierarchies form, separating not only one thought from another, but every thinker from every other thinker, hoping to erect one set of laws, one national identity, one definitive experience, a single economic model, a final all-encompassing theory, a total physics, an absolutely precise unit of measurement, the ultimate sub-atomic particle, the origin of the universe, the creation of life, the end of time, the biggest box-office hit, the true hero, the greatest hitter, and the almighty god. Indeed, the idea that subjectivity can be defined as always and everywhere the same can also be seen as part of this masculine drive to homogenise. Fixed identities and universal values ignore the complexity, plurality, inconsistency and ambiguity of subjectivity, imprisoning us in the apparent duty of being a stable, fixed and authentic self.

Yet it is crucial to recognise that masculinity does not confess its need to establish unitary principles of truth, being and order. It presents them as inevitable and necessary parts of pragmatic human dealing with the material world. Masculinity simultaneously advances and generalises its priorities while concealing them. Hélène Cixous, in her article 'The Laugh of the Medusa' (Cixous 1976), was one of the first to argue that, despite their control of the signifying system and their intense self-regard, men had little to say about their own sexuality. To a psychoanalytic reading of culture, it is the penis that operates to unify power, truth and order. Yet display of the engorged or erect penis remains controversial, and is one of the key definitions of pornographic representation. The erection is therefore emblematic of masculine power: it operates most effectively when concealed. Perhaps this helps to explain why shameless celebration of the penis, such as you find in the writing of Jean Genet, is unwelcome to almost all theoretical positions. Its very graphic quality is discomforting to conservatives, while its celebration is unwelcome even to queer theorists.

MASCULINITY, CINEMA AND THE GAZE

This issue of psychoanalysis, gender and visibility has been taken up in a major contribution to film theory by Laura Mulvey in her article 'Visual Pleasure and Narrative Cinema' (1975). Mulvey's aim is to analyse the process of watching movies in terms of Freud's definition of scopophilia, or the pleasure of looking, popularly called voyeurism. Freud argued that the human gaze was a form of non-genital sexual activity. Mulvey discovers that, especially in Hollywood cinema, film-makers have designed their films for a masculine gaze, producing the female star and the female body as objects of visual fascination. She traces this fascination back to the Oedipal boy's interpretation of the female body as castrated. She writes:

> Ultimately, the meaning of woman is sexual difference, the visually ascertainable absence of the penis, the material evidence on which is based the castration complex essential for the organisation of the entrance to the symbolic order and the law of the father. Thus the woman as icon, displayed for the gaze and enjoyment of men, the active controllers of the look, always threatens to evoke the anxiety it originally signified. The male unconscious has two avenues of escape from this castration anxiety: pre-occupation with the re-enactment of the original trauma (investigating the woman, demystifying her mystery), counterbalanced by the devaluation,

punishment or saving of the visual object (an avenue typified by the concerns of the *film noir*); or else complete disavowal of the castration by the substitution of a fetish object or turning the represented figure itself into a fetish so that it becomes reassuring rather than dangerous (hence overvaluation, the cult of the female star). (Mulvey 1989, p.21)

Here, Mulvey argues that the representation of female bodies and characters, both within film and in the culture that surrounds it, are subordinate to the desperate meaning-making procedures of the masculine subject. Men are preoccupied with the female body as the already-castrated.

The anxiety that the representation of this body triggers is to be met in one of two ways: the woman is displayed graphically (even nakedly, in the analogous case of print pornography, where intense interest is shown in the representation of women's genitals), and then shown to be completely vulnerable to masculine truth by being saved, corrected or enclosed in the web of either rightful punishment or consummating desire. On the other hand, as Freud argued when he sought an explanation for the sexual obsession of some male subjects for particular objects, men can deny the reality of castration by pretending that the woman does indeed have a penis. This can be either in another part of her body or a piece of clothing (shoes being the most famous comic example). Alternatively, as Mulvey argues here, woman's whole being can be interpreted as a phallic fetish object, a (screen) goddess or idol. Whatever the interpretation, woman functions here not as a category of living people, but as a representation alone, whose function is to reassure or encourage the subjective self-definition of masculinity.

THE HOMOSOCIAL

This model of the female as a token of exchange in masculine meaning-making returns in a very different form in Eve Kosofsky Sedgwick's theory of the *homosocial*. As with many of the theories of masculinity we are dealing with, this argument is commonly seen to belong to another, if related, domain—in this case, queer theory (see Chapter 8), for which Sedgwick's book *Between Men: English Literature and Male Homosocial Desire* (1985) is considered a founding, if not the founding, text.

Sedgwick draws on a motif in the structuralist anthropology of Claude Lévi-Strauss, specifically his understanding of the exchange of women as the fundamental defining principle on which human society is built. In *The Elementary Structure of Kinship* (1949), Lévi-Strauss had written: 'The total relationship of exchange which constitutes marriage is not established between a man and a woman, but between two groups of men, and the woman figures only as one of the objects of exchange, not as one of the partners' (Lévi-Strauss 1969, p.115). This pattern is still clearly visible in what in some Western societies is called the traditional marriage ceremony, in which the bride is accompanied into the church by her father (or some suitable older male relative) who 'gives her away' to her husband. The bride is formally exchanged between the nominal male representatives of separate families. Sedgwick advances this micro-drama as a model of gender relations. She draws on the literary criticism of René Girard, who sees the same motif repeated consistently in narrative:

> What is most interesting for our purposes in [Girard's] study is its insistence that, in any erotic rivalry, the bond that links the two rivals is as intense and potent as the bond that links either of the rivals to the beloved: that the bonds of 'rivalry' and 'love', differently as they are experienced, are equally powerful and in many senses equivalent. (Sedgwick 1985, p. 21)

As a narrative of erotic rivalry progresses, the female love-object is often depersonalised and set aside, as a token romantic discourse gives way to the intensity of a male protagonist's confrontation with a male rival. Woman becomes not an equal partner in an open-ended human relationship, but a mere prize in the struggle for dramatic triumph and resolution between the hero and his nemesis.

In this way, successful winning of the woman becomes not merely a sign of victory, but the symbol of all types of literal and abstract ascendancy: the hero's moral superiority, his higher truth, his role in assuring social order through a future free of corruption, and so on. This de-realisation of the feminine thus leads to an image of social progress and the consolidation of truth as a showdown between men. What is fought over is radically feminised, presenting a picture of the humdrum day-to-day world of social sustenance and support as a feminine zone, whose perimeters are policed by a necessary inter-masculine violence. Men inhabit the fringes of this world, committed to an endless, charismatic grudge match in which they attain a momentary orgasmic ascendancy, while remaining interpersonally ineffectual. It is this man-to-man bond, forged in a rivalry that usually leads to the death of one, that Sedgwick defines as 'homosocial'.

Fred Pfeil, in his *White Guys: Studies in Postmodern Domination and Difference* (1995), sees the homosocial bond played out in what he has dubbed the 'male rampage' films of the late 1980s and 1990s, the *Die Hard* and *Lethal Weapon* series in particular. An especially striking example is the climactic scene in the first *Die Hard* movie, when pseudo-terrorist gangster leader Hans Gruber—believing he has finally won—recalls a joke made earlier by rival cop-hero John McClane:

> [L]aughter is joined, first by the big square-shouldered thug who is the only member of Gruber's gang remaining, and then by McClane himself, as his wife Holly, still literally in Gruber's clutches, stares around in shocked bewilderment: for that laughter of Gruber and the thug is no longer contemptuous, no more than McClane's seems merely strategic, but *exuberant*; for just that one scant second, all three men, all three outlaws, compose a community no woman can enter, and share a joy no woman can know. (Pfeil 1995, p.12)

McClane's wife, Holly Gennaro, is reduced to the mere passive token over which the men are fighting. The struggle between rivals is not merely a narrative cliché, however. In this scene, it becomes an insight into the relationship between men. As the feminine, in all its meanings—sexual prize, hearth and home, embodiment of weakness and innocence—is bracketed off to one side as less than dramatically interesting in its own right, the relationship between rival men flourishes in a moment of correspondence and mutual understanding—indeed, of recognition—which transcends and belittles the feminine, despite the fact that the men will pursue each other to a violent annihilation. Indeed, this recognition is exalted by the fierce higher equality that final showdown always provides. Men, sworn to kill each other, emerge on to a unique plane of superhuman daring that they need share with no one, especially women. The hubris of their laughter as they stare death in the face, as the cliché has it, exalts them, separating them into a uniquely masculine domain of otherworldly heroism. In this masculine dream-space, men let their enemies recover their fallen weapons, refuse to shoot them in the back, tend their wounds so a fair fight can resume, and so on ad infinitum.

What we have here is a crucial gender inflection of the modern literary trope of the double. A common motif in proto-modernist fiction, the double or *doppelgänger* dramatised the confrontation between a protagonist and a counterpart who is his near-identical reflection or complement. In Dostoyevsky's story *The Double* (1848), for example, a troubled clerk meets a man who is an exact replica of him, and even shares his name. The nightmare process by which this double supplants him in every aspect of his life is, of course, a metaphor for the breakdown of the individual psyche. Its inevitable end is madness and institutionalisation. Versions of this doubling are legion in twentieth-century culture. Individuals discover their own meaning in a fierce engagement with a rival or opposite. In the showdown that has been a mainstay of film from the Western, through the *film noir*, to the male rampage film and the contemporary action thriller, this doubling results in the death of one of the pair. The hero and his double are set aside because they are attaining a higher level of personal significance. In fact, however, what the hero confronts in his double is not anything other to him, but some unrecognised aspect of his own nature: his evil twin, the rival who has seduced the woman he is in love with, the enemy who knows his own most desperate secrets, and so on. The double then enlarges the character of the hero by bringing out into the open his own dark hidden truth. By bringing the confrontation between the hero and his own secret double nature to a climax, texts raise the hero's subjectivity to a higher level, giving it a mysterious, even myth-like, sanctity that is linked to the aura of death. In sum, then, the purpose of the rivalry between the hero and his double is to create the image of a single superhuman subjectivity that sees its own evil nature in itself, and destroys it, usually by immersing itself in the dark and non-moral world of a uniquely raw and visceral masculine violence. In this way, the hero incorporates the darkness of villainy in himself, even as he destroys the individual villain who seems to be its vehicle.

If we translate this doubling into the homosocial bond, as Sedgwick has formulated it, we can redefine the structure of masculinity in this way: the two men fighting over the trivialised woman, or the symbolic feminine in general, are really a single giant and inclusive masculine subject wrestling with, but also indulging in, its own abject desire—a masculine subject, in other words, that seeks both to purge the world of violence and to bring violence into the world, to purify the world by really rubbing its face in the destruction that it is relieved is possible. The confrontation between McClane and Gruber in *Die Hard* sets the two men apart in a unique male-to-male bond. These two are the decision-makers, the rival driving forces behind whatever happens. Their activity renders everyone else passive. In turn, to justify their separation from the rest, they must engage in a verbal and tactical duel in which they are the only two players who count. They dominate not only the action, but also the language of the film. Their words count for so much more than anyone else's. They communicate with one another by phone, each one's small disembodied voice niggling at the other's self-respect like the voice of self-doubt. In order to match Gruber, McClane must rise to levels of atrocity and violence, joking as he kills, sworn to the other's thorough annihilation. He must become his double, absorbing Gruber's immorality within himself.

This is the endgame logic of all homosocial bonds. In marginalising the feminine as passive and amorphous, men recognise in the rivals they must defeat the other side of their own complex nature. To be victorious, they must lose everything except their hard military bodies. To do good, they must enact their own evil. To save the innocent and vulnerable, they must be endlessly calculating and malicious. These contradictions are summarised in Pfeil's description of male rampage heroes as 'wild yet sensitive (deeply caring yet killing) guys' (Pfeil 1995, p.5).

This contradiction is not to be seen as dramatic irony, or even as the compromise you have to make to do good in an evil world. Homosocial doubling dramatises a complexity at the heart of masculinity itself, where we find no Lacanian unifying principle of control and order, but contradiction. The male hero is good and evil, soothingly peace-loving and mindlessly violent; he destroys things in order to save them; he loves and even wants to support his (female) partner, but the only equal he respects is his villainous (male) double. He incorporates within himself both the idealistic (he loves democracy and the family) and the abject (he exults in fighting while injured and will laugh as he kills your brother). He fights for the social conventions that abominate bad guys, but finds his true place by living, as they do, outside of quiet Christmas family gatherings and cocktail party niceties. In this way, it is almost as if he says yes to every value—the nice *and* the nasty, the progressive *and* the reactionary, the honest *and* the criminal. No ideal or capacity falls outside his range.

I have written elsewhere (Mansfield 1997) of this capacity of the modern masculine to include everything in its domain, to be both sides of every coin. In the end, this ability to be both something and its opposite ends in a peculiar relationship to power that I understand as masochistic. The (male) masochist organises and directs someone to have power over him. In this way, he is both powerful and powerless in a single act. The thrill of this scenario is the simultaneous efficiency of the power he needs to stage-manage it, and the sincerity of the desperation with which he seeks to be a passive victim. This simultaneous power and powerlessness seem to summarise the sort of contradictions we have outlined above, of the masculine hero whose world-saving success depends on his ability to include the violence of his homosocial double within him. The hero enacts a ruthless power, but only in the service of ideals which are determined for him. In *Die Hard*, as McClane fights to save his wife, he comes increasingly to believe that he should have been more supportive of her career and ambition. His male rampage is presented incredibly as somehow part of his pro-feminist learning curve. He takes control yet submits to the values other people make.

It is tempting to read this contradiction as mere pretence on the part of the film-makers, who are cynically paying lip-service to liberal feminist platitudes. However, I see this contradiction to be the core of the sort of masculinity they seek to represent—one that is both naked masculine brutality, but is also listening and self-critical. This contradiction, however, is not progressive in any left-wing liberal sense. It is just part of the contradictory nature that masculinity has embraced in an attempt to reconfigure its power. The single, unified, phallic power of the patriarchal is so simple and naked, so easily outmanoeuvred, that it has needed to be replaced by something more subtle—in my reading, by a masculinity that is contradictory and inclusive, that exercises power while appearing to disavow it. In short, it is a masculinity that is masochistic.

MASCULINITY AND FEMINISM

Nowhere is the contradiction increasingly evident in masculinity more apparent than in some of the literature of the men's movement. We need look no further than one of its classics: Robert Bly's *Iron John*. Much has been written about the flaws of the argument of this book, especially its nostalgia for a more or less unknown pre-Industrial age of familial harmony, and its brutally indifferent and ignorant plundering of world cultures for stereotypes and tropes of what the masculine has been and could be again (for a thorough criticism of these aspects of the book, see Buchbinder

1998, Ch. 2). What interests me here are two things: firstly, Bly's attitude to feminism; and secondly, his representation of the authority of gender as a defining attribute of the subject.

Bly opens with the claim that 'the thought in this book does not constitute a challenge to the women's movement' (Bly 1992, p.x). Yet the text consistently implies that the dominance of feminine influence over the boy-child is retarding in all cultures and there is an implication that a similar demasculinisation is happening in a public sphere wherever feminist values are successful. This contradiction between the disavowal of any hostility to the feminist and an attempt to counter feminism seems another example of the having-it-both-ways logic of contemporary masculinity. Its most significant form is in the contradiction in the present attitude towards the role of gender in defining social identity. The belief that men need stronger male role models is a common claim in the men's movement and related neo-conservative commentary. The future of the subject is dependent on its unambiguous location within the clear definition of gender according to a strict binarism: men make men. To be a man, one must imitate other men (see, for example, Biddulph 1995, 1997). This rigid separatism flies in the face of an equal neo-conservative push towards the abolition of the significance of sexual difference in an openly hostile gesture towards affirmative action. You must be gendered, but not.

This reinstated belief in the absolute value of gender in the construction of subjectivity (you must be made a man by men rather than a person by people) represents a capitulation to—or an attempt to recall—the authority of the gender binary system that work like Judith Butler's (see Chapter 5) has aimed to expose as historical and contingent. There is a deperate need to believe that gender binarism is naturally determined by the makeup of our bodies. This thinking is being perpetually reinvigorated in one form or another—most recently in popular representations of genetic research, pinpointing the irresistible micro-calculus that leaves us no choice but to be 'men' and 'women'. This science, however, remains enclosed within culture. As Butler's argument implies, we would not know to look for evidence of gender binarism if it wasn't already the dominant language of human self-definition, saturating as it does almost every dimension of social interaction. The masculine can be found in the human body, but we have to ask ourselves whether the biological signs of the masculine (the penis, in particular) are the things that give rise to masculinity as we know it; or are they the mere markers that a political-historical formation finds for itself retrospectively in the body? Are the genes that are seen to determine masculine behaviour the cause of that behaviour or the sign and sanction of it? Butler's argument leads to the conclusion that gender finds in science markers that explain why it needs to exist, rather than its simple and unavoidable origins. As the meaning of gender categories becomes more and more blurred, the anxiety with which their authenticity is defended becomes more and more intense. After generations of attempts to preserve models of the feminine (as sexually modest, socially passive or naturally mothering) that have lost their meaning, the *fin-de-siècle* project has been to try to reinvigorate some model of the masculine that is seen to be under threat. All signs seem to indicate—especially the desperation with which the rescue attempt is undertaken—that the old primitivist masculinism is merely the last head on the block.

FURTHER READING

Cixous, Hélène, 1976 'The Laugh of the Medusa' trans. K. Cohen and P. Cohen, *Signs*, vol. 1, pp.845–893.

Mulvey, Laura, 1989, *Visual and Other Pleasures* Indiana University Press, Bloomington.

Pfeil, Fred, 1995, *White Guys: Studies in Postmodern Domination and Difference* Verso, London.

Sedgwick, Eve Kosofsky, 1985, *Between Men: English Literature and Male Homosocial Desire* Columbia University Press, New York.

8 | Radical sexuality: From perverse to queer

W E HAVE ALREADY seen how gender and sexuality have been identified by modern and postmodern theorists as key determinants of subjectivity. Psychoanalysis has seen itself as overcoming silence and superstition in the scientific revelation of the true importance of the family and sexuality in the constitution of personality. On the other hand, Foucault and others have been critical of the prestige that has accrued to power/knowledge's inflexible categories of gender (you are either a man or a woman) and sexuality (you are either heterosexual or homosexual). To the former, the truth will allow us to recognise without shame the meaning of our desire. To the latter, any model of truth will re-imprison us in another tyrannical disciplinary order. Is late twentieth-century sexuality freedom or imprisonment, then; the end of a cruel dictatorship of morals and mores, or its most sophisticated version? The two strands of subjective theory we have been tracing—the psycho-analytic/subjective and the Foucauldian/anti-subjective—do not merely correspond to the two sides of this debate; they are more or less defined by the positions they take up in relation to it.

The first point to be made here is that sexuality, with which we will be concerned in this chapter, has been increasingly seen not just (or often not even) as a human attribute or impulse, but as a régime. Even Freud located the construction of subjectivity within the tightly knit power inequities of the bourgeois family, allowing each position in the Oedipal triangle to be read as a specific coordination of gender and power. In turn, even the genitals of both men and women attained a more than symbolic political meaning. The development of gay and lesbian, and latterly queer, theories of culture has only intensified the understanding of sexuality as a political issue, involving hierarchies, oppressions, institutional mobilisation (police, doctors, courts) and all sorts of violence, from petty abuse and humiliation to physical attack and murder.

As many theorists have noted, this sexual politics is not unconnected with other political formations: political parties often adopt a wholly predictable attitude towards sexual issues, consistent with their line on economics and community relations, and a focus on the issue of sexuality inevitably draws theory into the intricate entanglement of race, gender, class and other politics. Eve Kosofsky Sedgwick wrote in *Between Men*, one of the most influential founding texts of queer theory:

> Our own society is brutally homophobic; and the homophobia
> directed against both males and females is not arbitrary or gratuitous,
> but tightly knit into the texture of family, gender, age, class, and
> race relations. Our society could not cease to be homophobic and
> have its economic and political structures remain unchanged.
> (Sedgwick 1985, pp.3–4)

Sexual identities and practices, therefore, operate at a uniquely sensitive pressure point in modern and postmodern culture. Much of the coordinated analysis of sexual and other politics remains to be done, yet it does help justify the application of the word radical to the most significant theorising of sexuality and subjectivity. My aim here is to give a broad overview of the different subversive impulses that have been discovered at this important imagined conjunction between the body, the self and others.

FREUD AND POLYMORPHOUS PERVERSITY

Radical is hardly a term ascribed to the work of Sigmund Freud these days, given that his theories are now often read as a prop or guarantor of the reigning system of what Adrienne Rich has called 'compulsory heterosexuality', bolstering not only the authority of the masculine, but the primacy of the 'normal' as the goal and measure of sexual development. Yet Freud did not simply abomin-ate and alienate the abnormal in an unthinking manner. He was keen to understand sexual 'perversion' as an inevitable part of human experience, where the normal is seen to be in a close and unstable relation with what it is supposed to surpass and exclude. This helps us understand why sexual conservatives are usually openly hostile to Freud. He writes: 'No healthy person, it appears, can fail to make some addition that might be called perverse to the normal sexual aim; and the universality of this finding is in itself enough to show how inappropriate it is to use the word perversion as a term of reproach' (Freud 1977, p.74).

Yet Freud goes on to distinguish truly pathological perversity from this merely ordinary type. Perversity is inevitable—as long as you don't have too much of it, it seems. Where the dividing line is to be drawn between the (oxymoronic) normal perversity and excessive perversity is a theoretical—indeed political—problem, influencing our understanding of how we should treat each other, and how analysts should treat patients. Freud's understanding of perversity is contradictory and unstable, therefore. Some critics, like Leo Bersani in *The Freudian Body* (Bersani 1986), have seen this contradiction as being at the heart of the Freudian project. According to Bersani, Freud's attraction to the range and dynamism of the contradictory, plural and perverse was at odds with his deeply conservative need to assimilate his ideas to the responsible and proper. The aim of contemporary psychoanalytic theory would be to reawaken the possibilities of a dynamic perversity.

But where does our compulsory perversity come from? Is it merely the inevitable failure of the Oedipal system to convince us, either consciously or unconsciously, to be good and to occupy the place deemed right for us? As Judith Butler has reminded us in a different context, conventions of behaviour and even of being and subjectivity can never simply be repeated in the correct and dutiful way power/knowledge demands. It is impossible to repeat our lines without making some—albeit accidental—variation to them. Yet Freud's understanding of perversity identifies another point of origin for normal abnormality: what is labelled 'polymorphous perversity'—Freud's theory of the sexuality of children.

Freud argued that childhood was loaded with a sexual potential that was uncentred and fragmentary. In contrast to 'mature' sexuality, which is supposedly focused on genital pleasure, childhood sexuality sought pleasure in an almost limitless range of physical experiences. Only at puberty did it obtain the focus and centrality we associate with adult sexual intercourse. This argument of Freud's has been most negatively received by those dedicated to the Romantic dream of childhood as innocent and pure. Yet Freud's argument now seems incredible for its rather chilling neutrality on the subject of paedophilia, and its ridiculous snobbery and sexism:

It is an instructive fact that under the influence of seduction children can become polymorphously perverse, and can be led into all possible kinds of sexual irregularities. This shows that an aptitude for them is innately present in their disposition. There is consequently little resistance towards carrying them out, since the mental dams against sexual excesses—shame, disgust, and morality—have either not yet been constructed at all or are only in course of construction, according to the age of the child. In this respect children behave in the same kind of way as an average uncultivated woman in whom the same polymorphously perverse disposition exists. (Freud 1977, p.109)

Usually, this anarchic perversity is connected with auto-erotism, masturbation, exhibitionism, thumb-sucking, the lips, voyeurism, petty sadism and so on, and reaches its height in the period from the third or fourth year (Freud 1977, p.92). Yet this universal perversity is to be understood as an inevitable result of the nature of the human body. In fact, Freud writes that 'any part of the skin and any sense-organ—probably, indeed *any* organ—can function as an erotogenic zone' (Freud 1977, p.157: emphasis in original), given the right amount of stimulation. Furthermore, 'any relatively powerful emotion' (1977, p.157) can quickly become sexual. Children are merely sensitive to this range of erotic possibility, and have simply not learnt to subordinate it to the necessary sanctions that Freud lists, in a telling order, as 'shame, disgust and morality'. These are what Freud defines as sexual maturity.

Yet this sense of the infinite sexual potential of the body, and even the emotions, remains with us, constantly accompanying the adult attempt to channel sexuality into very specific paths. Our normality is constantly being tested by a perversity that resurfaces in our sexual practices (the eroticisation of the mouth, food, clothing and so on), and finds itself reappearing in our quiet excitement at the movies, before an artwork or in dance. Indeed, an entropic perversity is like the huge and unshaped substructure of our psycho-corporeal lives, on which rests the fragile and narrow sexual disposition we are prepared to admit to. The balance is between a spontaneous and unstoppable shattering of the sexual self, and the attempt to control it by education and social pressure. Here, we can see the tension between a sanctioned and straightened normality, and an unpredictable and explosive carnival, loading each of us with an intense and compelling danger that parents, teachers, doctors, peers and partners—even we ourselves—wittingly and unwittingly seek to control. It is ironic that Freud's argument about the sexuality of children has been so rejected by those who want to see childhood as a uniquely innocent time. In the end, it has been another latter-day version of the same Romantic dream of childhood as natural and untouched that has taken up the idea of polymorphous perversity so enthusiastically. Counter-cultural theorists of the 1960s and 1970s used the same language as Freud to present sexuality as itself innocent and natural, only spoilt by a society and system that encouraged, on the one hand, shame and repression and, on the other, exploitation and cruelty. Left to develop on its own terms as a natural function, sexuality would not only flourish as a necessary and wonderful part of human experience, but would contribute to a loosening of cold and sterile social relations in general—the relations that were seen to underpin capitalism, colonialism and gender inequality.

Probably the most important version of this argument was the one that came to prominence in the gay and lesbian movement in the years after the Stonewall riots of 1969, proposing that when the contemporary heterosexist regime was overthrown, everyone would be able to express their natural polymorphous bisexuality. Statements like these about global social change are often treated with ridicule now, but what might seem rhetorically overstated or merely quaint has led to a thorough transformation of particularly bourgeois sexual mores in Western countries in the last thirty years, resulting in an astonishingly rapid and complete collapse of the authority of conservative doctrines on sex. Although sexuality can still be imbued with an unfocused sense of moral panic, particularly when associated with children, homosexuality, politics, celebrity or violence, coherent discourse about sex tends to worry more about the problem of power in sexual relations rather than any moral valuation of specific sexual acts *per se*. Issues of exploitation, inequality and consent have emerged as those of greatest importance. Even conservative commentators have transformed their judgments into these terms. It is worth remembering that this emphasis is relatively new. Less than a generation ago in Australia, for example, a husband could not be tried in court for raping his wife.

FOUCAULT AND THE HISTORY OF 'SEXUALITY'

Perhaps the most influential argument about sexuality since the 1960s—Foucault's multi-volume *History of Sexuality*—challenges the belief that the modern era has seen a progressive emancipation of sexuality from the constraints of traditional blind repression. Foucault argues that we have been seduced by what he calls 'the repressive hypothesis' (Foucault 1980a, Part Two), the belief that we are owners of a natural and spontaneous sexuality that has been repressed by society.

We recall that for Foucault (see Chapter 4), the individual is not a naturally occurring phenomenon that is then threatened or controlled by power. Indeed, he argued that the very fact that we connect the different aspects of our being to make a coherent entity called the individual is the first and most significant thing that power does to us, making us feel vulnerable to judgment, as well as responsible for our behaviour, appearance and deeds, and the imaginary coherent and autonomous subjectivity they are supposed to reflect. In the sexual domain, we have convinced ourselves that our sexuality, too, is a naturally occurring phenomenon that a blind and superstitious culture has sought to keep down. If only our natural sexual capacities could express themselves freely without the encumbrance of convention and inhibition, we argue, then we could discover true subjective freedom and fulfilment.

To Foucault, however, the very idea that we consider ourselves to have a quantifiable sexual nature—a 'sexuality'—is a manifestation of the same drive of the modern system of power/knowledge seeking another language with which to identify and organise us. Power operates positively to divide us into manageable units. Repression is a hopelessly expensive and inefficient way of controlling populations. Classifying individuals in their positive nature into certain manipulable categories, on the other hand, makes them visible and answerable for their behaviour and presentation. Instead of repressing our 'natural' sexuality, power/knowledge makes us infinitely conscious of it, as if it were a fixed and measurable thing. We talk of our sexuality as if it has a material reality, like one of our internal organs. Various preferences and practices are separated from others, and used to define some fixed attribute of our subjectivity.

In the twentieth century, as Eve Kosofsky Sedgwick has pointed out in *Epistemology of the Closet* (1990), the thing that counts in sexuality is object-choice only:

It is a rather amazing fact that, of the very many dimensions along which the genital activity of one person can be differentiated from that of another (dimensions that include the preference for certain acts, certain zones or sensations, certain physical types, a certain frequency, certain symbolic investments, certain relations of age or power, a certain species, a certain number of participants, etc. etc. etc.), precisely one, the gender of object choice, emerged from the turn of the century, and has remained, as *the* dimension denoted by the now ubiquitous category of 'sexual orientation'. (Sedgwick 1990, p.8)

How has it happened that the infinite zone of human physical possibility has been so colonised by a specific way of conceiving of the erotic, as a governing, defining attribute of subjectivity?

Foucault's answer impugns the Freudian approach as part of the wider drive, firstly, to classify human sexual behaviour into strict categories, and then to use it *hermeneutically*—or, in other words, as a way of interpreting the total of an individual's behaviour. Thus it became possible to read the slightest gesture or preoccupation as having a sexual meaning, or having some sexual complex as its origin. Foucault characterises this process as the drive of 'the will to knowledge' (Foucault 1980a). A *scientia sexualis* (or science of sex) was born (see Foucault 1980a, Part Three), which contrived a map of human sexual practices and categories that could then be used to define individual subjectivities, and intervene in them according to the same old logic of scientific authority and medical emergency. Sexuality was invented as a way of making subjectivity always and everywhere pathological.

According to this argument, therefore, our era is not one that has learnt to express sexuality and discuss it freely. Instead it has made sexuality infinitely important—even desperate—not merely as a site of pleasure and emotion, but as a source of meaning, anxiety and identity. In Foucault's terms, one of the significant developments of modernity is the substitution of an 'analytics of sexuality' for a 'symbolics of blood' (Foucault 1980a, p.148) in the defining of the individual subject. Locality, nationality, family name and class have lost their ability to define us, yet in our individuality, markers of health, hygiene, correctness and sexuality have become the most visible ways in which we are classified, and through which we classify each other. 'In the space of a few centuries,' Foucault writes, 'a certain inclination has led us to direct the question of what we are, to sex' (Foucault 1980a, p.78). In sum, the classification system of the *scientia sexualis* does not *repress* our free and individual desire, as implied by the counter-cultural 'repressive hypothesis'; it *makes that desire a marker of our imagined interior nature.* When Foucault critiques 'sexuality', therefore, he is not dreaming of a place where we will not be pigeonholed, where we can 'be ourselves', but identifying this very notion of subjectivity as the pretext on which power/knowledge leans in order to monitor and administer us.

The manifestations of this in modern culture are legion, from the intensely normative display of compulsory heterosexuality in TV sitcoms like *Friends* to practices as diverse as the architecture of the family home, in which rights of access to (and the searching of) the teenager's bedroom is linked to social pressure on parents to monitor their children's use of their own bodies in masturbation or sexual experimentation. Everywhere, sex is going on and everywhere, it is confessed and judged. Foucault's response to this pathologisation of sexuality has been to call for a 'different economy of bodies and pleasures' (Foucault 1980a, p.159), as a way of allowing erotic practices to become accidental and insignificant. As it turns out, this is not necessarily a call for a return to some earlier age of sexual innocence, whether that is conceived of as another historical era, or as a pre-socialised dimension of the individual personality, like the enthusiastic calls for the liberation of 'polymorphous perversity'. Both of these tactics seem to imagine that human sexual and physical practices could one day be free of power. Yet the later volumes of *The History of Sexuality*, which study the relation between sexuality and subjectivity in Ancient Greece and Rome, show how different political and cultural formations merely deploy sexuality in different ways, never quite producing it in some imaginary depoliticised space. This is enough, however, to subvert any claim from the scientists of sex that some truth about sexuality can be defined over and above politics and history.

The influence of Foucault's argument has been immense, particularly on the burgeoning field of queer theory. David Halperin, in his *Saint Foucault: Towards a Gay Hagiography* (1995), has described the introductory volume to *The History of Sexuality* as 'the single most important intellectual source of political inspiration for contemporary AIDS activists' (Halperin 1995, p.15). Foucault's argument has been combined with other influential writing to question the relation between sexuality and identity, and inevitably between identity and politics. This has been seen as the defining idea of the queer theory movement (Jagose 1996, p.125).

WITTIG AND THE 'STRAIGHT MIND'

There have been several significant influences on the queer theory movement, one of whom is Monique Wittig, whose writing on the sex/gender distinction we have already met in Chapter 5. Wittig's most important contribution to arguments about radical sexuality has been her disconnection of gender and sexuality. In her essay 'The Straight Mind' (1980), she argues that the discursive institutions that define sexuality map every relationship and subject on to the conventional polarity of heterosexuality. In its crudest form, this appears as the characterisation of each homosexual relationship in terms of an active/masculine partner and a passive/feminine one. In the history of the science of sex, this took the form of the theory of inversion, which has been thoroughly analysed in Teresa de Lauretis's *The Practice of Love: Lesbian Sexuality and Perverse Desire* (1994), where homosexuality was interpreted as a disjunction between your biology and your gender: lesbians were defined as mannish women, for example. This insistence not only on sexuality, but all human subjectivity, as a distorted or displaced version of the universal schema of the heterosexual takes a specific—if dominant—formation and turns it into an absolute 'natural' standard. Wittig sees this imperialistic heterosexuality appearing at the level not only of jargon and role-playing ('butch/femme') but also in the simple commonsense terms male and female. In order to free themselves from their subordination to this heterosexual régime—the logic of 'the straight mind', as she calls it—gays and lesbians should reject the labels 'men' and 'women', and indeed the difference that has been much celebrated by post-structuralist theorists:

> The concept of difference . . . is only the way that the masters interpret a historical situation of domination. The function of difference is to mask at every level the conflicts of interest, including ideological ones.
>
> In other words, for us, this means there cannot any longer be women and men, and that as classes and categories of thought or language they have to disappear, politically, economically, ideologically. If we, as lesbians and gay men continue to speak of ourselves and to conceive of ourselves as women and men, we are instrumental in explaining heterosexuality. (Wittig 1992, pp.29–30)

Wittig concludes her essay with the statement '[l]esbians are not women' (1992, p.32). This statement challenges the very logic by which lesbianism is defined (women who love women), thus drawing attention to the interdependence of the categories 'gender' and 'sexuality' in conventional understandings of our relationships. Yet if both gender and sexuality are specific cultural constructs, what reference points do we have for naming our desires and planning our self-presentation?

In *Gender Trouble,* Judith Butler deals with this issue in her discussion of Wittig's (and beyond that, as we have seen in Chapter 5, Simone de Beauvoir's) sceptical treatment of gender. She sees Wittig's rejection of heterosexual imagery for homosexual subjects as reductive and limiting, and maintains that gay culture has thrived on the parodic reappropriation of once-abusive terms, like dyke, queer and fag (Butler 1990, p.122). The categories that Wittig saw as the attempt at a forced heterosexualisation of homosexuality have recycled through gay culture to draw attention to the artificiality of all gender identities—the fact, perhaps, that heterosexual women aren't women either.

Gender is played out under the auspices of fixed roles divided into two opposite propositions: the 'masculine' and the 'feminine'. It is romantic and naive to hope for some new ideal category that would free us from this binary and project us into a (polymorphous or bisexual) beyond where our desire could roam free. Instead, the result of the new self-consciousness about gender that Butler's argument provides is that we recognise the contrived system within which we must live. Our response should be to dramatise this artificiality, to recognise that we are ever and always in subversion of it, by our failure to repeat properly the script compulsory heterosexuality lays down for us.

QUEER: POLITICS WITHOUT IDENTITY

The discovery of a politics still possible without the fixed categories of identity on which social politics in the late twentieth century has usually depended is one of the key attributes of queer theory. Again, it shows that not only gay and lesbian issues, but gay and lesbian thinkers, are at the vanguard of considerations of gender, sexuality and their historical meaning. This is not to say that queer is uncontroversial within gay and lesbian politics which traditionally have relied on a positive identification of a gay constituency (homosexual people) for their justification. Queer's rejection of both gender and sexual identities complicates the neat delimitation of any such constituency, and there has been much fierce debate between those who see practical politics as dependent on fixed identity, and those queer theorists who draw on Foucault's argument that sexual categories inevitably aid the logic of power (see Jagose, Ch. 8).

Queer theory is thus unhappy with the simple project of activism seen to dominate the gay and lesbian movements of the 1970s and 1980s, the aim of which was to secure the civil rights of an oppressed minority. Instead, a more intense politics can be found in the savaging of identity altogether, and through that, a reconsideration of the reigning culture of subjectivity. For example, Sue-Ellen Case's 'Tracking the Vampire', an essay that appears in the first of two special editions on queer theory of the feminist cultural studies journal *differences*, edited by Teresa de Lauretis, sees queer as attacking the very metaphysical assumptions on which Western culture depends, specifically the distinction between the living and the dead. Human life would seem to be incontrovertibly contained by the rejection of the dead as our entirely alien other. Yet we have seen how similar unquestioned assumptions about gender and sexuality have been critiqued as the product of cultural and political forces, and therefore are not inevitable.

In Case's argument, the separation of life and death is entangled in the politics of sexuality—specifically in the homophobic condemnation of gay and lesbian relations as sterile, and therefore hostile to the social ascendancy of the family. The family, Case reminds us, is an economic unit as well as the engine room of a society's gender and sexual values, and transmits its meanings down a line of property inheritance that is traditionally male. This transmission of property along blood lines is itself analogous to the metaphor of blood connection still used to define racial inheritance. Blood, with its link to property, race, HIV and menstruation, is a uniquely potent rhetorical site in the debate over gender and sexuality. Connections between blood's different themes overlap and commingle with one another in charged ways. Case's essay is an attempt to disentangle these lines and to see how their fundamental determinant is the unquestioned life/death binary that links the generative and heterosexual with health and life, and the sterile and homosexual with contamination and death. The horror genre cliché, the lesbian vampire, deconstructs this opposition. In fact, the contradictions of lesbianism in homophobic discourse are exemplified in the denotation of the vampire as the 'living dead'.

Queer practice, when viewed in these terms, is not merely a

lifestyle choice or a personal preference. It is a complicated cultural and political transgression. Case writes:

> Queer sexual practice, then, impels one out of the generational production of what has been called 'life' and history, and ultimately out of the category of the living. The equation of hetero = sex = life and homo = sex = unlife generated a queer discourse that revelled in proscribed desiring by imagining sexual objects and sexual practices within the realm of the other-than-natural, and the consequent other-than-living. In this discourse, new forms of being, or beings, are imagined through desire. And desire is that which wounds—a desire that breaks through the sheath of being as it has been imagined within a heterosexist society. Striking at its very core, queer desire punctures the life/death and generative/destructive bipolarities that enclose the heterosexist notion of being. (Case 1991, p.4)

It is hard to imagine a more thoroughly radical reconsideration of the meaning of sexuality than this, where what is at stake is not merely the free choice of your sexual object, but the metaphysical underpinnings of our relationship to life, death and being itself.

Indeed, this is a mere part of a movement that has seen experimentation at the margins of sexual pleasure as the possible frontier of human self-reinvention. Foucault saw in sadomasochistic (SM) practice a way of forging new subjective values across and beyond the sanctioned norm. SM has become the site of intense political controversy concurrent with the queer movement: some argue that it tests the structure of subjectivity and intersubjectivity in dangerous yet productive and optimistic ways, while others maintain it merely repeats the logic of a violent society from which progressive practice should try to separate itself. I have argued elsewhere (Mansfield 1997) that masochism unlocks the meaning of contemporary power relations in masculinity's attempt to reinvent its ascendancy in the postmodern era.

In the attempt to sabotage the authority of sexuality as a category of subjectivity, Foucault's work has encouraged an explosion of studies of the significance of the sexual in contemporary society and culture. Behind the assumption that our sexuality is dictated to us by Nature lurks a complex set of power relations, social norms and dominations. This is one of the places in which the problem of the subject can be experienced most acutely, where our most deeply felt irresistible desires embody contingent political forces. For both the subjective and anti-subjective approaches to subjectivity, the sexual has always been a defining issue. Indeed, the era of the subject is the era of sexuality. Each approach would have its own explanation for this. For psychoanalysis, the construction of the subject is always entangled in the hidden sexual politics of the family. For Foucault, the parameters of modern subjectivity have always been traced by a discourse that saw in sexuality both a way of defining individual life and of intervening in it. The complex history of both of these approaches may have made us more sceptical about our culture's discourses on sexuality, but so immersed are we within their categories, insights, dangers, politics and pleasures, that it is impossible to imagine a theorisation of subjectivity without them.

FURTHER READING

Foucault, Michel, 1980a, *The History of Sexuality Volume 1: An Introduction* trans. Robert Hurley, Vintage Books, New York.

Freud, Sigmund, 1977, *On Sexuality* trans. James Strachey, Penguin Books, Harmondsworth.

Wittig, Monique, 1992, *The Straight Mind and Other Essays* Beacon Press, Boston.

9 | Subjectivity and ethnicity: Otherness, policy, visibility, colonialism

THE 1990S HAS seen a violent upsurge in the politics of ethnicity and related issues: nationality, migration, refugees, community rivalry and so on. Yet at the same time as ethnic identities have become more and more a site of struggle, the means by which ethnicity is defined have become less certain. The twentieth century opened in the West with an obsessive emphasis on race as the determining attribute of human subjectivity: you were a member of a racial group before you were anything else, according to the eugenicist orthodoxy. The separation of races became a common priority of politicians and social administrators: miscegenation was seen as a dilution of racial destiny and both a symptom and cause of national decline. This belief had its logical expression in the Nazi Holocaust, the South African policy of Separate Development (Apartheid) and the forced removal of part-Aboriginal children from their parents (known in Australia as the Stolen Generations). It is absolutely crucial to notice in these examples that with modern ethnic politics we are not dealing with the spontaneous and dis-organised rivalry of one loosely formed community with another, nor centuries-old antagonism between neighbouring language or religious groups.

In fact, the dominant and most typical racism of the twentieth century has been government policy, drawing on the authority of a race science positioned not at the margins, but in the mainstream of Western thought. In the modern world, racial politics are not merely an extension of community hostilities and mindless tradi-tional prejudices. They are part of the disciplining of populations, gaining what authority they have from their coordination with legitimised institutions of learning and administration. In turn, racists in the street have drawn on the rhetoric of community management to endorse struggles and hatreds, complaining of ghettos, preferential treatment and so on.

In fact, even though it survives in social debate, 'race' is a term with almost no meaning, as commentators have long pointed out (see, for example, Appiah in Gates 1986). Through the twentieth century, liberal theory has progressively replaced it with the term 'ethnicity', though as we shall see, this is itself not unproblematic. Given the relativity of these terms, this chapter will not be about how your subjectivity is determined by your race and ethnicity. This would merely be a way of repeating the very artificial categories that now seem so problematic. Instead, it will discuss how these specific cultural and political issues have appeared in discussions about the self.

RACE, THE VISIBLE AND THE ENLIGHTENMENT

The politics of race revolve around the endless play of visibility and invisibility, emphasising—in a Western context at least—the visible markers of racial difference, from skin colour to the bone structure of the face. Hortense Spillers has described this in relation to African-American history as 'the politics of melanin' (Spillers 1987, p.71). Exhibitions of the Jewish racial 'type' in the Nazi period also drew on the visual as a way of defining racial differences. In ostensibly liberal societies, like the free market postmodern West, ethnicity is seen to exist only in those minority groups that bear visible markers of difference. According to this logic, white people do not have ethnicity, which is only an issue for minorities.

This denial is not merely the result of a secluded suburban culture, however. It can be traced to the heart of the very universal principles on which modern liberal societies depend. European Enlightenment thinkers saw themselves as able to speak for humanity in general, and believed that ethnicity was a restriction for non-Europeans only. In his introduction to *'Race', Writing and Difference* (1986), Henry Louis Gates Jr gives examples of this racially specific definition of the human. Scottish Enlightenment philosopher David Hume argued in 1753 that, because they had no arts and sciences and no 'ingenious manufactures', Africans were 'naturally inferior' to Europeans (Gates 1986, p.10). The Enlightenment's establishment of the higher human qualities (the arts and sciences, for example) automatically creates a hierarchy amongst peoples. If the highest human qualities are defined, then those who do not share them are inevitably less human. 'Nature' is then called upon as an endorsement of these values.

What we see here, therefore, is not the mere petrifaction of a prejudice of an eighteenth-century man, but the fact that the universal humanism which is purported to be Western thought's most significant achievement absolutely depended on creating hierarchies of racial superiority and inferiority. This sort of statement is everywhere in the Enlightenment, from Kant's 'so fundamental is the difference between [the black and white] races of man . . . it appears to be as great in regard to mental capacities as in colour' (Gates 1986, p.10) to Hegel's belief that since black people had no history, they had no humanity (Gates 1986, p.11).

The administrative history of racism in the modern era can be traced to these definitions of what is higher or lower in human behaviour (reason versus tradition, science versus emotion, evidence versus intuition and so on) which divide humanity into those 'peoples' who belonged to a productive future and those who did not. Indigenous populations were seen to belong to the past, and the influence of indigenous 'blood' in mixed-race children needed to be countered by their forced induction into 'higher' values. At the other extreme to this liberal-assimilationist model, the Nazi-genocidal program of racial purification dreamed of racially defined hierarchies of future dominant and subordinate, pure and contaminated races. The Nazi racial holocausts were the defining event of twentieth-century history, especially where race relations are concerned. In the West, they forced societies long built on racial hierarchies and stereotypes to emphasise their liberal humanist traditions and to claim that racial prejudice had always been an eccentric and minority viewpoint, the domain of the unenlightened and vulgar. This reaction did not result, however, in the end of racial policies, even in the most avowedly liberal democratic societies. Segregation and assimilation remained common practice at least into the 1970s.

CULTURE AND ETHNICITY

The discrediting of race-based thinking also caused a change in theory and terminology. In the second half of the twentieth century, human differences have increasingly come to be understood not in terms of race and blood, but culture and ethnicity. According to discussions of ethnicity, differences in values, behaviour and belief are not part of the individual's natural inheritance, determined by their membership of a racial group, but part of the culture into which they are inducted by family life, language and education.

This idea of culture as a crucible in which the individual is formed entered the human sciences in the work of British anthropologist Sir Edward Burnett Tylor (1832–1917) in his *Primitive Culture* (1871). This usage answers many of the problems posed by the narrow and potentially murderous concept of race. Culture and ethnicity are part of the flux, change and development of history, in a way that race is not. Cultures change and adapt; race is usually seen as a part of the unchangeable logic of nature. Culture and ethnicity also help to explain the way individuals' responses are not merely a reflection of their individuality, but are conditioned by established beliefs and practices that form the context in which they live. This explains why since the 1980s the term 'culture' has been generalised to explain the often-intangible value-systems that underprop institutions, organisations and workplaces. New chief executives almost invariably speak of a corporation's (healthy or unhealthy) 'culture'. The police, the bureaucracy, the universities similarly all have unique 'cultures'.

There have long been critics of this way of understanding human practice. Theories of culture often end by seeing individuals as completely enclosed by a set of pre-existing values to which they must become subordinate. For some conservative critics, this leads to a reduction in individual moral responsibility. To others, it results in a fatalistic and pessimistic image of culture as an immoveable burden that leaves us no freedom for dissent, negotiation and subversion. American anthropologist and cultural critic James Clifford has written: 'Since the mid-nineteenth century, ideas of culture have gathered up those elements that seem to give continuity and depth to collective experience, seeing it whole rather than disputed, torn, intertextual, or syncretic' (Clifford 1988, p.232). According to Clifford, we do need a term like culture to explain patterns in human behaviour that are neither generically human nor specific to the individual. Yet we also need to recognise cultures as internally unstable and riven, with perimeters that are unmappable and contested.

BOURDIEU AND HABITUS

One of the most important theorists to rethink the way culture determines subjectivity and behaviour is Pierre Bourdieu (b. 1930). Bourdieu's theory of habitus originated in the anthropological fieldwork he undertook in Algeria in the early 1960s, and was first fully developed in *Outline of a Theory of Practice* (1972). This work signalled Bourdieu's shift from anthropology to sociology, and later publications such as *Distinction* (1979) are not studies of ethnic as much as social groupings. I introduce the concept of habitus here as a way of signalling the instability and complexity that inevitably arise in any understanding of culture and ethnicity as determinants of social practices—and indeed subjectivity.

The pretext for the development of the concept of habitus was Bourdieu's dissatisfaction with the developing orthodoxies of structuralist anthropology, typified by Lévi-Strauss's understanding of marriage practices as a structured exchange of women. This sort of analysis reduced society to a fixed arrangement of constant and impersonal practices that were predetermined and inflexible. In turn, they satisfied the Western anthropologist's need to produce models of social behaviour as structured and stable arrangements of knowable and predictable acts and relationships. These relationships are seen to be purely *synchronic*: each action, each offering and exchange, is seen to take place as if simultaneously, fulfilling an already known and established pattern. One party's proposal of marriage, another's response to the proposal, the negotiations over dowry, property and timing, and the ceremonies themselves are all thus reduced to a single practice. The time that separates the various components of the arrangement is overlooked. In this way, according to Bourdieu, the agency of the various participating groups and individuals is ignored. What they do is automatic and leaves no room for surprise, innovation or disjunction.

Bourdieu's aim here is not to reinstate the idea of the free and autonomous individual, acting according to original and personal ideas and judgments. However, the role of the players in something as complex as a marriage arrangement has to be seen as *strategic* as much as it is merely the mindless dramatisation of inherited rules and norms. To understand social behaviour, therefore, the observer has to recognise how it only appears fixed and regulated from the outside. On the day-to-day level of regular social exchange, an element of tactical improvisation is always present, or at least always experienced by the participants. Hence, how participants represent their own practices, how they put conventions into operation on each particular occasion—how they may postpone or bring forward an offer or response, how they may actually phrase a communication or hesitate in delivering it—become important indicators of how social relationships are proceeding.

The various strategic options that become available to participants do not emerge from nowhere, however. Social behaviour arises in the context of what Bourdieu calls a 'community of dispositions (habitus)' (Bourdieu 1977, p.35). Our social practices are not the result of simple conformity to inherited rules of social behaviour—even if, over time, their regularity starts to make them appear that way to an outside observer. Instead, we draw on a range of possible strategies that appear to be available to us, while selecting from a range of possible outcomes that the world-view of our social and cultural context in a particular stage of its history allows us to see. We have no sense that our choices are fixed into trans-historical principles or rules. Although they are limited by our social and cultural context, they appear to us to arise as the inevitable circumstances of our behaviour, and our relationship to them is not experienced as cultural, ideological or religious, but as practical. The statistical consistencies that arise therefore indicate that these strategies emerge from a collective and dynamic—indeed, open-ended—history of possible behaviours, 'systems of durable, transposable dispositions' (Bourdieu 1977, p.72). It is these systems that Bourdieu calls 'habitus'.

The concept of habitus thus grasps the complexity and paradoxical nature of culturally and socially located behaviour. It shows how our freedom is determined, and how our spontaneity is made available to us. Bourdieu writes of habitus as:

> principles of the generation and structuring of practices and representations which can be objectively 'regulated' and 'regular' without in any way being the product of obedience to rules, objectively adapted to their goals without presupposing a conscious aiming at ends or an express mastery of the operations necessary to attain them and, being all this, collectively orchestrated without being the product of the orchestrating action of a conductor. (Bourdieu 1977, p.72)

The aim here is to find an alternative way to understand social behaviour that neither abolishes subjectivity (by seeing our choices as made for us by fixed social structures) or idealises it (as the source of purely free individual choices). Habitus is a set of possible practices and ways of perceiving those practices, attuned to a particular situation in a world inevitably made up of material situations and relationships.

Habitus is thus an enactment of the material and economic conditions of a given society—its class structures, for example. Individual behaviour is nothing other than 'a certain specification of the collective history of [a] group or class' (Bourdieu 1977, p.86). Each social group or class enacts a set of dispositions and practices that reveal its own particular habitus. Much of Bourdieu's subsequent work has analysed how practices such as education and art allow individuals to differentiate themselves from one another according to significant knowledges, tastes and inclinations. This process of separation and hierarchisation understands the priorities and values of a social group as kinds of symbolic or cultural capital that individuals can accrue, whereby we are able to distinguish ourselves from one another, to both validate ourselves in terms of our habitus and validate the habitus itself. Symbolic or cultural capital is in turn as important for Bourdieu as the material capital that Marxist social theory has always seen as the key to social structures.

FANON AND THE POSTCOLONIAL SUBJECT

Bourdieu concludes that it is the political context of the subject in the most general sense that produces the range of its possible behaviour. This also holds true when this political context is determined by violence and intrusion rather than by tradition and hierarchy. The most explicit example of this sort of structured violence is colonialism. Frantz Fanon (1925–61) produced a seminal contribution to the understanding of subjectivity and its relationship to the cruel politics of colonialism in *The Wretched of the Earth* (1961) and *Black Skins, White Masks* (1967).

Fanon presents the subjectivity of the colonised as a direct product of the colonial system: 'it is the settler who has brought the native into existence and perpetuates his existence' (Fanon 1967, p.28). 'Native' subjectivity, therefore, is not a pre-existing thing that encounters the coloniser with an underdeveloped consciousness and an undercivilised emotionalism, that must adapt or submit to a more advanced European civilisation. Psychological studies still influential in Fanon's time made just this sort of claim when they tried to deal with mental illness and high rates of crime in colonial Algeria, where he worked as a psychiatrist (Fanon 1967, pp.243–44).

This determination to see the native at an earlier stage of development is, to Fanon, part of the political culture of colonialism, which abominated the native as 'the enemy of values . . . the deforming element disfiguring all that has to do with beauty or morality' (Fanon 1967, p.32). This dehumanisation of the colonised is not a mere fictional trope able to satisfy the prejudices of the colonising and justify their presence in someone else's country. It remakes the settler and the native in turn as types of subjects, bearing completely different moral and cultural legacies: the colonised is unstable, irrational and inarticulate; the coloniser, on the other hand, is seen as a stabilising force, bearing the transcendent discourses of enlightened humanity that cannot only rationalise the need for colonial domination and subordination, but also drown out the particularities and specificities of local culture with the thunderous and confident universal statements about the progress of humanity. This sense of the necessary submission of the local and particular before the inevitable and universal recurs in more recent rhetorics of globalisation, which have also been interpreted by some theorists as colonising.

Colonialism operates therefore at the level of subjectivity. Fanon writes:

> Because it is a systematic negation of the other person and a furious determination to deny the other person all the attributes of humanity, colonialism forces the people it dominates to ask themselves the question constantly: 'In reality, who am I?'
>
> The defensive attitudes created by this violent bringing together of the colonised man and the colonial system form themselves into a structure which then reveals the colonised personality. This 'sensitivity' is easily understood if we simply study and are alive to the number and depth of the injuries inflicted upon a native during a single day spent amidst the colonial regime. (Fanon 1967, pp.200–201)

The colonial regime needs certain types of subjectivity in order to justify itself in moral terms and in order simply to operate in practical terms.

The reduction of native subjectivity to the irrational also anticipates any resistance by prefiguring it as emotional. Fanon's solution here is violence. Only in violence can the native discover the sense of subjective meaning that can stabilise the world and build freedom. 'At the level of individuals,' Fanon writes, 'violence is a cleansing force. It frees the native from his [sic] inferiority complex and from his despair and inaction; it makes him fearless and restores his self-respect' (Fanon 1967, p.74). Colonialism operates, therefore, not only on the level of a material exploitation and a military administration that can only be resisted by organised force. Violence is liberating, not primarily because it is able to destroy the structures of a colonial régime, but because it causes a revolution on the level of the subject, who can throw off the degradations and debasements of colonial culture and replace them with a purposeful and historically charged sense of itself and national possibility.

SPIVAK AND SUBALTERN STUDIES

Fanon's evocation of violence is indicative of the critical phase of decolonisation that he was experiencing first hand in Algeria, where massacre and torture had become routine. Later anti-colonial and postcolonial theorists have echoed his themes, though in a completely different political context and thus in different terms. An important example is Gayatri Chakravorty Spivak's analysis of the representation of subjectivity in the work of the postcolonial Subaltern Studies group.

Spivak brings their conception of the colonial subject into contact with the decomposed and deconstructed subject of the postmodern West. In the work of Subaltern Studies, the political action of an oppressed social group is represented as if it is the coherent action of a single collective subject. This is consistent with traditional radical rhetoric which talks of the working class or the colonised as if they are an undifferentiated single formation, little different from a single autonomous agent. There are obvious problems with this way of representing a mobile population: internal differences are suppressed in the name of a single program of action which automatically ranks participants as more or less loyal, or more or less attuned to the collective project.

Yet the post-structuralist paradigm of a fragmented and unstable subject that has become so favoured in Western countries refuses to recognise the specificity of the situation of the colonised subject as identified, for example, by a commentator like Fanon. The colonised were obliged to occupy 'the space of the Imperialists' self-consolidating other' (Spivak 1987, p.209). Colonialism produced a set of specific subject positions geared to its needs. Western intellectuals like Jean Baudrillard may well talk of arriving not 'at the point where one no longer says I, but at the point where it's no longer of any importance whether one says I or not' (Baudrillard cited in Spivak 1987, p.209). Spivak argues that this sort of declaration can only be made by way of a 'sanctioned ignorance' of the history of colonialism. Colonised subjects become merely old-fashioned, locked in an earlier subjectivity of oppression, expression and resistance, or else they are not recognised at all. The Subaltern Studies group, therefore, must remain committed to subaltern populations as subjects of their own history. Baudrillard's entropic subject is not a reflection of the position in which they find themselves, or the subjectivity that their historical experience has determined for them. The irony is, of course, that here the supposedly radical rhetoric of the Western transgressive intellectual performs the same function as the imperialism it nominally scorns, relegating the non-Eurpoean other to a less advanced stage of development. Global culture, whether it is the Internet or cultural theory, therefore repeats the colonising strategy, despite its loud announcement of new possibilities for a new freedom that defies history and the boundaries of national identity and experience.

PSYCHOANALYSIS AND ETHNICITY

What is the relationship between ethnicity and the two rival approaches to subjectivity that I have used to structure the argument of this book? I want now to look briefly at two writers who treat issues of racial identity in firstly a psychoanalytic and secondly a Foucauldian context.

Psychoanalysis has long been criticised for its universalism. Critics have argued that Freud saw the Oedipal complex as common to all human societies, thus ignoring cultural and ethnic difference. Gates has also drawn attention to the way Freud used traditionally racist and imperial metaphors to represent the sexual life of adult women as a 'dark continent', a phrase connected with the European definition of pre-colonial Africa as pre-civilised. The article I want to refer to here—Hortense J. Spillers' 'Mama's Baby, Papa's Maybe: An American Grammar Book' (1987)—is later and deals not only with Freudian but also with Lacanian motifs. Spillers' achievement is to show how the experience of a particular community challenges the terminology and conclusions of psychoanalysis.

Spillers' argument starts as a reconsideration of the Moynihan Report, whose full title is *The Negro Family: The Case for National Action*, written by Senator Daniel P. Moynihan and published by the US Department of Labor in 1965. Moynihan argued that since the United States was predominantly a patriarchal society, families centred on the mother, like those of African-Americans, were at a distinct disadvantage (Spillers 1987, p.66). Spillers reads Moynihan's argument as an indictment of the black American family in the guise of trying to help it. Behind the logic of Moynihan's judgments lies an understanding of the family consistent with the Lacanian image of a psycho-social and linguistic structure defined by masculinity. The black family, by not conforming to the apparently inevitable logic of this order, fails both itself and the society to which its progeny should be trying to attune themselves:

> According to Daniel Patrick Moynihan . . . the 'Negro Family' has no father to speak of—his Name, his Law, his Symbolic function, mark the impressive missing agencies in the essential life of the black community, the 'Report' maintains, and it is, surprisingly, the fault of the daughter, or the female line. This stunning reversal of the castration thematic, displacing the Name and the Law of the Father to the territory of the Mother and Daughter, becomes an aspect of the African-American female's misnaming. (Spillers 1987, pp.65–66)

With the establishment of the Lacanian norm of the patriarchal family as the cornerstone of moral value and economic efficiency, any family that operates otherwise is seen to be dissenting and doomed. The implication is that black women are responsible for this bad 'choice'.

Yet Spillers' article shows that the crisis of the black family identified by Moynihan is traceable to a system that set the ownership of property above the rights of family: slavery. In fact, for black families to be judged according to a family normativity that centuries of slavery systematically destroyed is incredible, if not laughable. Under slavery, the relations between parents and children threatened to challenge the relations between owner and slave. Such competing allegiances on the part of the slave would have undermined the absolute authority of the owner (Spillers 1987, p.75). Consequently, the middle-class, father-dominated family that the Moynihan Report sees as inevitable is only available under certain historical conditions, and to certain people.

Similarly, the categories of procreation, gender and sexuality that Freud discussed as if they were given by nature are only available to those who can live within carefully protected social, political and economic boundaries. In social systems like slavery, not only is the relationship between parent and child governed by the bond between owner and slave, but also the relationship between the subject and itself. Freudian psychoanalysis seems not to question the assumption of the individuals' ownership of their own bodies, and consequently their direct relationship with their own pleasure, sexuality and gender. The slave's pleasure and sexuality, however, are governed by systematic practices of rape and forced child-bearing. The distribution of gender identities is equally subject to a system of forced labour where physical torture and the slave market are ever-present realities. Spillers writes: '[U]nder these arrangements, the customary lexis of sexuality, including "reproduction", "motherhood", "pleasure", and "desire" are thrown into unrelieved crisis' (Spillers 1987, p.76).

Moynihan's argument, therefore, is willing to *see* certain aspects of African-American experience, but not others. Spillers connects this with the issue of race and visibility that we have touched on above. Skin colour divides the human population into groups that justify the broadest and most inflexible generalisations, setting the characteristics of one group (the 'White family') against another (the 'Negro family'). '"Ethnicity" in this case freezes in meaning, takes on constancy, assumes the look and affects of the Eternal' (Spillers 1987, p.66). Meanings can be spun endlessly out of these merely specular identifications: 'the human body becomes a defenseless target for rape and veneration, and the body, in its material and abstract phase, a resource for metaphor' (1987, p.66). Spillers is not arguing here for the individual's transcendence of social categories like ethnicity, but merely trying to show how the truth of ethnicity is not generated out of 'objective' observation; rather, it is the product of cultural practices and politics that choose to recognise some—usually visible—things and not others. Skin colour is always visible, but the psychological legacy of generations of torture is not seen and remains unmentioned (1987, p.67).

In the end, the twin pillars of psychoanalysis—the normativity of the middle-class family and the individual subject's identification with its own body and pleasure—are thrown into question by this visual economy. The first appears only available under certain historical circumstances, and thus generalisations like Freud's can only really be useful in specific societies. We should not be blind to this specificity, even if the theorist's context mirrors our own. In the case of the second, aspects of the body chosen and weighted by culture and politics become more important in defining the individual subject than anything that the subject can really call its own:

> This profitable 'atomising' of the captive body provides another angle on the divided flesh: we lose any hint or suggestion of a dimension of ethics, of relatedness between human personality and its anatomical features, between one human personality and another, between human personality and cultural institutions. (Spillers 1987, p.68)

The visible marker of skin colour defines the slave not as an autonomous individual, but as part of a specific economy, of the buying and selling of labouring flesh. This economy separates the subject from itself, making any sense of individuality or autonomy completely negligible in the face of the slave-market and the visible markers that define it.

The logic of the visible that governs this economy, defining who will and will not be slaves, is not unique to this uniquely cruel system. It is part of the political logic of the visible that is everywhere in Western meaning-making. We have noticed it earlier in Laura Mulvey's analysis of cinema (see Chapter 7). It is at the heart of psychoanalysis itself, and its theory of gender, which distinguishes so emphatically between the visible male and invisible female genitals. Indeed, Spillers calls US slavery 'one of the richest displays of the psychoanalytic dimensions of culture before the science of European psychoanalysis takes hold' (Spillers 1987, p.77). To psychoanalysis, gender and the membership of social formations from the literal family to the amorphous symbolic order are defined by the visible. Here too, despite the assumption psychoanalysis makes that subjects can be identified with their pleasure, we see an economy of visual markers dividing individual subjects from one another and defining our pleasure for us. A whole cultural tradition that makes a selective reading of the visible field the key determinant of identifications and meanings flourishes in fields as diverse as slavery and therapy.

RACE AND POWER/KNOWLEDGE

The issue of race threatens the authority of psychology by drawing attention to its involvement with politics. In her study of the relationship between psychology and race, *Beyond the Masks: Race, Gender and Subjectivity* (1995), Amina Mama analyses psychological studies of people of African descent living in the United States and United Kingdom in order to show how supposedly scientific analysis reflects the shifts in racial politics going on at the same time. Mama thus analyses psychology as a discourse intersecting with social and cultural factors, not as a science gradually clarifying a fixed set of facts. Her sceptical approach to 'truth' is thus broadly like Foucault's, seeing the models of black subjectivity that are produced by psychology not as better and better insights into the true nature of what it is to be black, but instead, as facilitating the work of social administrators (in the case of those theories that treat blackness as if it is a pathology that needs some sort of therapeutic help), or as justifying the social mission of black radicals (by providing 'objective' evidence for the psychological results of racial oppression).

In the United States, the twentieth century has seen a range of attempts to read African-American experience in terms of racial politics. At first, white psychologists analysed black subjectivity in terms of the damage done to black subjects by slavery. 'These construed the Negro as a psychologically tormented individual whose entire identity was dictated by white racism' (Mama 1995, p.47). Later theorists explained black subjectivity in terms of a uniquely black negative self-concept. This idea, particularly as it emerged in the work of black psychologists Kenneth and Mamie Clark, fitted with the emergent politics of the civil rights movement, and formed part of a submission on racial desegregation to the US Supreme Court (Mama 1995, p.51).

As Foucault has shown with the theorisation of criminality, the history of such modelling of subjectivity has to be traced through struggles over power, as well as through deliberations on knowledge, and can be seen as the place where the two are not separate. Given what is at stake in these political struggles, it is no surprise that radical as well as conservative activists look to the authority of science as a way of articulating their cases. Mama goes on to analyse the psychology of nigrescence, coordinated with the Black Power movements of the late 1960s, that argued strongly for a positive, proud relationship between the black subject and itself.

Mama's study draws attention to the political entanglements on which knowledge depends for its claim to relevance and seriousness. Her fundamental point about these studies, however, is that they always insist on understanding black subjectivity as defined by white racism, thus 'ignoring the existence of the diverse cultural referents available to many black people' (Mama 1995, p.52), and usually presenting black people as passive in relation to their oppression. She says of those original studies of the 'Negro' damaged by slavery:

> Nowhere in [this] work is there any acknowledgment of the various collective (cultural) responses to the long black history of oppression, or in fact that they might have had any experience apart from that of racism. Racial oppression itself is inadequately conceptualised as monolithic, total and homogeneous in its effects. The nuances and intricate set of social etiquette and behaviour, of betrayal and collusion, of inversion and resistance that constitute racism as a social process are barely touched upon. (Mama 1995, p.48)

This reduction of the variety of black experience to a single model is partly the inevitable result of one group being treated as an object of analysis. But it is also inevitable if you assume that all-inclusive statements about subjectivity are possible, that there is a single black, white, Asian, Russian, Parisian, Serbian, or British subject about whom definitive statements can be made. This assumption is never questioned in the works that Mama analyses (Mama 1995, p.43). In the case of racial politics—which are a uniquely potent site of ruthless official policy on the one hand, and endless struggle on the other—we can see why power and knowledge remain locked together: before it can act, even before it needs to know whether (as in our present example) the black subject is damaged, has a negative self-concept or whatever, power (and the forces that contest it) must make us believe that there is a single quantifiable object on which to act. Power needs knowledge, because knowledge can justify the idea that there is a thing (the 'subject') to be organised, categorised and measured, that human subjectivity is not an irreducible field of differences that continually counter and defy reduction to a single description. Social administration and politics alike need to believe that the subject exists.

HYBRIDITY

This issue becomes particularly acute when we move away from the simple categories of ethnic identity, where you are one thing and not another—black *or* white, Asian *or* Australian—and deal with the charged contemporary issue of cultural hybridity, where the issue of ethnic history remains highly important without being reducible to the fixed, known categories of ethnic identity which policy and prejudice are used to.

Hybridity as the mixing of apparently separate objects and identities is an issue that shows the way distinct zones of postmodern politics and culture overlap and intersect with one another. One of the most influential contributions to the debate, Donna Haraway's 'A Cyborg Manifesto' (1985), links the industrial image-scape of technology with the dangerous hall of mirrors of ethnic politics. In Chapter 11, we will deal with this article in detail to show how anxiety about technological change inherits some of its vehemence from earlier hysteria about racial mixing.

For the purposes of the present discussion of subjectivity and ethnicity, the issue or image of hybridity has functioned to show how models of stable racial and ethnic identity have always been more symbolic than real, more arbitrary than natural. Pure ethnic identities exist nowhere other than in political rhetoric. The reality of a globe structured by mass migration to its New Worlds, by reverse migration to its once boom-time metropolises and almost compulsory internal migration within states as people chase work, social advancement, love, cheap real estate, anonymity, physical safety and sunshine, is one of an accelerating intermixing of once meaningful local and ethnic labels to the point where an older rhetoric of stability and purity functions as a flimsy fantasy. This is apparent in the generality of the twentieth century's ethnic categories like 'black', 'white', 'Aryan', 'indigenous', 'Asian'—terms which define a moment in contemporary politics only, and in which more specific village, familial, tribal or language identities disappear.

With the long shadow of Nazism and its latter-day revivals as their prime antagonist, postmodern theorists have delighted in showing the inevitable hybridity of both human culture and even human DNA, in what Pnina Werbner has described as a contemporary 'reflexive global heterophilia' (Werbner and Madood 1997, p.17), or 'love of otherness', an arm's length celebration of ethnic difference that we see in the marketing of 'world music', multicultural carnivals and movies like *Baraka* (1992). The battle continues between those who require some image of ethnic or national essence to stabilise their place in the world, and those who celebrate the relativisation of all identities in a carnivalesque and cosmopolitan dream of human reconfiguration and reinvention. Again, a link between the rhetoric of the ethnic and the technological remaking of humanity should be noted.

Werbner raises the issue of whether such hybridity holds the utopian promise it may seem to, even if it is finally successful in discrediting languages of national, communal and racial purity that have underpropped the twentieth century's horrific history of racial policy. The irony and difficulty of hybridity, according to Werbner, is that it is both normal and transgressive, that it defines the day-to-day reality of our lives in its many forms (cultural, ethnic, and technological) but is still seen as a threat, still 'experienced as dangerous, difficult or revitalising despite its quotidian normalcy' (Werbner and Madood 1997, p.4).

Even though their status remains so deeply questionable, rhetorics of stable ethnic identity remain with us, as do their counterparts in the fields of gender and sexuality that the work of Judith Butler and queer theorists have done so much to relativise. Yet in much contemporary culture, these identities function in perpetual inverted commas: alive but in suspended animation, as part of the landscape of subjective life, but never its truth. This is exemplified in the work of artists who quote but mock the categories of identity that their more earnest allies, enemies or parents want to apply to them. Novelist Christos Tsiolkas (b. 1965) captures some of this sense of active yet suspended identity in the words of Ari, the narrator of *Loaded* (1995):

> I'm not Australian, I'm not Greek, I'm not anything. I'm not a worker, I'm not a student, I'm not an artist, I'm not a junkie, I'm not a conversationalist, I'm not an Australian, not a wog, not anything. I'm not left wing, right wing, centre, left of centre, right of Genghis Khan. I don't vote, I don't demonstrate, I don't do charity.
>
> What I am is a runner. Running away from the thousand and one things that people say you have to be or should want to be. (Tsiolkas 1995, p.149)

Here, as with queer theory, we don't have some claim for an authentic and essentially true individuality that pre-exists social categorisation, and that the narrator seeks to liberate. Ari is 'not anything', living in the shadow of defining categories whose residual efficiency persists despite their artificiality and lack of credibility. Beyond hybridity, however it is defined, lies the abandonment of the politics of identity that dominated the 1960s to the 1980s, demanding that oppressed groups identify wholistically with their oppression, that postcolonial societies as diverse as Papua New Guinea and Australia discover a new nationalism, that we appear in society in terms of identities that can negotiate a new social contract of tolerance and inclusiveness. As Ari's imagery points out, this democracy of identity is giving way to the chaotic invention of the subjective line of flight, hurling itself out of the shadow of identity into an unknown and perhaps unrepresentable future, in an unclimactic liberation hedged by endlessly renewed excitations but without the collective optimism Enlightenment rationalists promised would always accompany human advancement.

FURTHER READING

Bourdieu, Pierre, 1977, *Outline of a Theory of Practice* trans. Richard Nice, Cambridge University Press, Cambridge.

Fanon, Frantz, 1967, *The Wretched of the Earth* trans. Constance Farrington, Penguin Books, Harmondsworth.

Mama, Amina, 1995, *Beyond the Masks: Race, Gender and Subjectivity* Routledge, London.

Spillers, Hortense J., 1987, 'Mama's Baby, Papa's Maybe: An American Grammar Book' *Diacritics* Summer, pp.65–81.

Spivak, Gayatri Chakravorty, 1987, 'Subaltern Studies: Deconstructing Historiography' in *In Other Worlds: Essays in Cultural Politics* Methuen, New York and London, pp.197–221.

10 | Deleuze and Guattari: Rhizomatics

THE WORK OF Gilles Deleuze and Felix Guattari is about the most inventive and adventurous in recent philosophy and cultural theory, combining a transgressive, avant garde impulse with both scholarly erudition and an encyclopaedic range of reference. Analysis of recent developments in philosophy, computer science, mathematics, linguistics and biology is juxtaposed with an outrageous repertoire of imagery and a completely iconoclastic attitude to the great names of European culture. Their aim often seems to be the demolition of the sacred cows not only of Western academia, but also of the apparently obvious and commonsense logic on which we normally depend. Less bold theorists may dream of the loosening of the straitjacket of inherited modes of subjectivity. Deleuze and Guattari imagine the complete abandonment of any idea of coordinated selfhood. To them, the self is merely the collection point of infinite and random impulses and flows (to use their terms, *lines of flight* and *machinic assemblages*) that overlap and intercut with one another, but that never form any but the most transitory and dynamic correspondences. The breadth of their project, even of its two-volume centrepiece, *Capitalism and Schizophrenia* (Volume 1, *Anti-Oedipus*, appeared in 1972, and Volume 2, *A Thousand Plateaus*, in 1980), defies easy summary. The aim of this chapter is to provide a detailed analysis of the introduction to the second volume of that work, the chapter entitled 'Introduction: Rhizome', which provides a sense of their central themes and style.

For the purposes of this book, the work of Deleuze and Guattari occupies an important relation to the two strands into which we have divided modern and postmodern theories of the subject. The obvious alliance is to the Foucauldian analysis of the subject and its interrelationship with power and discourse, although there are significant differences. Foucault's rigorous scepticism about the status of subjectivity was grounded in the radical philosophical rhetoric of the early 1960s, which announced that subjectivity was doomed, even 'over', as a way of modelling human experience. Foucault's early papers, such as his discussion of Georges Bataille, 'A Preface to Transgression' (Foucault 1977), repeatedly argued this point. As his career progressed, however, Foucault modified this line, arguing that subjectivity was contingent upon the requirements of cultural and political structures as they changed through historical time. Subjectivity had no absolute, universal or consistent content, but it did appear as a regular position in cultural production and social life. Deleuze and Guattari never departed from the more radical argument that subjectivity itself does not exist.

The other strand of our analysis has, of course, been the psychoanalytic tradition. One of the main themes of Deleuze and Guattari's work is a critique of psychoanalysis. They do not simply attack Freudian and Lacanian thought, however. Instead, they mount a whole alternative theory of the unconscious and its function, which they name *schizoanalysis*. Schizoanalysis challenges the fundamental logic of psychoanalysis, but on its own terms. It does not simply reject the main Freudian motifs but, as we shall see, adjusts them to a completely different understanding of the core philosophical concepts of structure, identity, meaning and truth. The work of Deleuze and Guattari therefore stands as a key indicator of the way recent discussions of the self have progressed. It draws on all contributions to the discussion, critiquing, even exploding some arguments, while adapting and developing others, all in the service of a highly original, humorous, at times productively irrational drive to re-plot the horizons of cultural, aesthetic and psychological possibility (if, in fact, they believed in culture, aesthetics and psychology).

THE SUBJECT OF ABSOLUTE KNOWING

Deleuze and Guattari's prime focus of attack is the set of assumptions that underlie the hierarchical systems of meaning and truth that structure European knowledge, politics and morality. Each time we articulate ideas about the nature of the world, we make assumptions about the nature of truth, the subject who seeks it out and the methods of representing it. For example, reality is commonly assumed to be consistent and knowable. From the casual judgments we each make in our day-to-day lives, to the rushed sketches of journalists, to the patient experiments of empirical science, an often-uninterrogated assumption is dramatised: that the world has certain qualities and quantities, that they relate to one another in predictable proportions, and that they can be known. In turn, the relations between the elemental fragments that fill the universe can be modelled by mathematical, geometrical, at all times stable structures that provide intelligible ways of calculating the nature and meaning of events.

Standing opposite these knowable structures is an observing or analysing subject, accumulating a meaningful picture of the world, coordinated with the work of others in a vast collective, human enterprise. In a sense, the subject of human knowledge is one impersonal and trans-historical phenomenon, most eloquently rhapsodised in the work of influential German idealist philosopher G.W.F. Hegel, especially in his most widely read text, *The Phenomenology of Spirit*. Hegel's work has been hugely influential in non-English speaking Europe, and is the most common unnamed antagonist of recent philosophical critique. His influence in Anglo-American academic circles has, until recently, been most commonly channelled through Marxism, which developed firstly as a critique of Hegelianism.

Hegel imagined that human beings were developing in a collective enterprise of simultaneous self-critique and transcendence, whose ultimate goal was a complete self-consciousness, analogous to the self-awareness of God. The destination of this historical ascent was, in Jacques Derrida's terms, 'the subject of absolute knowing' (Derrida 1981, p.219). Every moment of the human quest for truth is an attempt to contribute to the invention of this huge common subject. As we learn, analyse and discover, each of us is partaking of this massive collective enterprise, with the goal of total knowledge as its imaginary end. The subject of absolute knowing is the ideal thinker, the hypothetical essence of human endeavour, simultaneously gaining greater and greater knowledge of the world and of itself. In the same way that our intellectual and cultural work assumes a knowable world, it also assumes a structure larger than each and all of us, that is capable of grasping the knowledge human work is garnering in one massive superhuman act of god-like intuition.

What propels the process of knowledge onwards, however—what makes it work and progress, if you like—is an efficient system of representations. Not only can we know the world, but we can also produce our knowledge in transmissible form. We have developed ways of picturing reality that ostensibly transcend time and place and enter a stream of human communication that is the fundamental measure of our march towards total self-consciousness, the goal Hegel had defined for us. These representations are usually understood as the passive reflections of the true nature of the world as we have uncovered it. As such, they stand opposite the world as its image, but remain subordinate to its more dense reality.

STRUCTURES VERSUS MULTIPLICITIES

It is the simplicity of the division of the world into coordinated parts—fixed truth, knowing subject and simple representation—that the theory of the rhizome seeks to subvert. The latter describes these traditional ways of understanding the human place in things as systemic, committed to hierarchies, structures and truth. Deleuze and Guattari write:

> There is no longer a tripartite division between a field of reality (the world) and a field of representation (the book) and a field of subjectivity (the author). Rather, an assemblage establishes connections between certain multiplicities drawn from these orders, so that a book has no sequel nor the world as its object nor one of several authorities as its subject. In short, we think that one cannot write sufficiently in the name of an outside. (Deleuze and Guattari 1987, p.23)

Our days are structured around the clear and systematic separation of events and relations into stable units. From the dynamism and flux of the phenomena that surround us, we insist on discovering a single thing that acts (the human subject) and an object that it is acting upon (reality). We seem to want to live in a world of neat separations and known quantities. Change, mobility, relationship, ambiguity, mixture are all seen as secondary and derivative. They are something that happens to stable, fixed entities after they come into contact with one another.

Deleuze and Guattari aim to see the complexity, the mixture and interpenetration of things as primary, as the fundamental basis on which we live and in which all things subsist. When we imagine that the truth of an object is to be found in its invisible internal structure, we are giving in to the dream of our culture that there is a final and absolute truth about each and every thing in the world. We want to believe that the purpose of our dealing with things is to find their fixed essential nature, to turn it into knowledge so that we will be free to move on to the next analysis. Yet, according to Deleuze and Guattari, our interaction with the world—and indeed the interaction of the various things in the world with one another—is not to be understood in terms of internal structures, no matter what they are. Instead, being is to be conceptualised in terms of the endless and multiple involvements that enwrap things in the world in an inevitable, albeit dynamic and transitory interrelationship—in the 'assemblages' that establish 'connections between certain multiplicities'. This is what they mean by the repeated assertion that our attention should be drawn to the outside or exterior. It is not in the excavation of stable structures that things are to be understood, but in the immersion in the endless play on and of surfaces.

ARBORESCENCE

The key metaphor used to explicate the contrast between the older understanding of a world built out of stable identities and one involving dynamic interconnections is the contrast between the arborescent (or root system) and the rhizome. Let us first see how Deleuze and Guattari characterise the arborescent system, and the key example of it, psychoanalysis, before we go on to describe what it is they seek to supplant it with.

Deleuze and Guattari complain in a bemused tone of the absolute dominance of the tree as a metaphor in Western thought (Deleuze and Guattari 1987, p.18). It is clear that trees occupy an intense symbolic position in Western religion, from the Tree of the Knowledge of Good and Evil in the Book of Genesis to the cross of the Crucifixion (commonly described in Medieval poetry as a tree) to Druidic and Scandinavian naming systems, the dance around the Maypole and the forest cults of New Age ferals. Outside of religion, metaphors of root, trunk, branch and fruit dominate our descriptions of everything from the structural theories of linguistics to the design of economic models and international telephone systems. Our families—whether conceived in terms of the distribution of a father's surname through the channels of procreation and immigration, or of species through evolution across macro-historical time—are all usually imaged in terms of trees. As with all metaphors that have become uncontested and obvious, the reasons for this usage are often seen as simple. Things grow and diversify the way trees do, we believe. But what assumptions and investments are preserved uninterrogated in this sort of metaphor?

Our faith in this metaphor segments the tree into its meaningful parts: the essence and meaning of the tree flow from its invisible roots. In this sense, it has a single, unified source, which can always be traced, even when it is invisible, concealed beneath the ground. It has a single trunk, and a unified and substantial body, which supplies the tree with its massive presence in the world. The trunk is the being of the tree, its intense reality. Out of this unified trunk, its multiple branches flow, at the end of which is produced its highest, most delicate and aesthetic—even its most useful and enchanting—part: its fruit and flowers. Yet this rich and colourful diversity is only ever an expression or phenomenon, whose higher reality and substance is always to be traced back to the trunk, and through the trunk to the *roots,* a word with almost unequalled charisma in the denotation of the source and meaning of anything, from the origins of a cultural form ('the roots of rock music') to an ethnic group (Alex Haley's seminal tracing of African-American identity in *Roots*) to an individual ('my roots are in the suburbs').

The tree, then, is a structured system where the parts not only coordinate with one another, but where a hierarchy of meaning and essential truth is implicitly established. That which is to be positioned as the undifferentiated massive substance of an entity— or moreover, that which can be located before this substance—is more loaded with truth and authority than that which is positioned as the fragile and differentiated, even unnecessary, end product. Deleuze and Guattari write: 'Arborescent systems are hierarchical systems with centres of significance and subjectification, central automata like organised memories. In the corresponding models, an element only receives information from a higher unit, and only receives a subjective affection along pre-established paths' (Deleuze and Guattari 1987, p.16). Everything in a tree system relies for its value on the meaning of other elements in the structure. This value is inevitably distributed into a hierarchy, which subordinates the value of an entity to another, *regardless of the function of that entity in any given relationship or situation.* Truth and value, then, are abstract, transcending the reality and requirements of any given event. The result of this is a massive reduction in potential and possibility.

PSYCHOANALYSIS AND SCHIZOANALYSIS

The limitations of the arborescent model can be seen most clearly in Deleuze and Guattari's favourite example of a retarding and inhibiting truth system: psychoanalysis. According to their argument, psychoanalysis consistently understands the truth of the subject to be traceable to its fundamental and fixed structures as they were set in place during the Oedipal phase. In turn, each individual's variation on the Oedipal configuration is subordinate to the larger, absolute model of psychological development under the sign and logic of the phallus—the 'phallus-tree', as Deleuze and Guattari jokingly call it (1987, p.17). This final and incontrovertible tracing of the individual subject to its roots, according to a pre-fixed truth, is classically arborescent in its unquestioned logic. In turn, its rigidity is dictatorial. Freud's case studies consistently force the individual unconscious into the straitjacket of Oedipal theory, blocking off any outlets and alternatives. The unconscious is to be traced back to its origins, not projected forward into its possibilities.

The latter is the imagined purpose of schizoanalysis, Deleuze and Guattari's ambitious alternative to, and parody of, psychoanalysis. Instead of seeing the unconscious as an immutable structure to be interpreted in terms of its imputed past, schizoanalysis sees the hidden and obscure dimension of subjectivity as a factory for the production of endlessly new and different desires. In short, the unconscious is not to be seen as a reflection of something lost or lacking, but as the production of the new and dynamic. In this sense, the unconscious is not a fixed and stable structure, but merely the collective term for an infinite number of uncoordinated and obscure desiring-machines, that are not merely replaying a pre-coded subjective truth that analysis seeks to reveal, but are seeking out endlessly new, plural and contradictory possibilities of interconnection, expansion and production. Instead of the maudlin, even morbid, desire of psychoanalysis, that is doomed to dream forever of recovering the ideal object that it has lost, schizoanalysis is projected forward into the invention of new interrelationships with what it does not know, even what does not yet exist. Subjectivity in schizoanalysis is not a structure, built around a stable and knowable quantity of lack, but an unmapped 'exterior' surface ever demanding new thrills of contact and relationship. Its most important locale is not the buried archive of dark and forbidden repressions, but the highly charged, hyper-stimulated open and excitable surface of the skin.

RHIZOMES

The image of the unconscious produced in schizoanalysis is perhaps the most dramatic example of the alternative logic Deleuze and Guattari propose: *rhizomatics*. What is the meaning of the rhizome, and how does it function as an alternative to the tree? In literal botanical terms, a rhizome is a type of stem that expands underground horizontally, sending down roots and pushing up shoots that arise and proliferate not from a single core or trunk, but from a network which expands endlessly from any of its points. Grass, for example, is rhizomatic. A tree grows upwards as an apparently single and purposeful formation, struggling to build its solid mass in order to crown itself with subordinate branches and flowers. A rhizome develops haphazardly from any point. Where a tree is a single vector aimed at a specific goal, the rhizome expands endlessly in any number of directions, without a centre. The multiplicities that are the tree's final achievement can be traced back to the trunk and roots as its origin and meaning. A rhizome, pushing in a number of directions at once, lacks this sort of unity. Its multiplicity is part of its nature, not its by-product. It is this set of contrasts that Deleuze and Guattari hope to develop when they use the two botanical structures as metaphors.

The rhizome is a model of the heterogeneous. Because it is a way of denoting the haphazard intersection of a number of lines, the rhizome links apparently disconnected impulses and forces, ones that are not only distinct, but that come from completely different orders.

Traditional Western thought (from Conservatism to Marxism) hopes to produce from a mobile and unstable set of multiple relationships a single authoritative and stable structure that will revalidate the model of truth which we began by outlining: a truth that depends on a stable, knowing and observing subject, a fixed and knowable object and a neutral system of representation. Yet these stabilities are an hallucination. Enfolded within each moment of analysis and observation are the many and transitory impulses that cross from subject to object, and from each of these to the text, passing their supposed fixed perimeters, linking whole dimensions of each in what Deleuze and Guattari call 'line[s] of flight' (1987, p.21) that ignore the ostensible fixed internal structure of apparently separate entities to produce new possibilities of assemblage. The observer does not reach out to the object or textualise it as an expression of a fixed and recoverable quantum of his desire. Connections are not to be understood in terms of origins and causes, which may enliven our humanistic debates, and set our egos aflutter as we attempt to assert our theory and interpretation against everyone else's. But these debates are a mere indulgence of our cult of the tree: our belief that through arborescent systems we will arrive at that moment of triumph and reassurance we call the truth.

The moment when a subject enters into relationship with an object in order to represent it is not a moment where the simple alignment of certainties gives dramatic form to the hidden fixity of a quantifiable self. It is one moment of touching where new connections and correlations cross between three apparently separate domains, linking them with new and different sequences of relationship and reinvention. The moment is to be understood in terms of the new assemblage created in interconnection, where the play of light, thought, sweat, dream, skin, signification, computing, all touch in a passing event of involvement and invention. This event is produced somewhere at some time, and to that extent is conditioned by history, science and politics, and out of their materials, but is as unique as all the other moments of interconnection going on at the same and at different times, with which it may or may not be linked.

In these interconnections, no higher purpose or unity appears. Similarly, the line that ostensibly divides one entity—or indeed one order—from another becomes permeable. An example Deleuze and Guattari give is the relationship between wasp and orchid. Inscribed within the orchid is the wasp that is part of its reproductive cycle. The wasp ceases to be a simple element of the insect kingdom as it spreads pollen, becoming a reproductive organ for the orchid. The orchid, in turn, exists at the limits of the wasp's own pattern of movements. They become not a system, because the crossover between them is never permanent or routine, but a rhizome, where the intersecting movements of whole different orders of being create a necessary yet transitory coordination. They form what

Deleuze and Guattari call 'a becoming-wasp of the orchid and a becoming-orchid of the wasp' (Deleuze and Guattari 1987, p.10).

BECOMING

'Becoming' is a crucial theme in the definition of the rhizome. In contrast to arborescent models, the rhizome does not seek to outline permanent structures as they exist across time and place. Instead, it sees the life of things in terms of an ever-changing and ever-renewed movement out of fixed forms into new possibilities. 'The rhizome operates by variation, expansion, conquest, capture, offshoots' (Deleuze and Guattari 1987, p.21). Structures and identities attempt to fix the truth in a knowable form. Yet nothing is ever in a state of permanent immovability. Everything is always crossing over into something else, decomposing and recomposing itself beneath the identities truth would like to erect.

This mobility is not the expression of things' internal nature, nor is it the result of prior causes that set change in motion. It is a permanent state of enervation and transformation constantly producing new modes of interpenetration and cross-mapping that change in turn into something else. A masochist who dons a bridle in order to be humiliated is not to be understood as acting out some buried childhood obsession (1987, p.155–156). He is becoming-horse, projecting himself out of the individual, sexual, masculine identity which arborescent logic uses to define and control him, into something else altogether: a rhizomatic interconnection between body, gear, script and other that defies the truth that measures him by 'medical', 'normal', 'individual' or even 'human' standards. The becoming-horse of the masochist does not respect the strict and paranoid distinctions that separate doctor from patient, desire from act, skin from leather, human from animal. In the end, what we encounter in this dynamic expansion of the possibilities of being is the fulfilment of one of the oldest missions of radical and post-structuralist philosophy since the 1960s: the complete abandonment of the whole idea of subjectivity. To Deleuze and Guattari, rhizomatic 'machinic assemblages of desire' means 'no subjectification' (1987, p.22). The masochist is forging new possibilities, not retrieving something from the archive of his interiority. The new assemblage he forms cannot be measured—as we always attempt to measure everything—in terms of what it means for the self. *Would I*

do it? Would I like it? What is he feeling, thinking, wanting, needing . . .?
This sense of isolated and self-judging selfhood has been left behind.

When we turn back on ourselves or judge the actions of another, we are trying to revalidate an autonomy and closure that we think we need to monitor in order to avoid the condemnation of doctors, family members, superiors and tabloid journalists. We are acting out our fantasy of the permanent visibility and vulnerability that Foucault saw as defining modern subjectivity. But this subjectivity is forced upon us, the product of power/knowledge and all-pervasive contemptuous institutions. What Deleuze and Guattari are proposing is that we cut ourselves adrift from this paranoid, introverted self-policing and reconceive of our being-in-the-world as an endless becoming new and otherwise.

It is important, however, to realise that the arborescent and the rhizomatic are not simply mutually exclusive opposites. This sort of binary 'either/or' logic restores the closed systems and hierarchies of truth that rhizomatics seeks to subvert. Arborescent modelling is, in fact, a selective reading of a rhizome. Each tree model is merely the attempt to suppress the unstable, plural and dynamic nature of things by emphasising one of its aspects or dimensions and pretending that that one feature summarises the meaning of the whole. For example, a family tree usually traces familial interconnections via one line of relationship, the tracing of paternal surnames probably being the favourite. Each child is positioned in a consistent line of derivation that represents the family as a sequence of simple and direct inheritance. Family relationships, however, could be more fully modelled as rhizomatic. Patterns of intermarriage and birth expand infinitely from any one point. Your birth connects you to two families via your parents; through them to four families via their parents and so on. The complexity of the picture is intensified by lines of flight conjoining you to siblings, cousins, their children, their partners, their partners' families, and so on to infinity. Yet the genealogies pored over and celebrated by family historians tend to ignore this complexity, and 'overcode' it, in Deleuze and Guattari's phrase (1987, p.9), by a simple tracing of inheritance along a single dimension. It is no accident that this single line of usually paternal inheritance connects with traditional masculine authority.

THE BODY WITHOUT ORGANS

In sum, then, the subjectivity of rhizomatics is no subjectivity at all. What best defines it is its *exteriority*: 'We think that one cannot write sufficiently in the name of an outside' (Deleuze and Guattari 1987, p.23). The human is not something to be defined in itself, either in terms of the values, rational faculties and sensibility that enchanted Enlightenment humanism, nor the predetermining interior structure to which Freudian psychoanalysis always returns. Instead, what we have conventionally understood as the human— and its traditionally most precious commodity, the individual— should be imagined in terms of the many and mobile relationships, interconnections and assemblages which orient its surface outwards, towards the world and the instabilities and contingencies that constitute it.

For Deleuze and Guattari, the inevitable extroversion of things is captured most effectively in the phrase they borrow from avant garde theatre theorist and author Antonin Artaud (1896–1948), the 'body without organs' (or BwO). Instead of always finding the scheme of the human body in its supposedly self-sustaining internal structures, the image of the BwO emphasises the random and endless play of connections and impulses on the surface of the skin. In turn, this metaphor is applied to all rhizomatic systems and eventually to the world itself. This is no extravagant repudiation of the truth of the biological functioning of structures like the human body. Instead, what is being challenged is the simple assumption that things are to be understood as autonomous and separate, holding their truth in their coordinated internal structure. Rhizomatics rejects the idea that we can ever arrive resolutely at the advanced separation of things from one another which is the minimum starting point for the traditional representation of the world as the collocation of autonomous units. Penetrating below the level of relationship is fake.

FURTHER READING

Deleuze, Gilles and Felix Guattari, 1987, *Capitalism and Schizophrenia, Volume 2: A Thousand Plateaus* trans. Brian Massumi, University of Minnesota Press, Minneapolis.

11 | The subject and technology

THE SOCIAL AND personal impact of technology has become one of the defining issues of the present. By technology, we usually mean information technology, specifically computing and all the industrial, commercial, entertainment and office procedures it now drives. We do not mean the plough, the book, the printing press or even the radio or telephone, each in its time the harbinger of massive social and cultural transformation, on a scale we can barely imagine. Our present anxiety about technology defines the new and coming as the fulcrum of some unforeseen change which may lead to an irreversible dehumanisation. The technology to which we have been acclimatised for decades, centuries and millennia seems to us to be perfectly in tune with what we imagine to be our true selves.

Some technology is even seen as definitively human. For example, Renaissance humanists identified the essence of the human with a piece of technology—the book, and the written word in general—which still in the high school teaching of literature is seen as a humanising phenomenon. Why are certain pieces of technology seen as humanising and others as dehuman-ising? Why is the technology of the past our greatest achieve-ment, and that of the future our greatest threat? It is never easy to find an answer to such questions without recourse to some all-encompassing ideology. I do believe, however, that we can detect in our linking of the question of our technology with the question of our humanity other telling anxieties that have been present in post-Enlightenment life: anxiety about speed and about hybridity, especially racial mixing.

It is too simple to say that these anxieties are autonomous and merely find a new way of expressing themselves in our worry about technology. Technological change, with its violence and social disruption, has brought these issues to prominence and given them a unique intensity. But at the same time, we are now so far from the time when human beings crossed the threshold from a pre-technological to a technological existence—if, indeed, we could say that human beings ever lived a pre-technological existence— that our present anxiety cannot simply be seen as a reaction to the invention and attractiveness of a few new gadgets. In sum, technology may cause some fear, but it is also the focus and expression of larger, older and more amorphous preoccupations.

How does technology connect with the debates about subjectivity that are the topic of this book? Before we go on, it is worth mentioning that the discussion here will not be a comparison between the psychoanalytic and anti-psychoanalytic models we have used to structure earlier chapters, though the idea that subjectivity is historically conditioned, and that the future will force it to transform itself, is a theme to which our discussion will return, especially when we deal with the idea of the cyborg. Suffice it to say every issue in modern and postmodern life is inevitably filtered through the terms that are the landmarks of the debate about the subject: humanity, individual will and agency, power, culture and experience. In what follows, we will see that the twentieth century's theorists of technology have seen that the dimensions of human experience, and the identity of humanity in general, are always at stake in the consideration of technology.

Nowhere is this more apparent than in the imagery of speed that has dominated our attraction to and fear of the new machine, and of technological innovation in general. In speed, the limits of the human body are constantly being reconsidered. With this remapping of limits comes also a reconfiguring of the scope of subjectivity, the conditions of feeling, of interrelationship between the self and society and, inevitably, the subject and its being in the world.

SPEED AND FUTURISM

It is misleading to talk of the speed of modern life simply as a focus of anxiety. Speed, with its adrenalin rush and smashing of imagined limits, has an irresistible charisma in our discourses of sport, power and technology. Its highest expression is the fetishisation of the speed record as a way of charting the limits of the capacity of both machines and bodies. To the Italian Futurists, whose most eloquent propagandist was the poet F.T. Marinetti (1876–1944), speed and specifically the motor car were the harbingers of a completely new humanity. Marinetti wrote in 1908: 'We declare that the splendour of the world has been enriched with a new form of beauty, the beauty of speed. A race-automobile adorned with great pipes like serpents with explosive breath . . . a race-automobile that seems to rush over exploding powder is more beautiful than the *Victory of Samothrace*' (Chipp 1968, p.286).

Speed here is the animating essence of new technology, giving it a spirit and life that will smash the softness of over-civilised Western flesh, initiating in its highest form, war, the 'dreamt-of metalisation of the human body' (Marinetti cited in Virilio 1998, p.3). Also destroyed will be the sentimental aesthetics of the West that still cling nostalgically to Classical models of beauty and form, embodied in a sculpture like the *Victory of Samothrace*. The machine and the speed it unleashes promise a future of purifying beauty that destroys as it builds, that will bring, according to its enthusiasts, an explosion that will shatter yet renew us. Speed, then, functions as a kind of sublime violence that brings an unparallelled thrill, but also a sense of human renewal, a renewal that will shatter the physical and sentimental limits of our subjectivity in order to make a wholly new experience of the world possible.

This theme of the future as an irresistible victory is one of the key rhetorical gestures of twentieth-century life. For Marinetti, speed is not just pleasure and excitement: it is also a kind of guarantee of change and disruption that mocks those who cling to tradition. According to Futurism, forces have been unleashed in our machines and the cities built by them that mean the future will decide things for us, smashing the pretensions of those who still imagine they can resist or control change. Here, as in the Fascist politics that eventually enlisted Marinetti, the Enlightenment idea of a rationally reflecting human subject as the guide and arbiter of history has been supplanted by large movements of impersonal force, beyond the reach of choice and doubt. It is here that the new subjectivity of the machine age will appear. This sort of recourse to the future as impersonal arbiter structures discourses as diverse as that of the freeway developers of the 1950s, the Marxist academics of the 1970s and the computer marketers of the 1990s. In discourse, the future is both an object of uplifting faith and a rhetorical weapon to tell your opponents that a new humanity is being born and that if it isn't obvious that they're wrong now, it soon will be.

We also see some of these values in the very different Russian Futurism. Kasimir Malevich (1878–1935), key practitioner and polemicist of Suprematism, one of the sub-movements in Russian Futurism, wrote in his 'Introduction to the Theory of the Additional Element in Painting' (1927):

> [T]he environment corresponding to [the] new culture has been produced by the latest achievements of technology, and especially of aviation . . . Futurism is not the art of the provinces but rather that of industrial labour. The Futurist and the labourer in industry work hand in hand—they create mobile things and mobile forms, both in works of art and in machines. Their consciousness is always active. The form of their works is independent of the weather, the seasons etc . . . It is the expression of the rhythms of our time. Their work, unlike that of the farmer, is not bound up with any natural laws. The content of the city is dynamism and the provinces always protest against this. (Malevich 1968, p.337)

Here there is a contrast between two types of human technology, one seen as linking industry (and the industrial working class itself seen as the embodiment of humanity), aviation and the city with the art of the present and future; the other linking nature, the farmer, the provinces and the past. The contest between these different technologies is being adjudicated not by how happy they will make us, nor what they will achieve, but simply by time: one is linked to the future, the other is not. Our preferences are to be decided not by our needs or desires, but by our unquestionable trajectory into an unknown future to which we are all subordinate, and that will decide things for us.

Crucially, Malevich sees the consciousness of industrial workers as part of the coordinated complex of forces that structure the machine's place in modern life. The human subject belongs to the machine, rather than being its inventor and master. Technology here is starting to take on the autonomy that, from *Frankenstein* to the *Terminator* films and beyond, has defined our anxiety about the human contrivance which is out of human control, challenging our safety and freedom. Yet our passivity in the face of the machine's promise of human reinvention has been as much embraced as reviled. Despite the huge ideological gulf that separated them, both Italian and Russian Futurism understood the technological not only as the bringer of a new age, but also as the forge of a new humanity and consequently another type of subjectivity. The machine is here an object of adoration and especially faith, the site of a promise of a new way of being in the world. A complex passivity in the face of the machine will define a new human life on the machine's terms. In an age which understands human life purely in terms of subjectivity, this renewal will always mean a transsubstantiation of the key elements of experience: a new strength wrought by prosthetics or genetic avant gardism, a new reach of human movement produced by both long distance and cyber-transport, a new pleasure brought by infinitely proliferating entertainment technology and a new social life offered by more efficient management of resources and time.

VIRILIO

One of the most influential of contemporary cultural theorists, Paul Virilio (b. 1932), has also focused on speed, but with a greater sense of ambivalence towards its promise. Like Marinetti, Virilio finds the meaning of speed in its relation to war. This reflects the Cold War context in which he was writing—his reputation rests on volumes that appeared in the 1970s and 1980s—but beyond that, the recognition that the demographic, cultural and technological conditions of postmodern life have been fundamentally determined by the exponential escalation of war, and its unparallelled ability to chaotically transform societies and populations. This seems an obvious point, but it is one that has been overlooked by many intellectuals, who see war as an irrelevant interruption to the progress of ideas and creativity, or at most, only a reflection and intensification of politics. To Marinetti and Virilio, in their very different ways, war has been the defining condition of twentieth-century life, and its meaning cannot be ignored. Marinetti's war was a war of the machine—the motorised vehicle, the tank, perhaps the aircraft. His dream, therefore, was of a subjectivity rigidified by the metalisation of the human body. Virilio's war is a war of nuclear deterrence, not only of massive retaliation, but also of the pre-emptive strike and instantaneous annihilation.

Speed, for Virilio, has not brought romance and thrill, but the complete remeasurement of human experience. The speed of response, the strategy of anticipation, the distance that ballistic technology reduces to nothing, all contribute to the complete

THE SUBJECT AND TECHNOLOGY | **153**

erasure of space as an issue in human existence. Speed has conquered space. The globe has been completely homogenised. Every point on the world's surface is in immediate contact with every other point. Every locality, and consequently everything and everybody, is instantaneously accessible—or, more accurately, vulnerable. In his most famous text, *Speed and Politics: An Essay on Dromology* (1977), Virilio writes: 'The invasion of the instant succeeds the invasion of the territory. The countdown becomes the scene of battle, the final frontier' (Virilio 1998, p.49). As a consequence, older 'geopolitical' models of the world that equated ascendancy with the ownership of territory, and that defined nations, states and peoples by where they were positioned on the globe, are giving way to a logic of unmonitored movement whose modulating principle is not the fixity of ownership, but speed whose ultimate achievement is absolute immediacy. Virilio writes: 'The violence of speed has become both the location and the law, the world's destiny and its destination' (Virilio 1998, p.57).

Virilio's reading of the technology of war as the incarnation of the contemporary logic of speed also applies to the information technology that has been a side-development of military research. The instantaneity of nuclear annihilation focuses military ascendancy in the speed of command and thus in the speed of decision-making and information transfer. In the period after the Cold War, the importance of information speed has shifted from strategy to economics and the media, as Mackenzie Wark has argued in his adaptation of Virilian thought to the media, *Virtual Geography: Living with Global Media Events* (1994). In this way, computerisation and economic rationalisation are an extension of the culture of war into the marketplace and the home. In *Critical Space* (1984) Virilio writes:

> The will to power of industrial nations implementing in practice the technologies of *total war* at the beginning of the century, is succeeded in this very moment by the theoretical implementation of a total involuntary war, by post-industrial nations investing more and more in information, automation, cybernetics, societies in which the utility of the labour force of humanity is declining, the *direct* responsibility of individuals to the advantage of the powers of 'anticipated' or 'deferred' substitution, power of the system of self-guided arms, of networks of self-programmed detection, *automatic answering machines*, which lead humanity to the confinement of desperate expectation. (Virilio 1998, p.69)

An automated warfare of total annihilation fought between missiles reduces human populations to a centralised commander-in-chief and a dispersed and passive population, which becomes merely a target. Marinetti's excitement at the idea of a hardened metalised soldier has been smashed by the massive increase in scale brought first by aerial bombardment, and later by the globalised threat of Mutually Assured Destruction. Marinetti still believed that technology would bring a new meaningfulness at the level of the individual subject: human individuals would be transformed by the speed of the war-machine. To Virilio, the speed of nuclear war marginalises the subject, whose decisions, locality and initiative no longer matter in a world where events take place at a speed no individual can match.

In the economic and social sphere, there has been a parallel transformation. Marxism was once able to believe that the industrial proletariat was the engine—indeed, the collective subject—of history, producing the future for itself out of its own labour and vision. The automation of response in nuclear retaliation, in computers pre-programmed to buy and sell shares at set levels, or even in the humble answering machine, dehumanises decision-making. The machine reduces human subjectivity to a series of alternatives. Once a pre-fixed path has been initiated, the soft and imprecise logic of human invention and spontaneity becomes irrelevant, inefficient, redundant. We turn our machines on, and stand aside as they open and close, advance or retreat, win or lose for us. In the end, we forget that the irrational, unpredictable and capricious may have led to less predictable, but more enlivening outcomes.

In the face of such developments we can see that the early post-structuralist idea that postmodern life would abolish the subject was not merely theoretical fantasy. Technology and the 'lifestyles' it brings challenge the idea of a free and controlling subject at the root of all decisions. Speed marginalises the subject, transferring war, economics—even entertainment—to a higher level, where the unreliability of the subject is eliminated as a threat to the efficient operation of systems. Our weapons, computers—even our video games—are faster and better than us. In video arcades, we are endlessly reassured of our failure by machines that will produce before our eyes the limit of our individual capacity. Other individuals will sit in the same seat after us and demonstrate pretty much the same failure too, and we even pay for it. The subject becomes simply the ever-exchangeable loser in the game, the one who turns on and off the answering machine, who watches the computer buy and sell. The marginalisation of the active subject reduces us to being a secondary part of the logic of the machine. Virilio writes:

> 'interactive user-friendliness' . . . is just a metaphor for the subtle enslavement of the human being to 'intelligent' machines; a programmed symbiosis of man and computer in which assistance and the much trumpeted 'dialogue between man and machine' scarcely conceal the premises: not of an avowed racial discrimination this time so much as of the total, unavowed disqualification of the human in favour of the definitive instrumental conditioning of the individual. (Virilio 1998, p.153)

Technology therefore threatens the very subjectivity we have inherited, by reducing our decision-making ability to a progressively narrowing range of choices. The reduction of space by speed gives the subject increasing access to the world. Equally, however, the globalised subject becomes infinitely accessible. No longer defined by locality, or even nationality, the subject is open to, even dispersed amongst, an endlessly proliferating number of information streams. We gain information instantly at the cost of becoming information ourselves, outside of any consideration of personal choice, as liberal political theory understood it. New possibilities open up to us, but only as they become technologically efficient, manageable and therefore standardised. The horizons of the subject are simultaneously expanded and reduced.

HEIDEGGER ON TECHNOLOGY

I now want to turn to two key thinkers who recognise technology's negative potential, but see in it a counteracting positivity: first, German phenomenological philosopher Martin Heidegger, and second, US socialist feminist Donna Haraway. Heidegger's discussion of technology comes from a lecture given in 1955, late in his career, entitled 'The Question Concerning Technology' (first published in 1962). The aim here is to discover the essence of technology over and above the machinic handling of the world that it appears to be.

Heidegger starts by arguing that technology is not merely a practical relationship to reality. Before anything else, it is the way that human subjectivity reveals the truth and potential latent in the world. In Heidegger's words:

The revealing that rules throughout modern technology has the character of a setting-upon, in the sense of a challenging-forth. That challenging happens in that the energy concealed in nature is unlocked, what is unlocked is transformed, what is transformed is stored up, what is stored up is, in turn, distributed, and what is distributed is switched about ever anew. Unlocking, transforming, storing, distributing, and switching about are ways of revealing. But the revealing never simply comes to an end. (Heidegger 1977, p.16)

The world contains various potentials concealed within it, what Heidegger calls 'standing-reserve' (1977, p.23). Humanity unlocks these potentials, changing them into a usable form, then storing them again as new potentials in an ever-renewing act of unconcealment and transformation. But human beings are not necessarily active in this process. It is not something we simply decide to do for ourselves. Heidegger does not believe that the world is merely inert material that human beings have total control over. Our attempts at revealing its potential are a response to a challenge (or 'challenging-forth') issued by the world, even by Being itself, that humanity takes up as its destiny. We are simply put 'in position to reveal the real' (1977, p.24). This goes beyond the simple question of whether it is our choice or chosen for us. In fact, to Heidegger, our situation is paradoxical: Being lays down this challenge for us, and by taking it up we attain the freedom and fulfilment that is our calling. He describes us as being 'gather[ed] . . . into ordering' (1977, p.19). In this way, we locate ourselves in the world and in Being itself.

There are two potential risks involved here. The first is that, by committing ourselves to ordering the world, we run the risk of identifying it purely and simply with rational structures. As a result, truth may seem to become for us simply a process of sorting the world into cold and fixed scientific categories. In this way, all forms of truth would become reducible to logical categorisation. God, however defined—and there is nothing conventional about Heidegger's God—may disappear here, or worse still, be understood purely in scientific or philosophical terms, not as an ineffable and transcendental mystery, but simply as the ultimate cause in a universe understood only in terms of cause and effect. Truth, then, would become debased, according to Heidegger, if we understood it purely in terms of the categories of our technological relationship with the world.

The second risk we run is that we too become mere potential for technological manipulation. The human itself is reduced to 'standing-reserve', and also becomes a mere object of ordering, losing subjectivity to become a thing to be endlessly measured, calculated and planned. In the end, human beings would live in a world where they would only encounter themselves, or versions of their own thought: a sterile humanism in which they would convince themselves that everything is their own work and that truth is knowable, rather than endlessly elusive, exciting and mysterious. In contrast to other rhetoric about the dangers of technology, Heidegger fears not a dehumanised world, where our own open-ended and creative values will be ruined by rational thinking, but a humanised one, where the mysterious and unknown otherness of the universe will be replaced by thorough and arrogant human calculation.

Heidegger does not merely see technology as a bringer of a narrow and reduced human life, however. We recall that the human relationship to technology is the result of a challenging-forth that humanity takes up. Technology, therefore, is not just a revealing and an ordering orchestrated by human beings; it is a 'granting' that we receive—in Heidegger's terms, a something we have not made. Technology is not simply a machinery of our invention, nor even a logical principle of our way of ordering the world. It is the enactment of a truth that we perform, but that has been offered to us. Our making of truth is not something that springs from our own inner genius. Revealing is not our method, but something that awaits us, and that needs us. Heidegger says, 'man [sic] is given to belong to the coming-to-pass of truth' (Heidegger 1977, p.32). We make our revelations not as a way of conquering a world that is fundamentally alien to us, but to show how we belong to the world, even in our apparent alienation from and conflict with it. This belonging *saves* us, according to Heidegger, restoring our relationship to the higher processes of truth.

This argument shows that the unnameable truth of Being that Heidegger saw as the highest pursuit of philosophy is not an alternative to the truth of ordering that we live out in our technology. He rejects the commonsense prejudice that pits us against the technological, science against religion, reason against passion, the human against the world. Technology's ability to reveal the truth of the potential of the world is also the world's calling out to us, its challenging of us to recognise truth as *our* calling.

Like all of Heidegger's work, this way of understanding technology always involves a consideration of subjectivity. The fact that truth offers itself to us signifies our belonging in the world. However, the consequent ordering and rationalisation that technology brings risks a total humanisation of the universe, ruining the subject's sensitivity to the mystery of God, and the reduction of the human population to a purely statistical meaning. What is at stake in technology, therefore, is not our inevitable doom if the machines get out of control, nor the logic of input and output, but what it means to be in the world, the world's meaning for us and the horizons of possibility for human experience: what shall we feel, what might we become?

HARAWAY AND THE CYBORG

While Heidegger offers a rare attempt at a metaphysics of technology, Donna Haraway's analysis is grounded in postmodern political history. Her main aim in 'A Cyborg Manifesto' (1985) is to challenge the traditional left-wing dependence on organic and essentialist models of humanity. These latter argue that contemporary social and economic conditions are dehumanising because they shatter our social interrelationships by intruding the profit motive into every aspect of human life: the love in our hearts, the beauty in our spirit, the labour of our hands are all cruelly subordinated to capitalism's insatiable will to maximise itself. Technology collaborates with this dehumanisation by accelerating the economy and society into ever less human dimensions, where the hands and eye of the individual worker are thrown on the junkheap by their inability to compete with the speed of microelectronic interfaces. According to traditional left-wing thought, therefore, technology is anti-human, and must be either controlled or countered by a culture that should recover its connections with its own inner truth and authentic values, and with Nature.

This is the argument that Haraway seeks to counter with the ambiguous figure of the cyborg. The cyborg is part cybernetic machine, part living organism. This breaching of the distinction between technology and nature is commonplace in postmodern life, and must be recognised as one of the products of multinational, militaristic capitalism—a result of the inventions and strategies developed to fight the Cold War. At the same time, however, it is only by recognising the radical potential of the cyborg's hidden side that there can be a proper engagement with the dominant institutions and values of the contemporary. To reject technology and seek nostalgic recourse in an idea of nature or a repressed authentic humanity is escapist. The cyborg in Haraway's usage alternates between being a model of the technologised reality of our present context, and a rhetorically useful metaphor. In her terms, it is both 'a creature of social reality as well as a creature of fiction' (Haraway 1991, p.149).

If we are to have an effective 'progressive' politics, we must recognise what the contemporary world has made of us. Haraway writes: '[B]y the late twentieth century, our time, a mythic time, we are all chimeras, theorised and fabricated hybrids of machine and organism; in short, we are cyborgs. The cyborg is our ontology; it gives us our politics' (Haraway 1991, p.150). It is only from where we are now, cyborgs in a technologised world, that our politics can begin, not from reference to some distant dream of our eternal nature that we imagine will save us from the debased present.

Haraway's argument poses two questions: firstly, why should we consider the cyborg as a description of our present state; and secondly, how can it aid our resistance to the status quo? In answer to the first question, Haraway argues that in the present, the traditional distinctions on which our definitions of our humanity have depended—between nature and the human, on the one hand, and between the human and the machine, on the other—have broken down. The persistent attempts on the part of science to discover something in human behaviour that definitively separates us from other living organisms, whether language or tool use or some behavioural patterns, have all failed. The question itself seems to worry us less and less as time passes. At the other end, the things that were supposed to separate us from our machines—our autonomy or creativity, for example—are becoming less and less exclusively ours. Haraway writes, 'our machines are disturbingly lively, and we ourselves frighteningly inert' (Haraway 1991, p.152).

The corollary Haraway draws from this is that our present culture is one not of essences and identities, but of overlaps and interfaces—of communication flow and systems management. She writes: '"Integrity" and "sincerity" of the Western self gives way to decision procedures and expert systems . . . No objects, spaces, or bodies are sacred in themselves; any component can be inter-faced with any other if the proper standard, the proper code, can be constructed for processing signals in a common language' (Haraway 1991, p.163). The body itself is now read as a machine. Genes are seen as codes, carrying messages. This is an image not of the individual body as a self-sustaining system, but as a set of shifting signifying surfaces turned not inwards towards a mysterious, untouchable and sublime essence, but outwards towards an ever multiplying number of possible interconnections.

Yet it may be argued in response to Haraway that this model seems to be one of contracting human horizons, of a dismantling and debasement, the triumph of technocrats and authoritarian planners over our individual wills and desires. Shouldn't we try to reinvent a model of humanity built around authentic definitions of the self, and stable identities? To Haraway, essentialist models of the human are not only out of touch with present realities, they have also collaborated with a self-serving Western mapping of the world according to its own needs and priorities. This goes for the radical/subversive tradition as much as for the capitalist/colonial one. The idea of the 'one who is not animal, barbarian, or woman; man, that is, the author of a cosmos called history' (Haraway 1991, p.156) is the highest product of Western theory, a belief that in either *laissez-faire* capitalism, white supremacist colonialism or even Marxist total theory, the West had discovered for the world the ultimate model of human interaction that could cover the globe with its truth, and its definition of what nature, the human, the good and the ultimate end of it all might be.

Here we arrive at the answer to our second question: what can the cyborg offer a radical politics? Haraway looks to the work of Chela Sandoval to develop a cyborg model of what the new political subjectivity is. Her answer is caught in the phrase 'women of colour' (Haraway 1991, p.156). Women of colour are doubly marginalised: ignored both by a predominantly white liberal feminism and by a predominantly male racial politics. According to Haraway, this phrase captures those who lie outside of the dominant white/male identity system. Women of colour represent not an identity, but the 'sea of differences' that all politics of fixed identities leave out. As such, it creates a generalised 'oppositional consciousness' (Haraway 1991, p.156) not hung up on its own essence and truth, but ever forging new coalitions and interconnections. These alliances at the expense of essences is the positive version of the cyborg's dependence on a logic of the interface and communication. The cyborg is forever inventing new interconnections and new systems to be part of. It is 'resolutely committed to partiality, irony, intimacy and perversity' (Haraway 1991, p.151). It is this invention of new and valuable interconnections that will make the cyborg (that product of the arms race and the globalisation of capital) some possible vehicle for productive change.

Technology cannot easily be separated out as something different from the human. If a computer and the system design that operates it are technology, is the hand equally a piece of technology, and the thought that makes it move? In the end, what crystallises in our anxiety about the different things that we call at different times the technological is a whole set of anxieties that may have little to do with the world of work, calculation and machines. The success of Haraway's argument is that she sees how these different domains—the machinic, the biological, the conceptual and the political—interconnect with one another, where technology as a material reality and as a cultural fiction are not separable. It is also telling that her discussion of technology includes discussions of racial politics in the evocation of 'women of colour' as a cyborg political subject. The cyborg is, after all, a hybrid, and hybridity stirs the fiercest racial anxiety (amongst European-derived cultures at least) as an image of decline, uncertainty and the immeasurable. Our anxiety about technology feeds on our anxiety about racial mixing, that Haraway's self-conscious politics cleverly inverts.

We can see an example of this anxiety in a book endorsed by right-wing Australian politician Pauline Hanson, which claimed that 'by 2050, Australia will have a President called Poona Li Hung, a lesbian of Indian and Chinese background. She is part machine—her neuro-circuits having been made by a joint Korean-Indian-Chinese research team' (Ackland 1998, p.23). We find combined here hysteria about technology, race and queerness. It is the direct opposite of Haraway's argument. The moral seems to be that although we need to be sensitive to the way the new enters our society and its politics, it never does so without reviving discourses that are not new, that have a deep and problematic purchase on our culture's soul.

FURTHER READING

Haraway, Donna, 1991, *Simians, Cyborgs, Women: The Reinvention of Nature* Free, London.

Heidegger, Martin, 1977, *The Question Concerning Technology and Other Essays* trans. William Lovitt, Harper & Row, New York.

Virilio, Paul, 1998, *The Virilio Reader* ed. James Der Derian, Blackwell, Oxford.

12 | The subject and postmodernism

THIS BOOK AND the ideas that it deals with are a product of postmodernism. The deconstruction of subjectivity in all its forms—from the post-Lacanian emphasis on the subversiveness of desire to the Foucauldian genealogies of disciplinary and sexual subjectivity—are definitively postmodern. Any list of the key postmodernist thinkers would invariably include Foucault, Kristeva, Irigaray, Virilio, and Deleuze and Guattari. Many of the others we have studied—Sedgwick, Butler, Mama, Spillers and Pfeil—take these figures as a reference point, deriving their own ideas either from their paradigms or from an analysis of their limitations. So postmodernism has been one of the unrevealed terms of our discussion from the start.

Now it is worth addressing postmodernism directly to begin some sort of overview of the theorisation of subjectivity as an historical event. As I will argue in the Conclusion, not enough attention has been paid to theories of the subject as a cultural/ historical artefact. Instead, virtual orthodoxies vie with one another for ascendancy in a debate whose imagined end is the definitive theory no one seems to actually believe in. Yet, for me, it is the fact that the debate has taken place, not its conclusions or eventual victors, that provides the best insight into the way we are.

MODERN AND POSTMODERN

What can the key theorists of the postmodern tell us about the subject? I will start by analysing two of the thinkers whose work put the term 'postmodernism' in the mainstream of intellectual debate: Fredric Jameson and Jean-François Lyotard. But firstly, what is postmodernism? The simplest definition of the contrast between the modern and postmodern would run something like this: modernism (whether you see it as the thought and culture of Europe since the Enlightenment, or merely in the first half of the twentieth century) felt that traditional ways of understanding the world and society had collapsed, and needed to be replaced by broad philosophical, cultural or political principles that could reinvent and reinvigorate humanity. To modernists, we were adrift in a changing world where tradition counted for less and less, and something had to be found (a national myth, a political ideology, a social plan, an economic model, a great aesthetic innovation) that would re-anchor us and provide us with some way of dealing with the future. To postmodernism, even this project has shattered to pieces. This shattering is interpreted either optimistically (modernism was authoritarian in its attempt to reinvent new and absolute principles by which we could live, and its demise in postmodernism frees up the infinite field of differences within humanity); or pessimistically (we have been abandoned in a junk-yard of values).

POSTMODERN SUBJECTIVITY AND LATE CAPITALISM

Let us turn now to the question of the postmodern subject. One of the most famous images of the state of the postmodern subject appears in Fredric Jameson's article 'Postmodernism, or The Cultural Logic of Late Capitalism'. Jameson is not an enthusiast for the postmodern. Yet, unlike other left-wing theorists of the early 1980s, when his article first appeared, he believes that postmodernism is not simply a fashion in art and theory. Instead he calls it a cultural dominant, indicative of the nature of late twentieth-century life and the changes that have created it.

Jameson argues that what characterises postmodern life is our lack of what he calls 'cognitive maps'. We now live in a world dominated by consumer, multinational or global capitalism, and the older theoretical models that we relied on to critique established systems no longer apply. Marxism and Leninism, for example, were developed under very different social conditions to our own—industrial and colonial capitalism respectively. Now we lack not only the confidence in these earlier ideological statements, but we have come to lack faith in ideological statements in general. This is because we feel ourselves adrift in the world without the reference points that nineteenth-century and modernist humanism provided.

Jameson uses an analysis of a key work in postmodern architecture, the Bonaventura Hotel in Los Angeles, to produce an allegory of what life is like in the contemporary world. Everything in the public spaces of this hotel is out of proportion with the human subject. We are either hurled through the roof to sky-high restaurants, severed from traditional streetlife by elevated walkways and condescending, alienating vistas, or cramped into maze-like shopping arcades. The person walking in the Bonaventura Hotel is immersed in a structure that never reveals its design, according to Jameson's analysis. We move from one context, perspective or dimension to another, more or less haphazardly. The modernist city, with its rationalised planning, its systems of mass transit, its central markets and high-rise office stacks, appeared alienating to those who believed human values were vested in natural, rural or town and village life. But it did provide the walking individual with a sense of its own context, with an overview and direction. Modernist writing is full of evocations of streetlife, from Baudelaire's stroller (or *flâneur*) to the heroic wanderers of James Joyce's Dublin in *Ulysses* (1922); even those modernist writers who were appalled by contemporary life, like T.S. Eliot in *The Waste Land* (1922), saw it played out on the scale of the pedestrian walking in the street. Now, in post-industrial, postmodern cities, the street is often evacuated, decayed and dangerous. The (bourgeois) individual who can afford it has withdrawn, if not to the suburbs, then to glass and metal towers with shopping, accommodation, multiplex cinemas, gymnasiums, offices and so on that remove the need to venture out into the street—towers very like the Bonaventura. Yet the imagined security these provide is at the cost of a disorientation, a lack of sense of place.

The subject lost in the Bonaventura is an allegory of the postmodern subject. Not only in the cityscape we now inhabit, but in the class and economic systems that direct our work and the national cultures that are supposed to define us, we lack the cognitive maps that would allow us to position ourselves in this world, to know where we are. This is true not only on the level of shared or public life. Our interior lives have become equally disoriented. We no longer *feel* as intensely as we once did. Jameson calls this dissipation of emotion the 'waning of affect'. He writes:

> As for expression and feelings or emotions, the liberation, in contemporary society, from the older *anomie* of the centred subject may also mean, not merely a liberation from anxiety, but a liberation from every other kind of feeling as well, since there is no longer a self present to do the feeling. This is not to say that the cultural products of the postmodern era are utterly devoid of feeling, but rather that such feelings . . . are now free-floating and impersonal, and tend to be dominated by a peculiar kind of euphoria. (Jameson 1993, p.72)

The aim of contemporary critique, then, is to start to redraw the cognitive maps that will allow the postmodern condition to be known, authentically felt and perhaps transformed. The postmodern subject, therefore, is a doubly disoriented one: it wanders in a world it cannot accurately conceptualise and its own interiority has lost its sense of intense feeling and meaningful place.

As we know, many recent theorists of the subject find little to complain about in this development. Jameson himself seems more attracted to modernist versions of cultural politics, especially those of Adorno and Horkheimer, and other members of the Frankfurt School, who in the mid-century, in the face of Nazism and the carnage it left in its wake, tried to come to terms with and renew the legacy of the Enlightenment (see Adorno and Horkheimer 1972).

THE DEMISE OF THE GRAND NARRATIVES

Other key theorists of the postmodern have no patience with the Enlightenment and its grand theories. One of the most significant is Jean-François Lyotard, in his influential text *The Postmodern Condition* (1979). This book arises from the attempt to explain how knowledge is validated in the contemporary world. Lyotard relies on a narrative model of validation. In other words, he argues that what we come to accept as the truth receives its authority when it conforms to larger stories of the human place in the world, that govern a given society in a given stage of its development. What is important is not whether something can be absolutely and objectively verified. Instead, facts, ideas, theories and knowledges are said to be true if they match or help develop the fundamental visions of the world that societies use to define themselves.

An example from the history of the modern West is the idea that society is—or should be—progressing through time towards maximum social justice and equality. Ideas are validated according to how effectively they contribute to or clarify this progression. The modern West has also liked to see history as a progression towards the maximum self-realisation of some abstract religious/aesthetic quantum called 'the human spirit' (where would sports commentators or art critics be without it?). In the late twentieth century, economic efficiency—understood simply in terms of the quantifiable equivalence of inputs and outputs over time, regardless of any other possible ascription of value—started to play the same role, especially as a way of assessing government policy. These paradigms that are used to value or devalue our ideas and decisions are called 'grand narratives' by Lyotard. To him, they define what was distinctive about *modernity*. The modern age, beginning with the Enlightenment, needed some macro-historical form that could make the human experience of time and society meaningful. The invention of such forms was perhaps a substitute for Christianity's loss of authority in Western society, a development that has steadily intensified over the last three centuries.

This search for larger narrative, or even mythic, structures as a way of regrounding human experience has been widespread in the twentieth century. The grand narratives that Lyotard identifies are hard for someone schooled in the debates of Western culture to disentangle from their view of what the world is and could be. Other attempts at restoring some sense of trans-historical unity to Western culture are more quantifiable, such as those that have relied on a sort of cultural primitivism, or that sought to strengthen the modern by reasserting the West's own perceived core heritage. These climaxed about the time of and soon after the First World War. Examples of self-serving primitivism are widespread in the West, and affected one another in diverse and contradictory ways. In the visual arts and music (for example, in the figuration of Picasso and in Stravinsky's *Rite of Spring*), non-European styles were understood as less encumbered by the denaturalising and excessive conventionality of the West, which was seen to be artificial and esoteric. Creativity outside of Europe was regarded as more vital, more in contact with a fundamental natural humanity.

In a different development in literature, major writers plundered Western culture itself for an image of its own raw authenticity or essential values, hoping to reconnect modern experience with the Classical or Christian heroism it had squandered. In *The Waste Land*, T.S. Eliot looked to the fertility symbolism beneath the bedrock of Medieval Christianity as a way of proposing the renewal of an essential European religious culture that could unify our experience and explain what really mattered to us. In *Ulysses*, James Joyce linked the random events of the contemporary urban day with the heroic wanderings of the ancient Greek warrior-hero Odysseus, in an ironic celebration of an essential continuity of both life and significance. What we see in such writers is a culture aspiring to universalise its own experience by drawing something out of itself, by looking not towards new horizons but to a simple hidden essence forever centring our experience, yet perpetually under the threat of loss and debasement. The grand narrative appealed to in these cultural artefacts was not some abstract human principle, but a core heritage—the 'West' itself. Modernist humanism has continued to speak of its role as not defending some argued truth that can be endlessly revalidated, but 'culture'—understood as the thing that contemporary life is perpetually compromising.

What is the relationship between these grand mythic ambitions and postmodernism? To Lyotard, the postmodern is not just an era, but an *attitude* of scepticism towards grand narratives. We do not see ourselves as progressing through history in promising modern ways, nor can we look nostalgically for what we imagine was meaningful for other peoples and times. Postmodern experience rejects earlier grand narratives for the destruction they have caused, in fact, rejecting grand narratives altogether. Postmodern life is defined by the crushing weight of the whole exhausted apparatus of an ostensibly heroic and ascendant culture still pressing down on us, still fomenting in an unconvincing way our tired ideological discussions, our increasingly careerist and spiteful public sphere, and our intensely corporatised 'arts'. To theorists of the postmodern, our experience is more conditioned by chance and accident than by these older, predictable and obsolete rhetorics.

What does this theorisation of the postmodern mean for contemporary subjectivity? The postmodern conception of the subject is positioned between the mirror-like presentations of Jameson and Lyotard. Both see a subject wandering, without the big picture overview of the human place in world-time that would help it locate itself: the longed for 'cognitive maps' of Jameson, and Lyotard's unlamented 'grand narratives'. By calling for some new representation of what this new world is like, Jameson seeks to revive our sense of what could be achieved by action, both in improving the world and recovering the potency of human feeling. Lyotard does not regret the passing of the grand narratives, connecting them with the massive top-down political planning of the absolute (Hitlerian and Stalinist) states that gave the twentieth century 'about as much terror as we can take' (Lyotard 1984, p.81).

Postmodern thinking draws on Lyotard's view of history to reject trans-historical models of what human society could and should be, even if they still structure our political rhetoric. We now live in a world where the only values present have been discredited, without having been replaced by anything else. All the tenets of both conservatism and liberalism are ridiculed without being buried, burned without being consumed, losing—like the grand narratives they are part of—any sense of authority or historical momentum while still remaining oddly central. Arrogance flourishes on every side, amongst those who don't want or need truth as well as those who still believe they haven't seen their truth superseded by anything better. In both art and theory, the liberation from grand narratives is relied upon for self-justification by those commentators who celebrate the mix of excitement and desperation, of ecstasy and self-destruction, of accident as both disaster and opportunity, that has come to be called postmodernism. How this cultural ferment will affect our politics remains to be seen.

POSTMODERN FEELING: PANIC, FEAR AND ACCIDENT

What defines the postmodern, then, is not a principle of meaning, but an uncertainty or interruption, at most a feeling. Contemporary theorists seem compelled to find and name postmodernism's distinctive feeling. It is hard to tell whether this longing for a label for the dominant mood of the present is a denial of Jameson's idea of the contemporary 'waning of affect' or a fulfilment of his belief that postmodern emotions are shallow and euphoric. This idea that an age needs to be defined by a feeling reinforces the dominance of the subjective as the measure of truth in late twentieth-century culture, something that many critics see as the clearest sign of postmodernism's failure to deal with the real world. For our purposes, this subjectivism indicates the centrality of the topic of this book to an understanding of the contemporary problem of meaning.

What is the dominant postmodern feeling theorists choose, then? Arthur and Marilouise Kroker argue it is *panic*: 'Panic is the key psychological mood of postmodern culture,' they write, 'panic culture . . . as a floating reality, with the actual as a dream world, where we live on the edge of ecstasy and dread' (Kroker et al. 1989, pp.13–14).

A fuller attempt to characterise the mood of postmodernism emerges in Brian Massumi's discussion of fear in 'Everywhere You Want to Be: Introduction to Fear', from the edited collection *The Politics of Everyday Fear* (Massumi 1993, pp.3–37). To Massumi, our fear is linked to our individual place in the contemporary economy. The act of purchasing defines our selfhood: 'I buy therefore I am' is one of the axioms of the present (1993, p.7). If we derive our identity from consumption, this means that it comes to us from the outside, and is not an expression of our interior reality or essence. Thus our identity is in an only accidental relationship with the self; it is external to us. In ourselves, we feel groundless and the accidents that come to us as purchases are an attempt to stave off our groundlessness. 'Identity is an act of purchase predicated on a condition of groundlessness' (1993, p.6). As human beings, we share the postmodern lack of fixed meaning that would, in theory, give us some sense of place in the world. This is the flawed, undefined state that we share. Our attempts to construct individual identity in the face of this groundlessness take the form of repeated purchases where we try to clarify some distinctive character that we can call our own: 'our generic identity . . . is the accident-form; our specific identity . . . is the sum total of our purchases' (1993, p.7).

Accident defines us both in our groundless state and in the purchases we use to compensate for it. We live permanently in the shadow of the 'imminent disaster' (1993, p.10):

> Society's prospectivity has shifted modes. What society looks toward is no longer a return to the promised land but a general disaster that is already upon us, woven into the fabric of day-to-day life. The content of the disaster is unimportant. Its particulars are annulled by its plurality of possible agents and times: here and to come. What registers is its magnitude. In its most compelling and characteristic incarnations, the now unspecified enemy is infinite. Infinitely small or infinitely large: viral or environmental. (1993, p.11)

HIV, the Ebola Virus, TB, drug-resistant golden staph, global warming, Y2K, the hole in the ozone layer, the collapse of biodiversity: in contrast to the strategic threats that fed the paranoia and policy of our grandparents (the triumph of the rival ideology, the spread of the alien race), our age is characterised by invisible, latent threats working quietly in the air we breathe and the bodies we inhabit. No national boundary protects us from these silent killers. No statistics can reassure us when or even if they will be contained. No scientific agency can protect us from the fear that the dangers we know of may only be the first amongst innumerable threats that have gained a foothold without our experts even being aware they exist: the thin edge of the wedge, the tip of the iceberg, the beginning of the end. Our fear is an hysterical conflation of the realistic and the fantastic. We cannot ignore these threats without desensitising ourselves to the complex world situation that is allowing their spread and development. On the other hand, we cannot believe in them without becoming suckers to the media's wanton and purely self-serving hyper-seduction.

The defining mood of the postmodern is fear, a fear that propels us into an incontinent consumerism that is in turn a kind of paralysis: '*Fear is not fundamentally an emotion. It is the objectivity of the subjective under late capitalism* . . . It is the most economical expression of the accident-form as subject-form of capital . . . When we buy, we are buying off fear and falling, filling the gap with presence-effects. When we consume, we are consuming our own possibility' (Massumi 1993, p.12). To humanism, in almost all its versions, it was the human *act* that defined our collective ascendancy: our spirit, our talent, our creativity, our will. The human race would clarify itself in its own history, lifting its head, extending its horizons, purifying its soul. In Massumi's view, and any number of other characterisations of the postmodern, the human act is reduced to an individualised, random and meaningless attempt to stave off a defeat that doesn't even bring the finality and pathos we can usually enjoy in our defeats.

That our acts can now be understood in this way shows how discussions of the postmodern are marking out an absence, perhaps of discredited and authoritarian systems, but an absence nonetheless. Love it or hate it, celebrate it or reject it, postmodernism evokes a simultaneously sanguine and sardonic rush that provides our contemporary frustration and stress with an intense, almost orgasmic, catharsis in the midst of an ever-renewing exhaustion. Theories of postmodernism are both a confession of defeat and a celebration of creativity and improvisation. We all succumb to an intensity of rhetoric—there is almost endless talk of loss, fear, anxiety, accident, panic, disorientation, groundlessness, defeat, solipsism, meaninglessness, paranoia, self-indulgence, indifference, debasement, paralysis—that, in the end, we may have become used to and that may not even worry us very much.

POSTMODERNISM AND THEORISING THE SUBJECT

What is at stake could be the status of intellectual debate itself, as it shifts from a detached and circumspect, universal and sophisticated vanguardism, showing us what our future might be or our essence truly is, to being merely one amongst an infinite and expanding number of content-providers needed to fill the ever-multiplying number of communication channels that we are led to believe we want, supplying documentaries screened cheaply overnight that can be videotaped. This has telling consequences for the material we have been discussing throughout this book. Do the theories of the subject that I have been outlining, and that I have argued are the defining cultural feature of modern life, reach their limit in the postmodern? Has their authority gone the way of all grand narratives, no longer the transcendental and dazzling systems to which we look for a meaning that will elevate, free and explain us, but the mere curious decorations of an aesthetic tradition of truth-fantasy, knowledge of which is our greatest boast, a bolster to our careers and a way of showing off? In other words, do our theories of the subject save us or simply feed our need for ever-new material?

The pattern of this book has been to divide modern theories of the subject into two broad, but not exclusive, camps. On the one hand, the subject is seen in Freudian terms: accidentally, yet somehow inevitably, the human becomes the intense focus of processes of identification and meaning-making that find in the body signs of stable identities and truth—gender, family role and sexual orientation. This process instils in the subject a structure to which all its adult behaviours can be traced. Our love, our work, our secret dreams and nervous habits all find in the Oedipal moment an individual truth that is at one and the same time unique to each of us, and also the materialisation of the priorities of (depending on which theorist you read) a class, a culture, a patriarchy or a language. The linchpin around which this theory turns is *desire,* which is seen as either a troublesome if inevitable spur to all human subjectivity; the irretrievable loss at the very heart of being; or an endlessly exciting emotional, physical, aesthetic and political force. You can take your pick: desire is claimed by both radicals and conservatives as both radical and conservative. In the twentieth-century mind, however, it occupies a uniquely charismatic place for its half-obscure, half-destructive, half-liberatory energy.

On the other hand, we have studied the cool theories of the subject that concentrate on *power*. Here, the subject appears merely as the focus of regulation, cruelly tricked by powerful cultural investments and the institutions that operate them into feeling permanently vulnerable to judgment and treatment. The individual is not a naturally occurring autonomous unit, nor even the construct of the body, gender and desire. It is the site of a pathologisation whose aim is to divide us up into endlessly manageable and knowable demographic units. Here, identity is neither liberating nor expressive of our selfhood, as much as a trap, something to be frustrated and deconstructed if we still believe in any possibility of freedom.

Both these models come from a high serious tradition of writing. Even at their most sceptical, they believe that the theorisation of subjectivity is either a progressive, therapeutic event or else a productively subversive one that will allow new possibilities of feeling and being. In the hands of the twentieth century's theorists of the subject, desire and power are serious things. To the postmodern cultural 'dominant', as Jameson calls it, they are endlessly expanding opportunities for marketing. As Massumi reminds us, 'the adjective of the eighties was "power" (as in "power lunch")' (1993, p.15). There was even 'power napping', if an executive felt like a snooze after his power lunch. Desire too feeds our entertainment with infinite possibilities of intense but trivial transgression, chaos and danger. In sum, desire and power operate for us in the postmodern, but residually—not as determinants or fundamentals, simply as a way of decorating our accidents with a simulacrum of seriousness, that is all to be forgotten next time round.

Perhaps, then, when we reach the end of the yellow brick road of theory, what we discover is not the truth of ourselves, or even the genealogy of our non-selves, but more possibilities to feed the only organ worth having in the postmodern era: the imagination. In our hyperactive fantasies—whether played out in front of the computer screen, in the office or in traffic—desire and power become mere opportunities for improvisation. We seek not the truth of ourselves but an open-ended number of possible experiences, as we dream of having it all. In fact, this dream has shifted in consumer/service-driven economies from being a slightly guilty, private secret to being an economically responsible duty. We have reached the stage where we not only can, but should try to, be just about anybody and everybody. As Massumi puts it, '"We" are every subject position' (1993, p.23). It is this experience of the subject as infinite and undefined that is discussed in the Conclusion, not simply as the present state of our subjectivity, but as the inevitable result of the fact that at a certain time in the history of the West, people thought the question of the I was one that needed to be broached using the full apparatus of science, theory and philosophy.

FURTHER READING

Jameson, Fredric, 1993, 'Postmodernism, or The Cultural Logic of Late Capitalism' in *Postmodernism: A Reader* ed. Thomas Docherty, Harvester Wheatsheaf, Hemel Hempstead, pp.62–92.

Lyotard, Jean-François, 1984, *The Postmodern Condition: A Report on Knowledge* trans. Geoffrey Bennington and Brian Massumi, Manchester University Press, Manchester.

Massumi, Brian ed. 1993, *The Politics of Everyday Fear* University of Minnesota Press, Minneapolis.

13 | Conclusion

WHY DID THE modern era become the era of the subject? Why, in the last few centuries, did the self become the focus of the most serious and esoteric theory? Why did this theory conclude that there was no spontaneous subjectivity, but only an obscure and shifting impersonal matrix of relationships, politics and bodies that determined our selfhood? It would be reassuring to find answers to these questions, even though Western intellectual life—like so much of the West's thrilling yet gruesome history—is littered with discredited ultimate answers, ridiculed total theories and murderous final solutions. As Lyotard points out in his work on postmodernism, we should beware of the destructiveness of big answers, even if we have to pay the price of uncertainty and open-endedness in our debates.

Yet the wrecked caravans and broken machines of those who have gone before may provide us with some partial answers. Caught up with the theory of subjectivity are other developments that it reflects and respects, that are perhaps not fully separate: the rise of capitalist individualism, for example, beckons to us as a possible root cause for the modern obsession with isolated interior life. A burgeoning free-market economy needed the autonomous individual as its fundamental social unit, separate from the communal and family identifications that could compromise the absolute freedom of movement of entrepreneurs, workers and capital itself (as a kind of free and autonomous inhuman subjectivity in its own right). Given this economic development, it was inevitable that Rousseau's free subject would appear. In turn, the dislocation, alienation and stress this subject would suffer because of forced migration, urbanisation and exploitation, would itself

174

find its theoretical reflection in theories of subjective or psychological disorientation, of loss and desire (in the case of psychoanalysis) or powerlessness and enforced rationalisation (in the case of Foucault).

There are other plausible explanations. Since Lacan and Foucault, subjectivity has been seen in terms of language. Roland Barthes argued in his first major work, *Writing Degree Zero* (1953), that from the middle of the nineteenth century on, Europe's literary culture became absorbed in the problem of language. No longer a vehicle of communication but 'a situation fraught with conflict' (Barthes 1968, p.83), language attained a social and subjective intensity in which the shifting possibilities of both political and interior life were somehow invested. Writers and thinkers needed to pay attention to the obscure and volatile machine with which all intellectual speculation, social planning and personal expression had to come to terms. An absolute explosion of textuality—from academic publication to compulsory literacy—meant that nothing existed unless it could speak or be spoken about. It is no surprise that such a culture of the word would find entwined in its subtleties everything that could be known and felt, down to the most atomic level of experience: the neurotic patient biting his nails in the therapist's waiting room and the citizen walking nervously in the visibility of the street.

The authority of truth has also been very much at stake in the modern era with the bitter rivalry between, on the one hand, a logical positivism (and popular adoration of the scientific model of fact) and, on the other, an absolute relativism (and popular scepticism towards any expert opinion). In the twentieth century, truth has been vulnerable to both mindless insistence and automatic cynicism. We simultaneously believe all we are told and nothing. Information hovers in a sort of suspension where it is useful but not completely credible. Nothing avoids having a use-by date. Chastened by our ever-apparent ignorance, and the ever-renewing obsolescence of what knowledge we do have, we turn in on ourselves as the only reliable locus of being. At the same time as the relativity of knowledge makes us nervous and solipsistic, we realise that theory, in its lust to saturate every corner of existence, from the nano- to the mega-, cannot stop itself taking our individuality as an object of analysis. We thus become both something to be explained and displayed, and the only thing that we feel sure really exists. In this way, the subject attains an absolute intensity of significance.

Each of these themes is tempting as an historical explanation for the modern era's obsession with subjectivity: the subject is either capitalism's ideology of the self, a mutation in the field of language or the only point where the problem of truth really bites. If you chose one of these explanations, you would be claiming that either capital or language or truth has its own autonomous history that determines or at least encloses other histories, the history of our self-consciousness about subjectivity being the one that matters here. But both the theorists we have outlined throughout the book and our own experience tell us that these histories are not separate, that they cannot readily be considered without one another, and that, as a consequence, erecting one as the infrastructure on which the others are based can only be a willing act of selection and assertion, usually for other reasons (we need a politics, we love language, we hope we will eventually find truth).

I argued in the introduction to this book that I did not believe that a final authoritative theory of the subject was possible or even desirable. This is why I have left these theories to stand or fall on their own merits, only arguing for or against them when it was necessary in order to clarify the comparison between them. I do not believe that these theories should be seen as an ascent towards an ultimate answer to the question of the subject. Instead, they need to be understood as an important cultural artefact, an historical development in which we can read the history of our politics, language and knowledge, but also our excitement, ephemerality and fear—in short, the changing quality of our experience. I drew on Foucault's distinction between metaphysics and genealogy to explain this approach: where a metaphysical method has the final elucidation of truth as its goal, the genealogical seeks to lay out the complex and incongruous sequence of processes and accidents that have led to the present, that do not tell us what we ultimately are but where we might actually be. I believe not only that the subject is best treated genealogically, but also that our theories of the subject should be treated in the same way. In other words, I cannot claim to know the fundamental reason why the subject became a theoretical problem for the modern era. The three possibilities sketched above must be seen each in its own way as a partial explanation.

Yet, even though we cannot find an ultimate answer, this does not mean we cannot generalise about this historical event. There are ways of *characterising* what the theorisation of subjectivity has been, which will contribute to our understanding of its significance.

We recall from Chapter 1 Heidegger's announcement of the end of the era of the metaphysics of subjectivity. This argument has been accepted more or less uncontested by theorists associated with post-structuralism, who in the last twenty years have been the driving force behind debates about subjectivity, in the humanities at least. Heidegger claimed that Western philosophy since Descartes had understood the fundamental nature of the human interaction with the world in terms of a consistent, self-identical and coherent entity called the subject. This entity processed its experience into knowledge, and its hypothetical goal was the maximisation of its self-consciousness. In turn, this subjectivity was seen as governed by some essential faculty or capacity—reason, perhaps, or simply thought, enlightenment, even imagination and love have been chosen over time as the core, defining attribute of the subject. This selection of a single essential element of subjectivity as its lodestone must be seen, of course, as recognition that interior life is complicated and amorphous, and full of surprises and accidents as much as it is of the accumulation of enlightenment and meaning. Something had to be chosen as the essence of subjectivity to stabilise its immense dynamism, to recover something that must be before, inside or above the endless flux.

To those coming in the wake of Descartes, knowledge, morality and society had to be formulated in terms of the subject first. The subject was either the point where truth and value were to be assessed, or the fundamental building block of all collective action and order. Truth had to be theorised in terms of perception, understood on the scale of eyes and hands. Morality was to be grounded in legally binding theories of personal choice and individual responsibility. Politics devised a social contract built on an individual's exchange of apparently natural freedoms for codified civil rights. To Heidegger, this metaphysics chose, more or less arbitrarily, one or other attribute of subjectivity as the transcendental truth of human life. The result was that more fundamental issues, like the question of Being, had never been properly addressed. Whether this is fair to Descartes or not remains debatable. The collection of essays *Who Comes After the Subject?*, edited by Eduardo Cadava, Peter Connor and Jean-Luc Nancy (Cadava et al. 1991) contains essays faithful to Heidegger's view, but some—such as Etienne Balibar's 'Citizen Subject' (Balibar 1991, pp.33–57)—dispute its representation of Descartes' role, not in order to vindicate him but to locate subjectivity in the history of the West's politics, rather than its metaphysics.

Whether true or not, Heidegger's view is now taken as orthodoxy. Perhaps what has been most influential about it is not its attribution of the metaphysics of the subject to one philosopher rather than another, but its insistence that subjectivity is not identical with human experience. Heidegger sees subjectivity as an historical phase, a development in the unfolding of philosophy that must inevitably be superseded. Very few of the theorists of the subject we have dealt with have done more than accept this part of the argument—subjectivity was an event in our culture, not our natural or inevitable state. As I have mentioned when discussing Deleuze and Guattari, the early work of some post-structuralist thinkers echoes this idea. A noted example is Foucault's discussion of the death of philosophical subjectivity in 'A Preface to Transgression', his discussion of Georges Bataille (Foucault 1977). Mostly this sort of heroic announcement has faded, yet the perception of the subject as having a fragile purchase on history remains.

I do not necessarily dispute the idea that subjectivity is enclosed by culture and history. Very few values and facts can escape their context, and in the humanities and human sciences—especially, but not exclusively—what is true for one generation is ridiculous fabrication to the next. However, when trying to see the theorisation of subjectivity as a cultural phenomenon in its own right, what is interesting is something quite different: *the subject has had its meaning endlessly theorised and proliferated only after being declared dead*. In other words, the subject has become an absolutely intense focus of theoretical anxiety at the same time as it is said to be over. Since it is more or less impossible to trace exactly what relationship philosophical and theoretical ideas have to the cultures they may or may not lead, reflect, ape, ignore or abuse, it is difficult to say whether our experience of subjectivity is equally contradictory. Yet everywhere in our art, our entertainment, our popular psychology and journalism, the self is represented as absolutely important but somehow insubstantial, even absent. We live out our subjectivity in a critical state of living death, a kind of suspended animation, where nothing is more important or serious, if only it would actually get around to feeling real.

This contradiction can be traced through the two groups of theories we have outlined in this book. For psychoanalysis, subjectivity has a design that can be measured and known—the family politics of the Oedipal drama produce a subject governed by the paternal phallus, the sign of authority and guarantee of meaning. Yet, as has been widely critiqued by later theorists like Irigaray and Deleuze and Guattari, the phallus operates only through its absence, the threat of castration. According to this myth-like structure, meaning simultaneously loads and unloads the subject, supplying it with a truth, but an absent one—a truth, in fact, that functions only in its absence. Subjectivity is a site of meaning, but a hypothetical one, that presses in on the subject, and that can even be recovered through his or her own words, or exhibited in bodily signs called symptoms, but that remains coherent and complete only in what individual subjects fail to be.

For Foucault, subjectivity is never spontaneous. Power/knowledge always intervenes between us and even our most intimate experience. At the end of his life, Foucault recommended that the best way of managing subjectivity was to be rigorously aware of the forces that had constructed our interiority for us, and then to undertake an aesthetic renewal of ourselves by experimenting with the infinite possibilities of feeling and the artifices of identity. Here, subjectivity is not only the intense site of feeling and desire it is for psychoanalysis. It is also the most acute political event. Yet both the subjectivity we are schooled in and the one that we create make us the ground of obscure truths that are forever being drawn away from us, an interiority that is constructed for us or even by us, but at a distance, part of an endless process of calculation. As in psychoanalysis, our intensity is most critical when it is indeed not ours.

Theory, therefore, is everywhere proposing the subject as both the most critical and important, but also the most elusive and abstract, phenomenon. In the end, these attributes cross-multiply with one another. Our subjectivity is critical only in its abstraction, important only in its elusiveness. The theories we have studied often seem to offer us insights into aspects of our experience: Kristeva's theory of abjection can be pretty convincing as an explanation for the way we gag at the skin on the surface of warm milk. Foucault is good on the anxiety we feel in relation to public codes of normality and health. Lacan's distinction between desire and demand captures something about our experience of consumption and sexuality. Yet, when we look for an overall statement about what theory can tell us about the modern subject, the truth may not be in an individual theory so much as in the fact of theory itself. Theory believes that our subjectivity is inseparable from a certain type of representation, one that automatically pairs our shapeless intensity with an endlessly elaborating formalisation. This confusion of presence and absence, the theorisation of a subjectivity that is supposedly dead, the inseparability of my feeling and someone else's ideas captures the paradox of post-postmodern life: where our experience could not be more desperate, even though it remains somehow removed, involved yet exempt, our own but out of our hands, here but somewhere else at the same time.

Perhaps we have merely returned to the fundamental point that Heidegger made: that what has counted is not the particular insights that different theorists have come up with—inspired and challenging as they may be—but the general fact that a phenomenon called the subject became a topic of discussion at all. This subjectivity was seen to be so serious that it needed to be endlessly discussed, yet so uncertain that it needed to be anchored by theory. In short, it defined everything about us—it was us—but we could not know it without thorough analysis and critique. It is this highly charged fragility that keeps us alive as well as interested as the postmodern era gives way to whatever future is awaiting us.

Glossary

abjection In the work of Julia Kristeva, the abject is that which challenges the subject's sense of fixity and stability (for example, flows that cross the perimeter of the body, such as blood, vomit, sweat and semen). Metaphorically, the abject extends to all transgression of boundaries, such as ambiguity and ambivalence.

arborescent *see* **rhizome**

body without organs Deleuze and Guattari adapt Antonin Artaud's phrase 'the body without organs' as a model of a subjectivity built on multiple surface flows, rather than a fixed internal structure.

castration In Freudian psychoanalysis, the boy-child attains masculine subjectivity by his response to the threat of castration. The penis is read as the sign of masculine authority, and the threat of its loss defines masculine culture. Girls and women are seen as already castrated, and psychoanalysis is thus criticised for depicting subjectivity as built on loss or lack, particularly in women.

corps propre In the work of Kristeva, subjectivity is identified with the limits of the body. She calls the image of the body as a closed system, impermeable to bodily flows, *le corps propre* or 'the clean and proper body'. It is this image of the body that is challenged by **abjection**.

cyborg The conventional term for a **cyb**ernetic **org**anism, creatures that combine technology (usually robotics) and biology. In the work of Donna Haraway, late twentieth-century human beings are cyborgs, poised between a lost myth of nature and a futuristic dream of perpetual technological revolution.

181

demand *see* **desire**

desire For Jacques Lacan, the entry into subjectivity in the **symbolic** order entails a loss of the intensity and unity of the **imaginary**. The longing for the return of this unity is called desire. However, because it is impossible to leave the symbolic and return to the imaginary in daily life, we experience desire in terms of trivial and transitory demands, which seem to offer satisfaction, but inevitably disappoint us.

Futurism Collective term for a set of modernist artistic movements which saw the future of humanity as attuned with technology.

gender *see* **sex/gender**

genealogy Michel Foucault distinguishes between two types of intellectual work: the genealogical traces the contingent development of thinking and representation of a certain topic, in order to understand how we picture ourselves. Metaphysics, on the other hand, aims to surmount images and representations to arrive at objective truth.

grand narrative Jean-François Lyotard defines the modern era as the era of the grand narratives. These understand human history as a collective progress through time to a specific goal, such as the maximum realisation of the human spirit, the creation of a free and just society or the perfect operation of society as an efficient economic machine.

habitus To Pierre Bourdieu, human interaction is to be understood not in terms of predictable and structured codes and rules, but strategies chosen from an historically derived range of possible practices. These practices form a 'community of dispositions' (Bourdieu 1977, p.35) or habitus.

homosocial Eve Kosofsky Sedgwick describes various male-to-male bonds as homosocial. The typical homosocial bond is the rivalry between two men for the same woman. The men see the bond between themselves as more important than the relationship with the woman.

humanism The collective term for ideas or philosophies that are human-centred. These usually assume a consistent and universal model of what is and is not human. Humanist theories are seen by postmodernism as overriding the differences between various social, ethnic, cultural and gender identities.

ideology In Marxist theory, especially that of Louis Althusser, ideology is the name for the representations promoted by a certain social system (usually capitalism) in order to disguise its inequalities.

imaginary For Jacques Lacan, subjectivity is inaugurated in the **mirror-stage** when the child first sees an image of the coordination of its body. This image remains in the subject's mind as its sense of wholeness and unity. When the subject enters the **symbolic** order, governed by language and identity, the imaginary is left behind, and becomes the object of **desire**.

mirror-stage *see* **imaginary**

modernism Collective term for either the philosophical orthodoxy of the West since the Enlightenment (defined by humanism, rationalism and grand narratives) or the dominant artistic movements of the first half of the twentieth century (defined by experimentation, aestheticism and the avant garde).

Name-of-the-Father For Jacques Lacan, the governing principle of the **symbolic** order is not the physical penis, but its sign or representation, the **phallus**. The phallus epitomises the principles of logic, order and patriarchal authority on which the symbolic is based. Whereas in Freud, the boy attains subjectivity by coming to terms with the father's control and ownership of the penis, in Lacan, subjectivity is attained when the child finds its place in the **symbolic** order, coming to terms with the linguistic version of the paternal phallus, the Name-of-the-Father, or **transcendental signifier**.

Oedipus complex In Freud, the boy-child must attain subjectivity by negotiating his way through his relationship with his parents, and their gender. This process—which involves a simultaneous rivalry and identification with the father, and a sexual objectification yet repudiation of the mother—is called the Oedipus complex, named after the king in Sophocles' drama who unwittingly killed his father and married his mother.

overdetermination In Freud, all aspects of human behaviour (and, by analogy, culture) are the result of intense, plural and complex unconscious influences. They are thus said to be overdetermined.

phallus *see* **Name-of-the-Father**

phenomenology The philosophical movement inaugurated by Edmund Husserl, including Martin Heidegger, Maurice Merleau-Ponty, Emmanuel Levinas, Alphonso Lingis and indirectly Jacques Derrida. To phenomenology, the world is to be understood in the way it presents itself to consciousness, rather than by scientific analysis into component units. Since the world is to be known only through acts of consciousness, reflection on subjectivity is a necessary part of all knowledge.

polymorphous perversity For Freud, human children find sexual stimulation in almost all physical processes. As sexual maturity develops, this polymorphous sexuality is overtaken by a sexuality focused in the genitals, one that is controlled by shame and morality. Yet we always remain sensitive to the infinite sexual possibilities of body parts and all sensual practices.

post-modernism The dominant Western philosophical and cultural movement since the 1960s. Postmodernism is characterised by its scepticism towards **grand narratives** (and authority in general), its belief that language is the structuring principle of human culture and subjectivity, and its commitment to difference.

post-structuralism The philosophical movement associated with Michel Foucault, Jacques Derrida, Julia Kristeva, Roland Barthes, Jean-François Lyotard and others. Structuralism tried to analyse the world in terms of stable and predictable structures (usually built on the Saussurian model of the sign in terms of **signified** and **signifier**). Post-structuralism sees the relationship between signified and signifier as unstable and unpredictable. Hierarchical principles of meaning, truth, essence and identity are thus seen as unfixed, incomplete and contradictory.

power/knowledge To Michel Foucault, power is not the instrument or possession of privileged people or classes. Instead, it is entangled with scientific and academic theories that classify the human population into manageable groups (for example, the criminal is distinguished from the law-abiding, the sane from the insane, the heterosexual from the homosexual and so on). In this way, we, as subjects, become prone to the simultaneous operation of power and knowledge, which are indistinguishable from one another.

psychoanalysis The movement inaugurated by Freud and including, amongst many others, Carl Jung, Alfred Adler, Melanie Klein, Jacques Lacan, Julia Kristeva and, as a dissenter, Luce Irigaray. The key influences on subjectivity, according to psychoanalysis, are gender and sexuality that produce a separation between conscious and unconscious minds, governed by imagery, language and **desire**.

repression For Freud, the key event in the **Oedipus complex** is the crisis when the **unconscious** is formed to contain material the subject is unable to deal with. This material is said to be repressed.

rhizome Deleuze and Guattari use the botanical term 'rhizome' as a model of the uncentred and non-hierarchical. In botany, rhizomes produce roots from a variety of junctions that develop in a variety of directions. The traditional model that is the alternative to the rhizome is the **arborescent**, or tree model, which emphasises a hierarchy of stable origins (roots), fixed identity (trunk) and meaningful end (fruit and flowers).

schizoanalysis Schizoanalysis is Deleuze and Guattari's alternative to and parody of **psychoanalysis**. Schizoanalysis sees **desire** not as an attempt to compensate for loss or lack, but as a dynamic and plural production of new horizons of being. Thus the subject is an open-ended producing, desiring machine, rather than a fixed knowable structure.

self *see* **subject**

sex/gender In conventional feminist theory, a distinction is made between the biological nature with which we are born (sex, divided into male and female) and the cultural identity into which we are educated (gender, divided into masculine and feminine).

signifier/signified In Saussurian or structuralist linguistics, the linguistic sign is divided into two parts: a material form, the signifier (marks on a page, sounds in the mouth), and a concept or meaning, the signified.

subject The term used to describe interior life or **self**hood, especially as it is theorised in terms of its relationship to gender, power, language, culture and politics, etc.

symbolic In Lacan's psychoanalysis, the symbolic is the order of language in which subjectivity is achieved. It is governed by patriarchal principles of hierarchy, meaning and order. The subject's entry into the symbolic marks its separation from the **imaginary**, to which it seeks to return by way of **desire**.

transcendental signifier *see* **Name-of-the-Father**

unconscious The hidden or obscure part of the mind where threatening psychological investments (usually dominated by violence and sexuality) are held by **repression**.

Bibliography

BOOKS AND ARTICLES

Ackland, Richard, 1998, 'Decision for Hanson has Disturbing Effect' *The Sydney Morning Herald*, September 17, 1998, p.23.

Adorno, Theodor and Max Horkheimer, 1972, *The Dialectic of Enlightenment* trans. John Cumming, Herder and Herder, New York.

Althusser, Louis, 1971, *Lenin and Philosophy* trans. Ben Brewster, NLB, London.

Appignanesi, Lisa ed. 1984, *Desire* Institute of Contemporary Art, London.

Balibar, Etienne, 1991, 'Citizen Subject' in Cadava et al., *Who Comes After the Subject?* Routledge, New York, pp. 33–57.

Barthes, Roland, 1968, *Writing Degree Zero* trans. Annette Lavers and Colin Smith, Hill and Wang, New York.

——1975, *The Pleasure of the Text* trans. Richard Miller, Hill and Wang, New York.

——1990, *A Lover's Discourse: Fragments* trans. Richard Howard, Penguin, Harmondsworth.

Bataille, Georges, 1982, *Erotism: Death and Sensuality* trans. Mary Dalwood, City Lights Books, San Francisco.

Bersani, Leo, 1986, *The Freudian Body* Columbia University Press, New York.

——1989, 'Is the Rectum a Grave?' in Douglas Crimp ed., *AIDS: Cultural Analysis, Cultural Activism* MIT Press, Cambridge, pp.197–222.

Bhabha, Homi K., 1994, 'Anxious Nations, Nervous States' in Joan Copjec ed. *Supposing the Subject*, Verso, London, pp. 201–217.

Biddulph, Steve, 1995, *Manhood: An Action Plan for Changing Men's Lives* Finch Publishing, Sydney.

——1997, *Raising Boys: Why Boys Are Different and How to Help* Finch Publishing, Sydney.

Bly, Robert, 1992, *Iron John: A Book About Men* Element, Shaftesbury, Dorset and Rockport, Mass.

Boundas, Constantin V. and Dorothea Olkowski eds, 1994, *Gilles Deleuze and the Theater of Philosophy* Routledge, New York.

Bourdieu, Pierre, 1977, *Outline of a Theory of Practice* trans. Richard Nice, Cambridge University Press, Cambridge.

——1984, *Distinction: A Social Critique of the Judgement of Taste* trans. Richard Nice, Routledge & Kegan Paul, London and New York.

Boyne, Roy, 1990, *Foucault and Derrida: The Other Side of Reason* Unwin Hyman, London.

Buchbinder, David, 1998, *Performance Anxieties: Re-Producing Masculinity* Allen & Unwin, Sydney.

Butler, Judith, 1990, *Gender Trouble: Feminism and the Subversion of Identity* Routledge, New York.

——1993, *Bodies That Matter: On the Discursive Limits of 'Sex'* Routledge, New York.

Cadava, Eduardo, Peter Connor and Jean-Luc Nancy eds, 1991, *Who Comes After the Subject?* Routledge, New York.

Case, Sue-Ellen, 1991, 'Tracking the Vampire' *differences: a Journal of Feminist Cultural Studies* vol. 3, no. 2, pp.1–20.

Céline, Louis-Ferdinand, 1974, *Rigadoon* trans. Ralph Manheim, Dell, New York.

Chipp, Herschel B. ed. 1968, *Theories of Modern Art* University of California Press, Berkeley.

Cixous, Hélène, 1976, 'The Laugh of the Medusa', trans. K. Cohen and P. Cohen, *Signs* vol. 1, pp.845–893.

Cixous, Hélène and Catherine Clément, 1986, *The Newly Born Woman* trans. B. Wing, University of Minnesota Press, Minneapolis.

Clifford, James, 1988, *The Predicament of Culture* Harvard University Press, Cambridge, Mass.

Dean, Carolyn J., 1992, *The Self and its Pleasures: Bataille, Lacan and the History of the Decentered Subject* Cornell University Press, Ithaca.

de Beauvoir, Simone, 1952, *The Second Sex* trans. H.M. Parshley, Bantam, New York.

de Lauretis, Teresa, 1994, *The Practice of Love: Lesbian Sexuality and Perverse Desire* Indiana University Press, Bloomington.

Deleuze, Gilles and Felix Guattari, 1977, *Capitalism and Schizophrenia, Volume 1: Anti-Oedipus* trans. Robert Hurley et al., Athlone Press, London.

——1987, *Capitalism and Schizophrenia, Volume 2: A Thousand Plateaus* trans. Brian Massumi, University of Minnesota Press, Minneapolis.

Derrida, Jacques, 1976, *Of Grammatology* trans. Gayatri Chakravorty Spivak, Johns Hopkins University Press, Baltimore.

——1981, *Dissemination* trans. Barbara Johnson, University of Chicago Press, Chicago.

——1987, *The Postcard: From Socrates to Freud and Beyond* trans. A. Bass, University of Chicago Press, Chicago.

——1991, ' "Eating Well" or the Calculation of the Subject: An Interview with Jacques Derrida' in Cadava et al., *Who Comes After the Subject?* Routledge, New York, pp.96–119.

Descartes, René, 1970, *Philosophical Writings* ed. and trans. Elizabeth Anscombe and Peter Thomas Geach, Thomas Nelson and Sons, Sunbury-on-Thames.

Descombes, Vincent, 1991, 'Apropos of the "Critique of the Subject" and of the Critique of this Critique' in Cadava et al., *Who Comes After the Subject?* Routledge, New York, pp.120–134.

Dollimore, Jonathan, 1991, *Sexual Dissidence* Clarendon Press, Oxford.

During, Simon, 1992, *Foucault and Literature* Routledge, London.

Elliott, Anthony, 1994, *Psychoanalytic Theory* Blackwell, Oxford.

Ellroy, James, 1995, *American Tabloid* Arrow, London.

Fanon, Frantz, 1967, *The Wretched of the Earth* trans. Constance Farrington, Penguin Books, Harmondsworth.

——1968, *Black Skin, White Masks* trans. Charles Lam Markmann, MacGibbon & Kee, London.

Foucault, Michel, 1967, *Madness and Civilization: A History of Insanity in the Age of Reason* trans. Richard Howard, Tavistock, London.

——1970, *The Order of Things* trans. A.M. Sheridan-Smith, Tavistock, London.

——1974, *The Archaeology of Knowledge* trans. A.M. Sheridan-Smith, Tavistock, London.

——1977, 'A Preface to Transgression' *Language, Counter-Memory, Practice* ed. Donald F. Bouchard, trans. Donald F. Bouchard and Sherry Simon, Cornell University Press, Ithaca, pp.29–52.

——1979, *Discipline and Punish: The Birth of the Prison* trans. Alan Sheridan, Penguin Books, Harmondsworth.

——1980a, *The History of Sexuality Volume 1: An Introduction* trans. Robert Hurley, Vintage Books, New York.

——1980b *Power/Knowledge* ed. Colin Gordon, Pantheon Books, New York.

——1984, 'What Is Enlightenment?' *The Foucault Reader* ed. Paul Rabinow, Penguin Books, Harmondsworth, pp.32–50.

——1985, *The History of Sexuality Volume 2: The Use of Pleasure* trans. Robert Hurley, Vintage Books, New York.

——1990, *The History of Sexuality Volume 3: The Care of the Self* trans. Robert Hurley, Pantheon Books, New York.

Freud, Sigmund, 1976, *The Interpretation of Dreams* trans. James Strachey, Pelican Books, Harmondsworth.

——1977, *On Sexuality* trans. James Strachey, Penguin Books, Harmondsworth.

——1979, 'A Child Is Being Beaten' *On Psychopathology* trans. James Strachey, Penguin Books, Harmondsworth, pp. 159–193.

——1984, 'A Note on the Unconscious in Psychoanalysis' *On Metapsychology* trans. James Strachey, Penguin Books, Harmondsworth, pp.50–57.

——1988, *The Psychopathology of Everyday Life* trans. James Strachey, Penguin Books, Harmondsworth.

Fuery, Patrick, 1995a, *Theories of Desire* Melbourne University Press, Melbourne.

——1995b, *The Theory of Absence* Greenwood Press, Westport, Conn.

Fuery, Patrick and Nick Mansfield, 1997, *Cultural Studies and the New Humanities: Concepts and Controversies* Oxford University Press, Melbourne.

Garber, Marjorie, 1993, *Vested Interests: Cross-Dressing and Cultural Anxiety* Penguin Books, Harmondsworth.

Gates, Henry Louis Jr ed. 1986, *'Race', Writing and Difference* University of Chicago Press, Chicago.

Grosz, Elizabeth, 1989, *Sexual Subversions* Allen & Unwin, Sydney.

——1990, *Jacques Lacan: A Feminist Introduction* Routledge, London.

——1994, *Volatile Bodies* Allen & Unwin, Sydney.

——1995, *Space, Time and Perversion: The Politics of Bodies* Allen & Unwin, Sydney.

Halperin, David, 1995, *Saint Foucault: Towards a Gay Hagiography* Oxford University Press, New York.

Haraway, Donna, 1991, *Simians, Cyborgs, Women: The Reinvention of Nature* Free, London.

Hegel, G.W.F., 1977, *Phenomenology of Spirit* trans. A.V. Miller, Clarendon Press, Oxford.

Heidegger, Martin, 1962, *Being and Time* trans. John Macquarrie and Edward Robinson, Basil Blackwell, Oxford.

——1977, *The Question Concerning Technology and Other Essays* trans. William Lovitt, Harper & Row, New York.

Husserl, Edmund, 1960, *Cartesian Meditations* trans. D. Cairns, Martinus Nijhoff, The Hague.

——1969, *Ideas: General Introduction to Pure Phenomenology* trans. W.R. Boyce Gibson, Allen & Unwin, London.

Irigaray, Luce, 1980, 'This Sex Which Is Not One' in Marks, Elaine and Isabelle de Courtivron eds *New French Feminisms: An Anthology* University of Massachussetts Press, Amherst, pp.99–106.

——1985, *This Sex Which Is Not One* trans. C. Porter and G. Gill, Cornell University Press, New York.

Jagose, Annamarie, 1996, *Queer Theory* Melbourne University Press, Melbourne.

Jameson, Fredric, 1993, 'Postmodernism or The Cultural Logic of Late Capitalism' *Postmodernism: A Reader* ed. Thomas Docherty, Harvester Wheatsheaf, Hemel Hempstead, pp.62–92.

Jardine, Alice A., 1985, *Gynesis: Configurations of Woman and Modernity* Cornell University Press, Ithaca.

Kant, Immanuel, 1929, *Critique of Pure Reason* trans. Norman Kemp Smith, Macmillan, Houndmills, Basingstoke.

——1987, *Critique of Judgment* trans. Werner S. Pluhar, Hackett Publishing Company, Indianapolis.

Kaplan, E. Ann, 1989, *Psychoanalysis and Cinema* Routledge, New York.

Krafft-Ebing, Richard von, 1965, *Psychopathia Sexualis* trans. F.S. Klaf, Staples Press, London.

Kristeva, Julia, 1982, *Powers of Horror: An Essay on Abjection* trans. Leon S. Roudiez, Columbia University Press, New York.

Kroker, Arthur, Marilouise Kroker and David Cook, 1989, *Panic Encyclopaedia: The Definitive Guide to the Postmodern Scene* Macmillan, Basingstoke.

Lacan, Jacques, 1977, *Ecrits: A Selection* trans. Alan Sheridan, Tavistock, London.

——1979, *The Four Fundamental Concepts of Psychoanalysis* trans. Alan Sheridan, Penguin, Harmondsworth.

Lévi-Strauss, Claude, 1969, *The Elementary Structures of Kinship* Beacon Press, Boston.

Lyotard, Jean-François, 1984, *The Postmodern Condition: A Report on Knowledge* trans. Geoffrey Bennington and Brian Massumi, Manchester University Press, Manchester.

——1993, *Libidinal Economy* trans. Iain Hamilton Grant, Indiana University Press, Bloomington.

Malevich, Kasimir, 1968, 'Introduction to the Theory of the Additional Element in Painting' in Herschel B. Chipp ed. *Theories of Modern Art* University of California Press, Berkeley, pp.337–341.

Mama, Amina, 1995, *Beyond the Masks: Race, Gender and Subjectivity* Routledge, London.

Mansfield, Nick, 1997, *Masochism: The Art of Power*, Praeger Press, Westport, Conn.

Marinetti, F.T., 1968, 'The Foundation and Manifesto of Futurism' in Herschel B. Chipp ed. *Theories of Modern Art* University of California Press, Berkeley, pp.284–289.

Marks, Elaine and Isabelle de Courtivron eds 1980, *New French Feminisms: An Anthology* University of Massachusetts, Amherst.

Massumi, Brian, ed. 1993, *The Politics of Everyday Fear* University of Minnesota Press, Minneapolis.

Metz, Christian, 1982, *The Imaginary Signifier* trans. C. Britton et al. Indiana University Press, Bloomington.

Moi, Toril, 1985, *Sexual/Textual Politics* Methuen, London.

Mulvey, Laura, 1989, *Visual and Other Pleasures* Indiana University Press, Bloomington.

Nietzsche, Friedrich, 1989, *On the Genealogy of Morals and Ecce Homo* ed. and trans. Walter Kaufman, Vintage Books, New York.

Oliver, Kelly, 1993, *Reading Kristeva: Unravelling the Double-Bind* Indiana University Press, Bloomington.

Pfeil, Fred, 1995, *White Guys: Studies in Postmodern Domination and Difference* Verso, London.

Rajchman, John, 1985, *Michel Foucault: The Freedom of Philosophy* Columbia University Press, New York.

Rich, Adrienne, 1996, 'Compulsory Heterosexuality and Lesbian Existence' in Mary Eagleton ed. *Feminist Literary Theory: A Reader*, 2nd edn, Blackwell, Oxford, pp.24–29.

Rivière, Joan, 1986, 'Womanliness as a Masquerade' in Victor Burgin, James Donald and Cora Kaplan ed. *Formations of Fantasy* Methuen, London and New York, pp.35–44.

Rousseau, Jean-Jacques, 1953, *The Confessions* trans. J.M. Cohen, Penguin Books, Harmondsworth.

——1968, *The Social Contract* trans. Maurice Cranston, Penguin Books, Harmondsworth.

Saussure, Ferdinand de, 1983, *Course in General Linguistics* trans. Roy Harris, Duckworth, London.

Sedgwick, Eve Kosofsky, 1985, *Between Men: English Literature and Male Homosocial Desire* Columbia University Press, New York.

——1990, *Epistemology of the Closet* University of California Press, Berkeley.

Silverman, Kaja, 1992, *Male Subjectivity at the Margins* Routledge, New York.

Spillers, Hortense J., 1987, 'Mama's Baby, Papa's Maybe: An American Grammar Book' *Diacritics* Summer, pp.65–81.

Spivak, Gayatri Chakravorty, 1987, 'Subaltern Studies: Deconstructing Historiography' *In Other Worlds: Essays in Cultural Politics* Methuen, New York and London, pp.197–221.

Tsiolkas, Christos, 1995, *Loaded* Vintage Books, Sydney.

Tylor, Edward B., 1958, *Primitive Culture* Harper, New York.

Virilio, Paul, 1998, *The Virilio Reader* ed. James Der Derian, Blackwell, Oxford.

Wark, McKenzie, 1994, *Virtual Geography: Living with Global Media Events* Indiana University Press, Bloomington.

Werbner, Pnina, and Tariq Madood eds, 1997, *Debating Cultural Hybridity: Multicultural Identities and the Politics of Anti-Racism* Zed Books, London.

Wittig, Monique, 1992, *The Straight Mind and Other Essays* Beacon Press, Boston.

FILMS

Alien, dir. Ridley Scott, 1979.

Baraka, dir. Ron Fricke, 1992.

Die Hard, dir. John McTiernan, 1988.

Silence of the Lambs, dir. Jonathan Demme, 1991.

Un chien andalou, dir. Luis Buñuel, 1928.

Index